THE
FRANCHISE
FOOTBALL
LEAGUE

1994
OFFICIAL
FANTASY
FOOTBALL
JOURNAL
AND
COMPUTER
GUIDE

DICK GIEBEL

THE
FRANCHISE
FOOTBALL
LEAGUE

1994
OFFICIAL
FANTASY
FOOTBALL
JOURNAL
AND
COMPUTER
GUIDE

DICK GIEBEL

A Fantasy Sports Properties Trade Paperback

A FANTASY SPORTS PROPERTIES PAPERBACK

Published by:
Fantasy Sports Properties, Inc.
PO Box 9805
McLean, VA 22102

FSPI, FBL, Franchise Baseball League, FFL, Franchise Football League, FBBL, Franchise Basketball League, Fantasy Basketball, FHL, Franchise Hockey League, and Fantasy Hockey are all registered trademarks of Fantasy Sports Properties, Inc.

Ultimate Football is a registered trademark of MicroProse Software

PRODIGY is a registered trademark of The Prodigy Services Company

The FFL software and trademark are registered in the U.S. Patent and Trademark Office Patent No. 4,918,603 Registration No. 1,687,798

The FBL, FHL, and FBBL software and trademark are registered in the U.S. Patent and Trademark Office. Patent No. 4,918,603 Additional Patents Pending.

ISBN 0-9636895-2-5

Printed in the United States of America by Peake Printing, Washington, DC

Cover Design by Chris Overton

May 1994   10 9 8 7 6 5 4 3 2 1

With grateful appreciation to DAVID GEORGE'S POWER SPORTS TALK, PRODIGY, and the FFL. Thanks for the opportunity to talk and write about Fantasy Football--life sometimes can be so grand!

★☆★☆ACKNOWLEDGMENTS★☆★☆

Special thanks go out to all of those who contributed their time and efforts to make this edition of the Franchise Football League's *Fantasy Football Journal* a success. Thanks for the support from my family: Cindy, Matt, Tim and Caitlin.

Thanks, kudos and appreciation go to David Warner and his ability to keep this project on its timetable--one day, Dave, we'll do a book on Rock 'n Roll! Thanks to Suzanne Carbonneau for correcting the incorrect and keeping the grammar sharp. I am grateful to Dave Dewenter for his splendid chapter on FFL software, and yes, sooner or later, even I will be a keyboard wizard. Thanks to Bill Kelly for the many hours skimming through the countless player names, making sure all the trades, free agents and roster moves were accurate--hopefully Bill's eyesight has returned. The editors and authors would also like to thank Chris Overton for her wonderful work on the cover of this book, and for being able to do so much on such an abbreviated schedule.

A special thanks to the gurus of the FFL, Pat and Cheryl Hughes: may their future projects be successful and their hard work pay off. A sincere thanks to David George & POWER SPORTS TALK SHOW--it's always a laugher with hosts Rudy Martzke, Larry Michael and Rick "Doc" Walker. A special thanks also to former hosts Tom George and Todd Whitthorne--pros like these two are difficult to find. Speaking of pros, it's been a treat working with Dave George (Producer) and Sharon D'Agostino (Director)--may all projects be so enjoyable. I would be remiss if I left out friends and advisors like Marty McGrath (Publisher) and Michael Goodman (Media/Publicity.) Also thanks to article contributors Larry Michael, Larry Weisman, John Weiss and Dave Douglas.

Thanks to the league members of the infamous HFL and congratulations to '93's HFL Champion "UNIFIED." Thanks so much to the many friends that I have made through PRODIGY and my weekly column. And lastly, thanks to you, the Fantasy Footballer--*may you forever run*!

★☆★☆CONTENTS★☆★☆

★**1**★
What is Franchise Football League?   **3**

★**2**★
Starting a Franchise Football League   **8**

Welcome to the seventh year of Franchise Football League's Fantasy Football! This *Journal* has become one of the leading sources for information and insight for fantasy "owners" trying to pick the winning franchise in their leagues. This year, we add another expert to our lineup--we are pleased to have Larry Michael, one of the finest NFL play-by-play announcers on radio today, adding his insight in the Team-by-Team Reviews section, which begins on page 36.

More and more, we at Fantasy Sports Properties are hearing from teachers, parents and coaches about the impact of fantasy sports games on children. In this often difficult world we live in, fantasy football has become an excellent motivator for young people, allowing them to interactively participate in something they love--sports--while at the same time building group camaraderie. Following the progress of the stars on their teams enhances their reading, writing and mathematical skills, while "critical thinking" skills--high on the nation's educational agenda--are used in analyzing players' performances throughout the season. If you or your league-mates have had similar educational experiences with fantasy football, please let us know--we'd love to hear about them. Please contact us at the address below.

Well, how about all the changes in the NFL this season?! They've moved the schedule back to 17 weeks (from 18 weeks last year) with only *one* bye week. Drafting last year was nearly impossible as it was hard not to have had a key backup out on bye during the same week as your regular starters. Two bye weeks were a bad idea, especially for fantasy leaguers, and we hope the NFL doesn't recreate that fiasco anytime in the future. I don't think pay-per-view can disrupt a draft, but following *your* players could get expensive--bad idea, too!

On a positive note, we do like some of the new NFL rule changes! The two-point conversion will add *more* scoring, which is always good! (By the way, if a conversion attempt is intercepted or fumbled and recovered by the other team, the ball is ruled dead, unlike in college, where the ball may be returned for two points. Go figure!) Also of note is that kickoff return yardage (and possibly kickoff return *scoring*) should increase dramatically, as teams now kick off from the 30-yard line and not the 35.

Speaking of *more* scoring, many of you who write in told us that player specialization was creating a difficult situation for fantasy drafting if you used the FFL scoring system last year. For example, Barry Sanders once was a premiere FFL star when he scored a lot of touchdowns. However, last year he reached the end zone only three times, despite another fine rushing year (1,115 yards) leaving many FFLers unhappy with his point production. In order to keep up with the times, and to resolve the problem of player specialization or "designated scorers," we at the FFL have also made some dramatic scoring changes. You'll find on page 17 the *new* Official FFL Scoring System, in which fantasy points are awarded for *yardage* by QBs, RBs, and Pass Receivers.

Additionally, we have teamed up with *Ultimate Football* from MicroProse to provide the leading football software game available. If you want the best in simulation, complete with outstanding graphics and up-to-date stats capability, this is it!

We think you'll be pleased with these changes, with this *Journal*, and of course with our indispensable software and downloading services (see the Appendix for more information). Remember, it only takes about five minutes to download stats into our program, versus many, many hours of manual transcription. Don't forget, by downloading, it's 99.99% accurate--the first time!

So once again, please feel free to write me with your comments or concerns, and have a great draft and a great year!

Patrick J. Hughes
President
Fantasy Sports Properties
PO Box 9805
McLean, VA 22102

ABBREVIATIONS

QB -	Quarterback	AZ -	Arizona Cardinals
RB -	Running Back	ATL -	Atlanta Falcons
HB -	Halfback	BUF -	Buffalo Bills
FB -	Fullback	CHI -	Chicago Bears
WR -	Wide Receiver	CIN -	Cincinnati Bengals
TE -	Tight End	CLE -	Cleveland Browns
PR -	Pass Receiver	DAL	Dallas Cowboys
K -	Kicker	DEN -	Denver Broncos
P -	Punter	DET -	Detroit Lions
S -	Safety	GB -	Green Bay Packers
FS -	Free Safety	HOU -	Houston Oilers
SS -	Strong Safety	IND -	Indianapolis Colts
DB -	Defensive Back	KC -	Kansas City Chiefs
CB -	Cornerback	RAM -	Los Angeles Rams
LB -	Linebacker	RAI -	Los Angeles Raiders
OLB -	Outside Linebacker	MIA -	Miami Dolphins
MLB -	Middle Linebacker	MIN -	Minnesota Vikings
ILB -	Inside Linebacker	NE -	New England Patriots
		NO -	New Orleans Saints
FG -	Field Goal	NYG -	New York Giants
PAT -	Point After Touchdown	NYJ -	New York Jets
Yds -	Yards	PHI -	Philadelphia Eagles
DT -	Defensive Team	PIT -	Pittsburgh Steelers
TD -	Touchdown	SD -	San Diego Chargers
Pts -	Points	SF -	San Francisco 49ers
AVG -	Average	SEA -	Seattle Seahawks
REC -	Receptions	TB -	Tampa Bay Buccaneers
NFL -	National Football League	WAS -	Washington Redskins
FFL -	Franchise Football League	NFC -	National Football Conference
		AFC -	American Football Conference

Introduction

      This is not one of those *boring* books driven solely on stats. This is a book that can be read by fantasy footballers and just plain football fans. I sort of look at this book as ZEN: THE FANTASY FOOTBALL WAY. Sure I'm being facetious, but I tire of those folks who put down anyone remotely connected with fantasy football.

      What I have tried to do in this book is have fun, and give you information on players who can enable you to win your league's championship. At the same time, I wanted a book that was informative and humorous--*this is what football should be!*

      I challenge anyone to find a more frank book on football that discusses NFL teams, the owners, coaches and players. This is not a kissup book to the NFL--this is a gut check, discussing the game and the players for 1994.

      As for the so-called critics and cheap-shotters who find fantasy football to be a hobby for dorks--I say, "Kiss-off!" The fantasy footballers that I encounter are some of the most knowledgeable football folks around. These men and women are not hung up (as some assume) on stats, stats and more stats. Instead, most are just plain knowledgeable fans who have a terrific understanding of the game *and the players.*

      I have a terrific respect for the many sportswriters and sports reporters covering the NFL. On the whole they do a great job reporting and keeping the public informed. But for some reason, a few seem to be always putting down fantasy football as if only airheads would enjoy such a game.

As for those disparaging remarks that certain sportswriters make in reference to fantasy football players, suggesting that we have just dropped in from Mars: excuse me...who do they think read their insipid columns? And let's call it like it is...have you seen some of these print and TV/radio reporters who knock fantasy football? These guys are the same doofusses who caught more than a few tosses with their faces *instead* of their hands in high school gym class.

So I hope you enjoy this book. To our many fans of the FFL and fantasy football we thank you for your support and friendship over the past six seasons. If this is your first time picking up an *FFL Journal*, I hope you find it entertaining, informative and fun! Thank you.

★1★

What is Franchise Football League?

WHAT IS FRANCHISE FOOTBALL?

Franchise Football is a game that allows you the opportunity to be the owner, general manager and head coach of your own NFL team. Now, don't tell me that you wouldn't want to replace a Jerry Jones in Dallas! Just once, wouldn't you like to trade shoes (and hairdos) with Jimmy Johnson and call the plays?

Then again, maybe even Jimmy Johnson would like to coach the Cowboys (again). Who's to say that Barry Switzer hasn't been boning up on the NFL over the last several years by playing fantasy football?

Well, for ordinary folks like you and me (who just weren't *fortunate* enough to be on an Arkansas high school football team with Jerry "Ergo My Ego" Jones like Jimmy Johnson) it doesn't have to be "just a fantasy." Now it can be fantasy football...the FFL way! You draft players, build your own team, and compete against other teams in your FFL league.

Imagine the feeling of matching your wits against your buddies, co-workers or family. Will your draft strategy work?

Who will be the emerging scorers for 1994? Which quarterback will lead the league? Will it be John Elway or Steve Young? Will Emmitt Smith continue to prove he is the best running back in the NFL? Will Jerry Rice continue to be the best receiver in football, or will he be challenged by Andre Rison, Michael Irvin or Anthony Miller? Which rookies will jump into the limelight? Who will be a bust? All of these questions must be faced, and decisions will have to be made as you take charge and draft a fantasy team.

Hey, no one said these decisions would be easy...but these kinds of decisions are fun. So why delay starting a league and miss the fun? The choice is yours, and the choice is simple: either spend another season frustrated as you watch some inept play calling, or call your own shots and see how you rate as an FFL team owner. Fantasy Football makes you put up or shut up! The FFL--you will never watch football quite the same way again. Enjoy!

GEE, I LIVE MY LIFE IN A CAVE AND MISSED THE BEGINNING OF THE FOOTBALL SEASON--CAN I STILL START A LEAGUE?

Part of the intrigue of drafting an FFL team is the great unknown. Drafting a fantasy team several days before the NFL season kicks off is exciting because there are still many decisions to be made by NFL coaches--decisions such as starting players or who will be cut, traded, or placed on injured reserve.

Therefore, the FFL suggests forming a league prior to the start of the NFL season. However, if by chance you have just now discovered the Franchise Football League program and fantasy football, by all means, join in! It's simple to just hold your draft and play an abbreviated schedule. On the plus side, you and your cronies will know firsthand who's starting full-time, who's hot and who's not. Also, you will know who's injured. So, starting late

4

shouldn't stop you. (After all, starting late certainly didn't hurt Emmitt Smith last season.) So play!

SO WHO DIED AND MADE ME AN EXPERT?

Well, now you have the opportunity to become something of an expert through Franchise Football League's fantasy football program. This is my sixth book on fantasy football, an endeavor which is akin to projecting the upcoming year's stock market. In other words, I attempt my very best at predicting just who will be top scorers and potentially explosive picks.

What I do is not rocket science, but my recommendations are well thought-out and researched. Sometimes I'm on and sometimes I'm not, but that's what makes this game so enjoyable. Also, it gives *you, the reader* some responsibility. Shucks, I'm a realist: besides this book, you probably have purchased several other football magazines or books. Combined with that knowledge, this book should provide you with the confidence that you are making informed decisions. I'm trying to make *you* the expert.

I've been playing fantasy football for 12 years, and I have *never* walked out of a draft with every player that I wanted. In my dozen or so fantasy league years I have begrudgingly developed the realization that my league-mates are every bit as astute as I am (although only I got the book contract).

Playing in my league are men and women whom I have learned to appreciate and with whom I have developed great friendships. It's funny, but the league that I play in now has expanded to over 30 people, residing all over the country. We only really see each other two to three times a year--but what a party, and what a great group. (I know I'm kissing up, but I may need to work some trades in '94.)

I know that this scene is replayed all over the country with FFL and fantasy leagues that have sprouted up over the last several years. I've been on countless call-in radio talk shows and have responded to many folks from all walks of life who have written me on PRODIGY, and the one constant is that you folks are not only knowledgeable about the world of sports, but a blast to talk and correspond with.

Also, it's quite evident just how popular fantasy football has become. Leagues are now part of the office, job site, universities and high schools, and are shared among families and friends.

I still remember the early days of playing fantasy football: only a few people understood the concept, and even fewer actually played. I still recall quizzical looks from those who were not playing and couldn't understand my enthusiasm over drafting players from NFL teams and cheering their every score.

I can remember sitting in the stands of RFK Stadium rooting for the Redskins against Dallas when I absentmindedly let out a roar as Cowboy great Tony Dorsett (who happened to be one of my FFL running backs) broke off a long run for a touchdown. I suddenly knew exactly how Miami kicker Garo Ypremian must have felt in the 1971 Super Bowl when he vainly attempted a pass (which looked more like a two-handed set shot), and the errant flub was picked off by Washington's Mike Bass for a touchdown. At that moment, the ex-soccer player looked mighty foolish.

Cheering for a Dallas TD in Washington in the late '70s was not an intelligent move--in fact, it was moronic. I quickly escaped the section of stunned and irritated patrons by urgently yelling, "Look, a fumble!" as I did a 360 and dove for the nearest exit. It was at that moment that I realized that I would never be watching NFL football quite the same...*ever again.*

STATS, DON'T FAIL ME NOW!

You've heard the saying "stats don't lie?" In fantasy football, they can be very misleading. For example, in 1993 Bobby

Hebert had a solid scoring season for the Atlanta Falcons, but in spite of his being re-signed by the Falcons, this season it still may be a challenge for him to compete for the starting job. Therefore, picking Hebert solely based on stats would be an incredible screw-up!

Overlooking Jeff George based on his woeful 1993 stats would be another knothead move. Forget that this guy has a split personality--I mean, in Atlanta this year the guy will have Andre Rison, Ricky Sanders and maybe even Deion Sanders as targets. (If Michael Haynes were still aboard, I'd be doing cartwheels.)

So what does one do? Well, amigo, it definitely depends on how your own league handles scoring. Basing your picks on stats works well if your league bases points solely on scoring. In a league just counting touchdown scoring, Thurman Thomas (BUF) will not be a great draft pick because he racks up tons of yards but not many TDs, but Eric Metcalf (CLE) would be a natural because he can score as a returner, runner and receiver. However, in a league that gives points based not only on scoring, but also for yards gained as well as for receiving yards--man, ol' Thurman suddenly looks like a *hot pick*! In leagues just counting TDs, certain players do little offensively (yards-wise), yet they score. In 1993, Marc Logan (SF) scored 7 TDs but gained only 280 yards. Yet, in a league that counts only TDs, he is a better selection than Rodney Hampton (NYG) who gained 1,077 yards, but scored only 5 TDs. Call me a dead-head fool-head, but in a thousand drafts, regardless of the scoring systems, I'm going to draft Hampton over Logan a thousand times.

Or, let's look at Eddie Murray: kicking for the 10 points-per-second, don't-blink-there's-another-scoring-opportunity-for-the-kicker Dallas Cowboys made Eddie "Money" Murray a great fantasy pick. B-u-u-u-t-t-t, remove him from the high-powered silver and blue sidelines (away from the Dallas Cheerleaders and back-slapping Jerry J.) and put him on the Philadelphia Eagles sidelines (standing next to the trainer and a bucket of Gatorade)--Hmmm, Eddie...been nice knowin' ya.

★2★

Starting a Franchise Football League

Occasionally, someone will ask me why one needs the FFL, the FFL software---or even my *FFL Journal*. Normally, upon regaining my composure after throttling such a nudnik, I explain it this way:

Thumbing through the sports pages today is like reading the obituaries. Players are dropping off teams and signing with others on what seems like a daily basis. Tracking all of these player moves is more difficult than keeping up with the latest Bill Clinton escapade.

So, if even keeping up with the rosters appears complicated, will it be too much of a hassle to form an FFL league and play fantasy football? My answer to this predicament is that the FFL provides an easy way to help you keep up! The beauty of fantasy football is that it makes you pay attention to the whole league, and not just your favorite teams. So get off that sofa, drop the remote control, grab some friends, and let's play fantasy football!

OK, OK! SIGN ME UP! I'M A ROOKIE...WHAT DO I DO?

Don't get intimidated by all of this--simply play fantasy football the FFL way. If you've never been part of a league, don't fret--starting one is a breeze. First of all, keep it simple and begin with people you know--family, friends and co-workers. One key suggestion for beginners: don't be overly ambitious and attempt to organize a 20-team league. Think simple; or, better yet, simply think! For the novice, large leagues are difficult to maintain successfully. My suggestion would be to stick with 8 to 10 teams at the start and, if successful, entertain expansion in the following year or two. It's best to select franchise owners who are likable, and, at the same time, fit the mold of fun-loving football fans interested in competing in a fantasy league for the entire season. This last point is important, because it only takes a couple of idiotic mental-midgets who lose interest during the season to bring down the entire league.

SETTING UP YOUR FANTASY LEAGUE

1. League Organization

Organize 2 to 16 "teams" to form your own league. A team can consist of one person or multiple partners, but a tip to the wise: try to keep your league down to 8 to 10 teams. Holding down the number of teams eliminates a watering down of your draft. Although you can start an FFL league with as few as 2 teams, the down side of a small league is that all the teams will be loaded with superstars, the scoring is higher, and there's less challenge and competition among team owners.

2. Select a Commissioner

Don't minimize the importance of a good commissioner. This is a time-consuming job consisting of keeping records, tracking weekly lineups and trades, and solving a whole lot of problems. The commissioner doesn't have to be a wizard or a know-it-all of fantasy football, just someone who can be firm in the handling of questionable scoring decisions, yet remain open-minded when dealing with franchise owners' concerns. Two big tips: it's best that the commissioner have the use of a computer; and choose a commissioner carefully--an order-taking wimp won't stand up and be accountable for important league decisions; on the other hand, a hard-headed bully will ruin your league.

3. Draft Day

Your commissioner sets up the league's fantasy draft. Tip: give plenty of notice but schedule your draft just prior to the NFL season opener. I realize many of you draft in late July or early August, but the problem I have with drafting this early is that many teams haven't made their cuts, players will get injured, and starters haven't been listed. Drafting later (just before Game 1) is a better move. The commissioner has the responsibility of running the draft on draft night. This is a time of celebration and exuberance--have fun and enjoy the draft!

4. Franchise Representation

By giving plenty of notice for the fantasy draft you will ensure that every franchise is represented. A missing franchise puts a damper on the draft, and having another franchise draft for the phantom team is both a drag and an inconvenience. It is difficult enough keeping track of who's drafting whom and deciding just what your own next move will be; adding the responsibility of drafting for another team is a complete bummer! Therefore, make it clear that all franchises are to be represented.

5. Draft Sequence

As a rule of thumb, an existing league generally will operate the draft just like the NFL--based on the final standings from the previous season. The last-place team receives the first pick, next-to-last gets the second pick, etc. Obviously, this sequence will give last season's champ the final pick in round one and the first pick in round two.

Example Sequence for 10 Teams

Round One	Round Two
Team #10 - 1st pick	Team # 1 - 1st pick
Team # 9 - 2nd pick	Team # 2 - 2nd pick
Team # 8 - 3rd pick	Team # 3 - 3rd pick
Team # 7 - 4th pick	Team # 4 - 4th pick
Team # 6 - 5th pick	Team # 5 - 5th pick
Team # 5 - 6th pick	Team # 6 - 6th pick
Team # 4 - 7th pick	Team # 7 - 7th pick
Team # 3 - 8th pick	Team # 8 - 8th pick
Team # 2 - 9th pick	Team # 9 - 9th pick
Team # 1 -10th pick	Team #10- 10th pick

Round three would lead off with Team #10 picking first--order reverses every round. If you are organizing a new league, just pick numbers from a hat--and sequence the draft.

1 - # 10 (first round)
10- # 1 (second round)
1 - # 10 (third round)

#10- #1 (fourth round)

Remember to reverse the order every round.

HOW TO RUN A SMOOTH DRAFT

1. Set The Draft Date

Just before the start of the NFL regular season, the league commissioner sets a date for the FFL fantasy draft. The commissioner must be prepared to list the players chosen round-by-round. An easel and a marker will help the commissioner or an assistant to record each round and will allow league members to review their choices.

2. Bring on the Dancing Weenies

Scientifically speaking, people are usually content after they've eaten, so try to coordinate your draft in conjunction with some kind of food and/or drink function, and you'll like the results. Don't try to eat at the same time your draft happens, though--talk about messy!

3. Prepare, Prepare, Prepare

You've already done a bit of this, because, after all, you *are* reading this book. Seriously, though, this is the time when you really must get your people up to speed on the latest roster moves, injury reports, etc. Give your league members enough materials so that they can't dare claim that they are unprepared. The last thing you want to have in a three-hour draft is questions like, "Is Sterling Sharpe available?" Nothing infuriates league commissioners (many of whom are tracking not only their own picks but everyone else's as well) more than these knucklehead questions. So, buy *lots* of this book, get a few magazines, newspapers, and maybe a *Sports Illustrated '94 NFL Preview Edition* or two.

Another helpful hint is to use the FFL program to print out NFL rosters for your league members to use. Bring lots of highlighters, markers, pens and pencils, extra paper, etc. Give them the feeling that this is professional draft, and you'll have a draft just like the NFL's...except it won't be at the Marriott Marquis in New York.

4. Don't Let The Draft Drag

To move the draft along, set up a time limit per selection. (For example, many leagues suggest one minute between picks.) If you don't set a time limit initially, your draft will drag and tempers will flare. Trust me, without a time limit per selection, your draft will become a nightmare. Have fun, but move the selection process along to ensure a successful draft.

5. Suggested Number of Players to Draft

4 Quarterbacks (QB)   2 Kickers (K)
6 Running Backs (RB)   2 Defensive/SpecialTeams (DT/ST)
6 Wide Receivers(WR)
2 Tight Ends (TE)

These are the numbers of players the FFL suggests to draft per team. This is not a hard-and-fast-rule, but with these amounts you will have enough players at each position to cover situations such as the always-wonderful bye week, or injuries, etc. Many existing leagues change these numbers slightly, so use them as general guidelines.

Supplemental Draft

Do you remember just how smart you felt immediately after the draft? Now, several weeks later, you begin to notice your team fraying around the edges. Do you know what you need to give yourself a fixer-upper? My friend, you need a quick trip to the Supplemental Draft.

Many leagues hold Supplemental Drafts to fix "mistakes" (or, shall I say, those humongous "reaches" that you hung your hopes on). Not only will the Supplemental Draft correct Draft Night flaws, but it also is helpful in cases where your key players are injured, or worse, benched. I recommend that you hold the Supplemental Draft after Weeks 5 or 6, in order to supplement rosters with NFL players not chosen at the outset. I also recommend that you set a draft limit of 6 players to be selected for each team.

One other reason to hold the Supplemental Draft is that it is a great opportunity to get the whole gang back together. This is also a good chance to make trades, or just to trade barbs and banter!

Weekly Starting Lineups

Each franchise must submit a 9-player starting lineup (8 players and one defensive/special team) to the commissioner prior to the kickoff of the first game of the NFL/FFL week. If no starting lineup is submitted, the commissioner will assume that the team has no lineup changes. The FFL recommends the following starting lineup requirement:

1 Quarterback	(QB)	1 Tight End	(TE)
2 Running Backs	(RB)	1 Kicker	(K)
3 Wide Receivers	(WR)	1 Defensive/Special Team	(DT/ST)

Some leagues will set Thursday evening as the time to call in their weekly lineups. Most commissioners, however, will give franchises until game time on Sunday to call in lineups. The commissioner should *never* accept any lineup change after games are in progress on Sunday! A good suggestion is to get an answering machine so each franchise can record his or her lineup. Believe me, if the commissioner takes every call, he or she will never get off the phone. And for the other franchise owners calling in lineups, a constantly busy phone line is a real drag. Therefore, it is imperative that the commissioner use a tape recorder/voice mail. This is the quickest and the most reliable method; besides, recorded lineup messages eliminate any confusion or errors--after all, you've got it on tape!

Trades and Waivers

As with real NFL teams, franchise owners can trade or transfer one or more NFL players from one franchise to another. However, all trades must be approved by the commissioner, and in order to play a traded player on that weekend, trades must be finalized in time for the weekly lineup exchange. No trades are allowed during the final four weeks of the season. (This is recommended to prevent real loser franchises from "selling" their talent to winning teams or teams in contention for the league championship.)

A franchise owner may also waive a player on his/her current roster and add a non-roster player up to a maximum of eight times during the season.

FFL SCORING SYSTEM

FFL scoring is based on actual plays made by NFL players each week during the NFL season. This is real scoring--not Nintendo. Only players listed as *starters* for each franchise receive points for that franchise. Points are awarded for rushing TDs, receiving TDs, passing TDs, points-after-TDs (PAT), 2-point conversions, field goals, and any TDs scored by defensive/special teams players, including safeties.

Also, the FFL has added performance scoring for yardage, receptions, interceptions, etc. Many leagues around the country have requested that performance scoring be added to make the FFL even more complete-- *and we've done it!*

Official FFL Scoring System

Regular Scoring Plays

	0-9 yds. Points	10-39 yds. Points	40+ yds. Points
QB pass for TD	6	9	12
RB run for TD	6	9	12
PR* catch for TD	6	9	12
DT** or ST, LB, DB return for TD	6	9	12

	1-39 yds. Points	40-49 yds. Points	50+ yds. Points
Field Goal	3	5	10

Two-Point Conversion

QB pass for conversion	2
RB run for conversion	2
PR catch for conversion	2
QB run/catch for conversion	4
RB pass/catch for conversion	4
PR run/pass for conversion	4

Bonus Scoring Plays

	0-9 yds. Points	10-39 yds. Points	40+ yds. Points
QB run/catch for TD	12	18	24
RB pass/catch for TD	12	18	24
PR pass/run for TD	12	18	24
K pass/run/catch for a TD	12	18	24

Performance Scoring

QB Pass Yds.	5 points beginning at 250 yds.	1 point for every 10 yds. thereafter
QB Rush/Rec Yds.	5 points beginning at 50 yds.	1 point for every 10 yds. thereafter
RB Rush Yds.	10 points beginning at 100 yds.	1 point for every 10 yds. thereafter
RB Pass/Rec Yds.	5 points beginning at 50 yds.	1 point for every 10 yds. thereafter
PR Pass/Rush Yds.	5 points beginning at 50 yds.	1 point for every 10 yds. thereafter
PR Receiving Yds.	10 points beginning at 100 yds.	1 point for every 10 yds. thereafter

Safety scored by a DB, LB or DT = **4 pts**. INT thrown/Sack received by a QB = **-1 pt**.
Point After Touchdown (PAT) = **1 pts**.   Sack made/INT made by a DB, LB or DT = **1 pt**.

Key: QB (Quarterback), RB (Running Back), PR (Pass Receiver), K (Kicker), ST (Special Teams player), DT (Defensive Team), LB (Linebacker), DB (Defensive Back), TD (Touchdown).

*Pass Receivers (PR) include wide receivers (WR) and tight ends (TE).

** If your league uses the defensive/special teams unit method (in which franchise owners pick an entire defensive and special teams unit rather than individual players), and any player from that unit scores a TD, the points are awarded to that franchise.

League Newsletters

Communication with league members is crucial, and the best means is through a weekly newsletter. You should keep league members up-to-date with weekly information on stats, scores and league standings. Generally, since the commissioner keeps track of the stats, he or she should also do the newsletter. Make sure you include the following:

* Weekly winner
* The past week's scoring results, team by team
* Year-to-date league standings
* Weekly head-to-head schedules
* Any league business (trades, roster changes, etc.)
* Any rules interpretations

TEAM vs. TEAM SETUP

While some leagues still prefer a system where there is one weekly winner based on the number of starting points for the franchise, many Franchise Football leagues now supplement their league with the team-vs.-team (or head-to-head) format in order to give more teams a chance to stay in contention and win. It also provides a playoff structure similar to the NFL's. For ease and convenience, the FFL has structured a 17-week schedule to be used by 8-, 10-, 12-, 14-, and 16-team leagues. This schedule is included in the FFL program, and can be printed out from within the software.

One bit of advice on setting up leagues--don't get overly ambitious and set up a 20-team league. Besides being overweening, a 20-team league completely dilutes your player pool.

★3★

The Draft

OFF-SEASON RECAP

I won't kick around the offseason Jerry Jones and Jimmy Johnson fiasco (you know, the one that led the two-time Super Bowl coach from a rigorous, 80-hour a week job with the 'Pokes to a year of boat-cruising and network-schmoozing) any more than has been done on countless sports radio shows nationwide. In fact, I won't even make *much* reference to Jerry Jones attempting to become an Al Davis *sans* the leisure suit and bulky medallion. I will, however, scoff at the selection of Barry "Wishbone-head" Switzer to be the new Dallas coach.

Hiring Switzer is Jones' idea of a final slap in the chubby face of the stiff-haired but otherwise brilliant Jimmy Johnson. Face it: if Switzer wins the Super Bowl, Jerry Jones will crow that he was right--anyone can coach and win with *his* Cowboys. Now before you throw a pity party for Switzer, the self-proclaimed "Bootlegger's Son," just remember that the man used to run up scores on the lowly opposition with relish. I can still hear the peachy-keen voice of Jim Lampley reading college scores on

Saturdays that went something like this: "Penn State 31-West Virginia 28, UCLA 24-USC 21, and Oklahoma 62-Florida Panhandle 0." A-h-h-h, yes-s-s-s, the proverbial *stacked deck*.

Switzer won't be sitting on any lead in the fourth quarter, *no sir-ree Bobby McGee*; offensively, he will approach the game with the same loving verve as Buddy Ryan. Don't expect to see the Cowpokes fall apart and unravel like Tonya Harding's pair of skate laces. Jones is correct. Jones is astute. The talent is deeper in Dallas than perhaps any other NFL city. Dallas will win, but it won't be the same without the George Allen-like intensity of Jimmy Johnson. My only hope is that Buddy Ryan wasn't *also* an Arkansas teammate of Jerry Jones.

So don't be fooled by Barry Switzer. He is not some down-and-out dolt who will be a puppet for Jerry "Limelight" Jones. Barry is a coach who survived his coaching days at Oklahoma by being an excellent *salesman* for his program. He recruited athletes--*not students*. He was in the game for the victories and the money. As a result, the Oklahoma program was under great scrutiny for stretching and breaking the NCAA rules which govern college sports.

After leaving Oklahoma, he didn't find colleges and universities attempting to woo him to coach their struggling football programs. You see, Switzer was a sad embodiment to many of all the ugly things that happen in college recruiting. What university president would possibly want to deal with a rule-bending powermonger, bent on winning *at any cost*? But Switzer has proven once again just what a true survivor he really is.

With this in mind, perhaps he will be a better *buddy* for Jerry than the more austere Jimmy. Dallas will win. Jones will win. Switzer will win. Gee, I wonder if Switzer can schedule Florida Panhandle for a few scrimmages?

PHOENIX...err, ARIZONA CARDINALS...AND BUDDY TOO!

Bill Bidwill is a twit. A pompous, bow-tie-wearing twit. (Imagine someone wearing a bow-tie in the middle of string-tie country...someone quick, call the fashion police!) Bidwill really yo-yoed ex-head coach Joe Bugel and, frankly, really demonstrated his shortcomings as an owner by canning the enthusiastic Bugel for the ever-caustic Buddy (Just who's buddy is he?) Ryan.

Unless you were residing in Biosphere II (or perhaps the Bidwill residence) you should be hip to the fact that Buddy Ryan is a walking time bomb and shouldn't be allowed around sharp objects or sharp people. I mean, throwing a roundhouse in the direction of *your own team's* offensive coordinator is not exactly a chapter out of a Leo Buscaglia book on hugging, loving, and just wanting to buy the world a Coke. You get the feeling that Buddy is not the kind of guy who would ever break into a verse of "We Are The World."

So why would Billy Bidwill hire Buddy? Has he turned in his bow-tie for a beanie with a propeller on top? Who will be Buddy's assistant coaches, Hannibal Lector and the happy-go-lucky Dr. Kevorkian?

I want to see hot-headed Gary Clark's reaction to Buddy's defensive backs nipping at Clark's annually sore hamstrings with hammerhead tackles during practice.

Well, no longer is it only the city of Phoenix that will suffer the embarassment of Bidwill's doofus strategies--now the entire state gets involved. Bidwill's latest dullard move is renaming the team the ARIZONA CARDINALS.

I guess this helps the paranoid Bidwill by cutting off any future NFL team moves to anywhere in Arizona. I guess this would grind to a halt any secretive desires from, say, Al Davis (who seems to have changed his motto from "Just *win*, Baby" to

"Just *move*, Baby"), and keep him from taking his team to Tempe, Mesa, or better yet...Tombstone.

Bidwill's the kind of guy who makes the other owners want to sign *his* room number to their pool bar bills. Can he really be as much of a sap as he appears by hiring the volatile Buddy Ryan? Is he that out of touch? Or maybe this Bidwill bozo is sharper than I'm giving him credit for. Maybe he has had enough, and now *the nerd* is going to get *his revenge* by sending his prized, vicious pit bull of a head coach to wreak havoc on the rest of the elitist NFL. Hmmm...*The Revenge Of The Nerds (part IV)*?

TWO-POINT CONVERSIONS

The NFL has decided to take a risk and add the TWO-POINT CONVERSION to the scoring possibilities for 1994. Already, coaches are talking about their disdain for such a madcap scoring (and coaching) nightmare.

Personally, I think the two-pointer is a great idea which should liven up the game a bit. Sure, no team is going to abandon its penchant for kicking extra points, but I can see it being utilized nonetheless. Picture this: a team is trailing 14-6 with 30 seconds remaining until halftime. The trailing team scores a TD to cut the score to 14-12. Instead of opting for the extra point, perhaps we see the two-pointer and a 14-14 score. Or another scenario goes like this: the game is in the fourth quarter with Buffalo leading Miami 20-9. Miami scores a TD with four minutes remaining, thus making the score 20-15. Miami coach Don Shula decides to go for the two-pointer. Miami is successful, and now the score is 20-17. Shula now can play for the tie and send the game into overtime. Last season the score would have been 20-16, and the Dolphins would have been forced to score another TD.

The real benfit of the two-pointer is that it gives fantasy players *another* potential scoring bonus. I mean, who is going to stop Emmitt Smith around the goal line? Emmitt's potential to be on the receiving end of this two-pointer benefit is obvious. The two-pointer will be a welcome addition to the NFL and the FFL.

DRAFTING PLAYERS FOR THE STRETCH RUN

When drafting players for your FFL team, the best move is to select players on teams projected to make the playoff run. Drafting Indianapolis Colts and Cincinnati Bengals usually won't help your team in the stretch run. Players from solid offensive powerhouses in the running for playoff spots are the guys you want on your franchise.

When I draft a kicker, I want one who will be called on to boot 50-yarders in December, when the stretch run to the playoffs is in effect.

IS THERE A DOCTOR IN THE HOUSE? THE INJURY FACTOR

It is sometimes difficult to read between the lines when NFL teams give injury reports on players. During the season, NFL teams must submit injury status reports on *all* players. Unfortunately, these reports are quite tainted. Coaches attempt to smokescreen the seriousness of certain players' injuries by listing a player as "questionable." In NFL circles, "questionable" means a player has a 50-50 chance of playing. It's funny, though, just how many "questionable" players *never* play for weeks. Then the players listed as "doubtful" (which means there is only a 30% chance of playing), suddenly and *very miraculously* get healed, and hallelujah...they play!

It also is decidedly difficult to figure out the health status of players who were seriously injured during the 1993 season. Right now, reports from teams with injured players such as Randall Cunningham (PHI), Fred Barnett (PHI), Terry Allen

(MIN), Vaughn Dunbar (NO), Lorenzo Neal (NO), Dan Marino (MIA) and Garrison Hearst (AZ) list them as recovered--but are they really? I have heard reports that there is concern over Hearst being capable of playing in '94. So you tell me, who's zooming who?

So, for this exhibition season, keep an eye on the latest status reports for players like Hearst, Cunningham, Barnett, Allen, Dunbar and Neal. It is crucial to be assured that these players are fully back and not suffering any lingering injury effects. If reports seem dubious, don't draft them, or at least don't draft them early-- you'll only be wasting draft choices and quite possibly your season.

OFF-SEASON BIG-BUCK FREE AGENT PICKUPS

One of the more embarrassing problems you'll encounter when drafting is, frankly, trying to figure out just which teams certain players ended up signing with during the off-season. I consider following these signings as another key to developing a winning fantasy franchise. First, if a team is willing to spend the bucks on a player, then it naturally leads one to believe that this player will play an integral role in the team's 1994 plans.

Forget the old team philosophy of building for the future-- today, it's the aggressive teams' chance to reload (provided of course they have room under the cap). It also helps teams that are decimated by injuries, have aging vets, or lousy draft selections (sounds like the FFL's Supplemental Draft).

The big key here is to *estimate* just what kind of effect a player will have on his new team. For example, Anthony Miller is a bullet of a receiver. His new team is Denver, which means he will be on the receiving end of Howitzer-armed John Elway. In my humble opinion, this season we will be watching many replays of Elway-to-Miller TD bombs. Therefore, the signing of Miller was a huge move, one sure to be picked up on by an observant FFL owner.

Now Michael Haynes, another fleet-of-foot receiver, left the fast track of Atlanta (and new Falcon QB Jeff George) to sign with the hardly-offensive New Orleans Saints. Maybe Haynes simply prefers cajun cooking, but can he handle playing with a team that thinks defense first and offense second? Or will Haynes' escaping the huge shadow of Andre Rison inspire him to want to be "the main target?" Hmmm, we'll see in '94.

1994 KEY PLAYER FREE AGENT MOVES

PLAYER	POS	NEW TEAM	OLD TEAM
Jim Everett	QB	New Orleans	L.A. Rams
Michael Haynes	WR	New Orleans	Atlanta
Merril Hoge	RB	Chicago	Pittsburgh
Ethan Horton	TE	Washington	L.A. Raiders
Vance Johnson	WR	San Diego	Denver
Erik Kramer	QB	Chicago	Detroit
Anthony Miller	WR	Denver	San Diego
Chris Miller	QB	L.A. Rams	Atlanta
Scott Mitchell	QB	Detroit	Miami
Eddie Murray	K	Philadelphia	Dallas
Blair Thomas	RB	New England	N.Y. Jets
Lewis Tillman	RB	Chicago	N.Y. Giants
Michael Pritchard	WR	Denver	Atlanta

OTHER PLAYER MOVES (Listed Alphabetically)

PLAYER	POS	NEW TEAM	OLD TEAM
Gene Atkins	S	Miami	New Orleans
Howard Ballard	OT	Seattle	Buffalo
Darrick Brilz	G	Cincinnati	Seattle
Jeff Carlson	QB	Denver	N.Y. Giants

25

PLAYER	POS	NEW TEAM	OLD TEAM
Tony Casillas	DT	Kansas City	Dallas
Ray Crockett	CB	Denver	Detroit
Rueben Davis	DE	San Diego	Arizona
Steve DeOssie	LB	New England	N.Y. Jets
Donald Evans	DE	N.Y. Jets	Pittsburgh
Jeff Feagles	P	Arizona	Philadelphia
William Fuller	DE	Philadelphia	Houston
John Gesek	C	Washington	Dallas
Dennis Gibson	LB	San Diego	Detroit
David Griggs	LB	San Diego	Miami
Myron Guyton	S	New England	N.Y. Giants
Ron Hall	TE	Detroit	Tampa Bay
Dwayne Harper	CB	San Diego	Seattle
Ken Harvey	LB	Washington	Arizona
Andy Heck	OL	Chicago	Seattle
Chris Hinton	OT	Minnesota	Atlanta
D.J. Johnson	CB	Atlanta	Pittsburgh
Jimmie Jones	DT	L.A. Rams	Dallas
Randy Kirk	LB	Arizona	Cincinnati
Bob Kratch	G	New England	N.Y. Giants
Lonnie Marts	LB	Tampa Bay	Kansas City
Robert Massey	CB	Detroit	Arizona
Tim McGee	WR	Cincinnati	Washington
Eric Moore	OL	Cincinnati	N.Y. Giants
Nate Odomes	CB	Seattle	Buffalo
Louis Oliver	S	Cincinnati	Miami
Gary Plummer	LB	San Francisco	San Diego
Walter Reeves	TE	Cleveland	Arizona
Kevin Ross	DB	Atlanta	Kansas City
Ray Seals	DE	Pittsburgh	Tampa Bay
Clyde Simmons	DE	Arizona	Philadelphia
Lance Smith	G	N.Y. Giants	Arizona
Michael Stewart	SS	Miami	L.A. Rams
Pat Terrell	S	N.Y. Jets	L.A. Rams

PLAYER	POS	NEW TEAM	OLD TEAM
Tony Woods	DE	Washington	L.A. Rams
Mike Withycombe	G	Cleveland	San Diego
Mike Zandofsky	G	Atlanta	San Diego

STAYING AT HOME (KEY PLAYERS WHO RE-SIGNED)

PLAYER	POS	TEAM
Bubby Brister	QB	Philadelphia
Tim Brown	WR	L.A. Raiders
Larry Centers	RB	Arizona
Ben Coates	TE	New England
Maurice Johnson	TE	Philadelphia
Brian Kinchen	TE	Cleveland
Harper LeBel	TE	Atlanta
Brett Perriman	WR	Detroit
Reggie Rembert	WR	Cincinnati
Matt Stover	K	Cleveland
Pete Stoyanovich	K	Miami
Scott Zolak	QB	New England

KEEP AN EYE ON PLAYERS ON A TEAM WITH A NEW HEAD COACH

OK, this part is up to you: *You* must keep up with the philosophies of new coaches Barry Switzer (DAL), Pete Carroll (NYJ), Buddy Ryan (AZ), June Jones (ATL), and Norv Turner (WAS). What is the mood? Are these teams going to challenge now, or rebuild for the future?

DALLAS COWBOYS

In case you missed my earlier diatribe on the subject, Barry Switzer now has taken over the Cowboys. Please don't buy all that nonsense that the 'Pokes are headed for the cellar. Listen, this is a quality team built by the J.J.s and will continue to roll into the 1994 season. Sure, Michael Irvin has voiced his opinion, and Irvin has a right to be concerned, being faced with Switzer and his love of the wishbone offense, but this is just Michael's way of letting his *new boss* know that he wants the ball. Switzer is crude, but not stupid--he'll still get Emmitt and Michael the ball and win a ton of games. Switzer will probably set scoring records in Dallas. With Ernie Zampese now the offensive coordinator, expect Aikman to spread the ball around and toss a career-high TD amount. My tip: don't shy away from the boys from Dallas!

NEW YORK JETS

Pete Carroll has been close to getting several NFL head coaching jobs over the past few years. He has always been known as a sharp defensive mind, so the real question is whether he can juice up the offense? Boomer did everything he could, but with players like Rob Moore and Johnny Mitchell coming up with nagging injuries, the "O" in the offense stood for "Oh No!"

I feel that the Jets primarily will still be a defensive team attempting to control the ball on offense. Expect a short passing game, and a "ground chuck"-type of running game with Johnny Johnson and Adrian Murrell. Expect a lot of 13-10, 17-13-type games. Don't look towards the Jets for those Barry ("I'll Bury Ya") Switzer-type of scoring bursts.

28

ATLANTA FALCONS

I never thought I would *ever, ever* make a statement like this: For some strangely confused reason, I am going to miss Jerry "Coupe De" Glanville--he was a fun guy! Unfortunately, it seems that Jerry is the type of coach who is good enough to build a team capable of making the playoffs, but just can't quite get *into* the playoffs to prove his team's talent. Today, the NFL is all about playoffs and money. Jerry simply ran out of time and the owners' patience.

So now enter June Jones, the Falcons' former offensive coordinator. Jones is one of the more creative minds in the NFL, and he *should* be able to take Atlanta into the playoffs. Jones toiled in Atlanta for many years as a backup QB, and later he worked his way up through the coaching staff. He has paid his dues and he has the inside knowledge and understanding of the complete Falcon team and management.

Jones also will have a super talent in Jeff George to head up his offense. If George grows up and stays healthy, he will be one of the NFL's finest quarterbacks for 1994. I expect to see George throwing deep and often to Andre Rison and maybe even Deion Sanders! This will be a very good club with the scoring potential matched by very few NFL opponents. Expect Coach of the Year accolades for June Jones.

WASHINGTON REDSKINS

Last season was a debacle for the Washington team and fans. Richie Petitbon really didn't have much of a chance, nor much of a team. A year later, ex-Dallas offensive-guru/phenom Norv Turner steps into the Capital City's hot spotlight. Turner has already made several decisions that have the look of a housecleaning sweep. With the exception of keeping LB Monte

Coleman around, it seems as if the Washington minds have decided to cut loose the vets and rebuild.

Expect Turner to simplify the Redskins' offense. (Hey, if you think about Dallas, it's mostly hand-offs and a couple of quick passes to the wideouts.) Expect more Reggie. *Much* more Reggie. Reggie Brooks was all set to be drafted by the Cowboys in 1993, but Washington nipped the pick just before Dallas. Turner will use Brooks *à la* Emmitt. The big question in Washington is who will be the quarterback? Mark Rypien has been let go, and the Redskins have signed former San Diego Charger John Friesz for a third of Ryp's $3 million salary. Although critics nailed Ryp pretty hard, it is important to remember that he played injured the entire season. He is a gutsy guy. Ryp lacks footspeed, but not courage--he could've been *the* key to Washington's offense in '94. He can still play, and will make a good backup for Vinnie Testaverde in Cleveland, where he signed in late April. So with Ryp gone, does first-round draft choice Shuler get the start, the way Bledsoe and Mirer did last year, or do they nurture their golden boy, and put Friesz in the lion's den? Good question, for in May, Turner announced he full well plans on starting Shuler in the Skins' opening game. Keep your eye on this QB battle...should be fierce!

ARIZONA CARDINALS

With Buddy Ryan and Barry Switzer in the same conference, you can expect all kinds of houliganism and bad attitudes displayed by these two. At least the media will get some great quotes and sound bites from these "terrible two."

Mark this down: Buddy will have a fierce-hitting defense that will be a major headache for teams to play this year. Also (keep marking...) *never ever* expect to see the Cards in the Run-and-Shoot offense. Expect a controlled offense that will get a lot of cheap scores due to Buddy's defense knocking the "how-do-ya-do" out of the opposition.

Steve Beuerlein should find comfort in wide receivers Gary Clark, Randal Hill and Ricky Proehl--this will be their second season together. Expect Garrison Hearst (if he's healthy) and Ron Moore to chew up a lot of yardage. Buddy hasn't inherited a sissy team of bozos--the Cards are a good team, soon to be better.

OFFENSIVE SCHEMES

This concept almost always gets overlooked. Why? The better draft wizards in fantasy football have the ability to select players who perform on teams that treat the offense like it is a *WEAPON*. I'm personally excited (...whoa, big fella...) over the prospects of John Elway and Denver dope-slapping the league again with some great offensive football. Elway should be throwing deep to Anthony Miller, Derek Russell, Mike Pritchard and the good-anywhere Shannon Sharpe.

Then there is the aforementioned Atlanta Falcons' squad with the nutty Jeff George and that cannon of an arm. As good as Elway-to-Miller will be this season, so will the George-to-Rison combo be electrifying. Both of these offenses will be among the league leaders in the point parade--followed by the 49ers, Cowboys and the Dolphins.

HELP...I WON MY LEAGUE...AND NOW I PICK LAST!

Never confuse winning your league championship with being popular--they are *never* the same. Oh sure, everyone puts on a good face and genuinely acts the role of the congratulating schleppers that they are. But let's wake up and smell the FFL lottery picks--you don't have one. In fact, if your league is like most, you get the dubious honor of selecting the last pick of the first round.

Now the good side is that you may also get the first selection of the second round. So, you definitely want to be prepared and have a strategy when making that double pick. To me, this is exciting, but you don't want to botch it up, since you won't see another pick for quite a while (the last pick in the third round.) The tip here is to think double(s) and prepare for the turnaround pick.

One tip for drafting anywhere in the draft is to make a mock draft. This will help you be prepared (and not surprised) when it's your turn to draft. One thing that always amazes me is how people can be stunned at their draft turns and take an eternity to make a selection in the third or fourth round. A *smart* franchise will be prepared, have three or four names ready each time they pick, and draft the top name available.

My last tip for you *numero uno* folks: don't come to the draft with a big head. You can forget receiving any sympathy for picking last. And don't ask anyone for lunch money--everyone knows you cleaned up in '93!

YO SATCHMO, I'M A NOVICE BUT I DON'T WANT TO GET SMEARED!!!

No need to develop an attitude and get all grouchy with me. OK, so you've never played this game before--no big deal (unless you play with the swarthy, deceitful, evil bunch of tyrants that I play with). First of all, you're doing the right thing by reading this book (a book report is optional for extra credit). Secondly, keep up with the exhibition season and know who has suffered a serious season-ending injury.

Now I know that sounds obvious, but basically this is how the game works. You don't need to be a ten-year fantasy veteran in order to win a league championship. You do need to be prepared, draft intelligently, and most of all, *be lucky*!

Yes my green, novice friends, despite the ultra-wise airs that league winners attempt to put on, the underlying goal is to keep away from injuries (to you and your key players) and be luckier than the rest of your league mates.

So for all of you new to fantasy football, good luck and remember to be prepared, draft intelligently, and enjoy the season. Remember, the point is to have fun.

BEWARE THE *RIPPLE EFFECT*

This is one of the most frightening events that occurs during a fantasy draft. The draft is in the second round and suddenly one of your competing franchise owners shouts out, *"I'll select Jason Elam...kicker for Denver."* These words seem to freeze in time, when suddenly the next franchise owner excitedly yells, *"We take Pete Stoyanovich, kicker for Miami."* The *Ripple Effect* is now "in the house."

Expect panic and mayhem as franchise after franchise begin hurling the names of all the top field goal kickers *way too early* in the draft. Kickers are key to your franchise, but you shouldn't go berserk and draft this kind of player in the second or third round of your draft.

The tip here is to prepare a draft plan--and stick to that plan! Don't let the flow or the *ripple* of the other drafting franchises affect your own draft plan.

SURVIVING PRESEASON FITS OF FREE AGENCY

Let's see if I've got this right: in 1993 Wade Wilson goes from the Falcons to the Saints, and this year he gets released. Bobby Hebert in '93 goes from the Saints to the Falcons and this year...he gets released, then ends up re-signing with the Falcons. This season, Chris Miller goes from the Falcons and ends up in LA LA Land. Jim Everett leaves L.A. and lands in the Saints marching band. Really now, wouldn't trading be an easier method?

By the way, do you think that Jim Rome of ESPN Sports (you know him, he's the guy who got roughed up by Jim Everett for calling him *Chris Evert)* will ever call Chris Miller...*Jim*?

Anyway, with free agency now so rampant, what does one do? Simple, keep track of the player moves (I've listed them earlier in this book) and assume that the newly signed free agents will be playing pivotal roles on their *new* teams. (After all, why else would they have signed them? Duh!)

Free agency has become the musical chairs of the NFL. In order to stay under the new salary cap, many veterans are now finding themselves looking for jobs, or accepting pay cuts. It is sad to watch an Art Monk (a 14-year veteran) leave the Redskins and perhaps break Steve Largent's all-time receiving mark in a city other than Washington.

Warren Moon left the CFL to become an all-pro in Houston. Now Moon is on his way to Minnesota, and, as Joe Montana did to KC in '93, will attempt to pump life in the offense of a team gearing for a playoff run.

Up until a few years ago, future Hall-of-Famers like Joe Montana, Art Monk and Warren Moon would have ended their careers in San Francisco, Washington, and Houston, respectively. With the new union contracts and the league-enforced salary caps, loyalty will soon go the way of the Dodo bird and become extremely extinct.

THE TIMELESS ONES

As I wrote last year, "with the impact of free agency, in a year we probably will not find older players still abundant in the

NFL." Well, this is a fact for this season. Instead of veteran players playing their final seasons (and making big bucks) in the sun of their home cities, they now find themselves out in the cold. I still believe that many veteran players soon will be forced to accept a major decrease in pay. Face it, an offensive lineman who hits the age of 33 may find himself accepting a contract at half of what he made the year before. And many will accept the pay cut, simply because in what other profession would they be making $200,000-$300,000 per season?

Who will be paying a veteran QB a million dollars a year to ride the bench? Forget it. The league will get younger, the vets will be phased out, and loyalty will be a lost thought...on both sides.

Still, allow me the opportunity to salute the handful of veterans who, despite their advancing years, dwindling paychecks, and aches and pains, still perform a cut above the rest and keep one step ahead of the greedy NFL *Grim Reaper*.

PLAYER	POS	TEAM	AGE
Steve DeBerg	QB	Free Agent	40
Joe Montana	QB	Kansas City	39
Vince Evans	QB	L.A. Raiders	39
Warren Moon	QB	Minnesota	38
Phil Simms	QB	N.Y. Giants	38
Eddie Murray	K	Philadelphia	38
Clay Matthews	LB	Cleveland	38
Matt Bahr	K	New England	38
Drew Hill	WR	Atlanta	38
James Lofton	WR	L.A. Rams	38
Art Monk	WR	N.Y. Jets	37
Nick Lowery	K	Kansas City	37
Monte Coleman	LB	Washington	36

★4★

Team-by-Team Reviews

If you've been sleeping through the first few chapters, well, you'd better pay attention here, because this section is packed with team-by-team reviews submitted by some of the most brilliant minds in the world of sports. (I say this because the pay I get them is peanuts!) Seriously, I am honored to have Larry Michael (Mutual Radio), Larry Weisman (USA Today), and John Weiss and Dave Douglas (NFL Films) give their perspectives on the NFL teams. In my opinion, these gentlemen are on the cutting edge of excellence in their fields.

Larry Michael has great football knowledge and *the voice* born for play-by-play. Larry Weisman's accurate written perspective on the NFL is always on the mark, and interesting to boot. And John Weiss and Dave Douglas's work with NFL Films is chock-full of solid subjects and some of the best commentary, shots and profiles around. In fact, Dave was responsible for NFL Films' first coverage of Fantasy Football!

I am honored to have their opinions as part of this year's *Journal*.

DRAFTING HEAD COACHES

One fun part added to the *FFL Journal* last season was an idea presented by *you, the reader*. (See...I really *do* listen, gang!) People had written in to suggest including head coaches as part of their leagues. This little addition added even more fun and helped tweak the game. Obviously, you don't want to draft a head coach who appears headed for the gallows--so even if this pick won't turn your season around, it could help out and allow you to squeak out a weekly victory in a close head-to-head game.

COACH	TEAM	PROJECTED '94 WINS	INSIDE SKINNY
George Seifert	SF	12	How many more years for Young, Rice and Watters?
Barry Switzer	DAL	12	Emmitt is still the best. Troy and Michael will lead.
Wade Phillips	DEN	12	Great offseason moves and Elway is due for a Super Bowl.
Mike Holmgren	GB	11	Played the same hand as Denver--Solid team.
Don Shula	MIA	11	Don and Dan can't wait for another year-- the time is now! `
Marty Schottenheimer	KC	10	Marty's season falls on Joe's shoulders.

COACH	TEAM	PROJECTED '94 WINS	INSIDE SKINNY
Marv Levy	BUF	10	Buffalo can never be ruled out, but health will be a concern.
June Jones	ATL	10	Strong defense and lots of "O," this team is a powerhouse.
Wayne Fontes	DET	10	Finally a solid offense besides just Barry Sanders.
Jack Pardee	HOU	9	He'll miss Warren Moon and, yes, Buddy Ryan too.
Bill Belichick	CLE	9	Strong defense, solid WRs and RBs--It's all up to Vinnie T.
Dennis Green	MIN	9	Warren Moon and some great "D" will pump life into the Vikes.
Buddy Ryan	AZ	9	Like him or not, he can whip a team up into a frenzy.
Bill Cowher	PIT	8	If someone stumbles, the Steelers have the might.
Art Shell	RAI	8	A real running game will go well with those speedy WRs.

COACH	TEAM	PROJECTED '94 WINS	INSIDE SKINNY
Bill Parcells	NE	8	Steadily improving--solid, but still a year away.
Dave Wannstedt	CHI	7	Erik Kramer will lend a steady hand, but the Bears are still rebuilding.
Dan Reeves	NYG	6	Just not enough offseason moves to shake loose in '94.
Norv Turner	WAS	6	Six wins would be a major move for this rebuilding team.
Tom Flores	SEA	6	Too much Denver and LA Raiders; these guys are another year away.
Bobby Ross	SD	6	Team will miss Butts, Miller and Lewis, but watch Means.
Chuck Knox	RAM	6	Nice draft; rebuilding, but they will rock with Bettis.
Sam Wyche	TB	5	Good offseason moves and a nice draft--I think Wyche could surprise.
Jim Mora	NO	5	If Jim Everett gels and if RBs can remain healthy...too many ifs.

COACH	TEAM	PROJECTED '94 WINS	INSIDE SKINNY
Pete Carroll	NYJ	5	Will be feisty, but in his first year, Jets will come up short.
Rich Kotite	PHI	5	Randall is the key--this team has lost just way too many players.
David Shula	CIN	5	Young Shula is building a competitive team--this team is no doormat.
Teddy Marchibroda	IND	4	I am not knocking the Colts--they'll be tough but still lose.

PROGNOSTICATIONS
Or...
"Just a Super Bowl Guess"

Just in case you were in a curious mood and asked nicely, "Excuse me, Geebs," (although my last name is Giebel, you also take it upon yourself to make us buds, and refer to me as Geebs), "according to your twisted little mind, who will win the Super Bowl?"

I always enjoy the opportunity to expound on who I think will win the Super Bowl. Now if I really and truly knew the outcome, I would be appearing on stage as *Psychic Houdini Giebel* and would be a weekly guest on the *David Letterman Show* or the *Tonight Show with Jay Leno*. Frankly, prognostications are actually just knowledgeable guesses. But what the heck, let's play the role of psychic and get on with my viewpoints and picks.

First of all, I would respond with the indirect pratter of "any team could win...blah...blah...blah." Then I would nod slightly (as if some divine insight suddenly intervened) and in a Zen-like controlled voice...I'd chant, "DALLAS...Dallas...dallas..."

Oh sure, they lost the best grass-floor general in football (Jimmy Johnson). Oh sure, they are now coached by Barry "Pile It on by 60 Points" Switzer. But hey, they *still* have Troy, Emmitt and Michael. And hiring Switzer isn't like Jerry Jones suddenly hired Dr. Kevorkian....

Of course, the season won't be a complete rollover; the San Francisco 49ers are still bobbing and will give the Cowpokes a real run. Everyone else in the NFC will once again be playing wild-card-level football. My surprise NFC challenger will be the Atlanta Falcons. QB Jeff George has a fast track and faster receivers, plus a running back who can gain some yards in Erric Pegram.

In the AFC, Denver is the team. *Period.* John Elway to Anthony Miller is a sure thing! Kansas City will once again prop up Joe Montana, who is becoming the Frank Sinatra of football. Joe can win, but can Joe survive? I can hear Joe mouthing the Sinatra line, "Will someone please get me a chair?"! Also, how many more yards and carries does Marcus Allen really have left in his legs?

Everyone has Jimmy Johnson looking over Don Shula's shoulder and primed to replace *The Don* after this season. I look for Don and Dan to make a real run for the AFC championship.

Buffalo once again will be cursed by the fans and the media if they come anywhere near a Super Bowl challenge, but I say, "Tough!" Quit griping about the Bills--everyone in the AFC has had the opportunity to dislodge 'em, Gener, yet no one has. Cleveland will make noise, but how serious can they be with Vinnie tossing the ball?

So without beating around the goal post, I look for a Dallas/San Francisco NFC championship game and a Denver/Miami AFC championship, with a Super Bowl contest of Dallas versus Denver. And the winner: Denver!

★☆★☆ARIZONA CARDINALS★☆★☆

by Larry Weisman
Sports Columnist
USA TODAY

Forget yesterday. The Arizona Cardinals may well be the team of today. New name, new coach (Buddy Ryan), new attitude (Ryan's). New approach.

Ryan, who spent last season as Houston's defensive coordinator and seemed on his way to oblivion after smacking another coach on the sidelines during a game, once again has landed upright. Cardinals owner Bill Bidwill first had demanded Joe Bugel produce a winning record or lose his job, then rescinded that ultimatum, but fired Bugel anyway.

Bidwill, at this advanced stage of the game, seems ready to commit to winning. The Cardinals haven't finished over .500 since 1984, haven't made the playoffs since 1982, last won the division in '75. They were suffering from drought long before moving to the desert in 1988.

With Ryan, change will come. The Cardinals lost their best pass-rusher, OLB Ken Harvey, as a free agent to Washington, but brought two other Ryan protégés, DE Clyde Simmons and LB Seth Joyner from Philadelphia. The Cards spent heavily to re-sign MLB Eric Hill and clearly plan to win with defense under Ryan, the man who put the "pug" in pugnacious.

QUARTERBACK

Steve Beuerlein put up decent numbers for the fantasy player but did less well in real life, which hurt Bugel. He had a shaky start in the opening day loss to Philadelphia, but really played

42

much better down the stretch when the Cardinals seemed convinced they could save Bugel from Bidwill.

Beuerlein threw a good number of short TD passes (6 in the 1-to-9 yard range) because the Cardinals didn't discover their running game until Garrison Hearst vanished and Ron Moore emerged. He's not likely to throw as often near the goal line, but Ryan has always liked a go-for-broke attitude and there's speed on the wings. Beuerlein could be a good sleeper pick as an FFL starter.

Backing Beuerlein last year was Chris Chandler, who was distinctly mediocre. He shopped himself as a free agent and has picked up a little interest from the New York Jets but was unsigned at press time. This is a need the Cardinals must fill, best with an experienced hand.

RUNNING BACK

Ryan wasted no time going nuclear on Hearst, the damaged second-year back. Ryan likes his players working out under his watchful eye and living nearby, but Hearst, recovering from knee surgery, wintered in Georgia. Bad idea.

Ryan hoped to trade Hearst, whose work ethic didn't meet the coach's standards, and stick with Ron Moore. That's a mixed blessing for fantasy GMs.

Moore rushed for 1,018 yards but his long run was 20 yards and 6 of his 9 rushing TDs were in the 1-to-9 yard area. He caught no TD passes and generally will give way to Larry Centers in passing situations. Moore only caught 3 balls while rushing 263 times.

Centers, the team leader in receptions with 66, scored no rushing TDs and three via the air, none very long. If Centers and Moore could be combined, they'd be a great pick. Separately, neither figures to break fantasy league records.

The Cards will take a healthy look at Chuck Levy, their number two pick, in this spot, but he has the look of a third-down back.

WIDE RECEIVER

The Cardinals possess great speed on the flanks. Perhaps they'll put it to better use this season.

Gary Clark came on after a slow start but shook free for only four TDs and could wind up as the third WR behind Ricky Proehl and Randal Hill. Proehl seems on the verge of becoming a real game-breaker. He had seven TD catches last year, with a long of 51, and gets great separation. Hill's pure speed makes him a threat, too, but he's always been erratic.

The Cards are thin at TE. Butch Rolle will be back but he has lost the goal line touch he had years ago with Buffalo when he caught 10 consecutive passes for TDs (spaced over several years). The Cards didn't throw much in that direction, and the other TE, Walter Reeves, went to Cleveland as a free agent.

When Ryan coached Philadelphia he had Keith Jackson at TE. Don't be surprised if the Cardinals pursue one via free agency or the draft and make use of him.

DEFENSE/SPECIAL TEAMS

Given Ryan's track record, be bold. Grab the Cards' defense early. Ryan stresses turnovers, always has and always will. He encourages the defense to take the ball away and run with it, to try to score and put a hurtin' on the enemy's offense. With a head-hunter S like Chuck Cecil, Simmons at DE, Seth Joyner at LB, and a collection of other young and aggressive D-linemen, Buddy Ball is here.

Philadelphia's special teams were never known for kick blocking. Johnny Bailey is a decent kick and punt returner who had one TD from a punt return last season.

The strength of this pick is that Ryan's defenses always key on turnovers and score on the offense. He hasn't failed before, and he won't here.

KICKER

Greg Davis had a weird year. He was eleventh among FFL kickers in scoring but he could have been way up the charts.

Davis made 4 of his 5 tries from 50 yards or beyond, but was only 4 of 10 from 40-49. Under 39 yards he was 13-13. If that sort of inconsistency doesn't drive you bats, take Davis. He'll be working with a better offense and better field position, and if he misses with any frequency, Buddy will fire him.

★☆★☆ATLANTA FALCONS★☆★☆

by Larry Michael
NFL Play-by Play Announcer
Mutual Radio Network

New head coach June Jones will stick with the four-receiver offense, otherwise known as the "RED GUN." This is a critical year in the offensive set, and first-year coach Jones will look for leadership from former Indianapolis quarterback Jeff George. Free agency has cost the Falcons one of the best deep threats in football, Michael Haynes, but the Falcons' offense still promises to be exciting. A big question mark for the team is the status of Deion Sanders. In this era of the salary cap, can the Falcons afford the $3 million luxury of one of the league's most electrifying players?

QUARTERBACK

Jeff George is looking for a fresh start at the Georgia Dome. His leadership abilities, his commitment and his toughness have all been questioned; the only thing that *hasn't* been questioned is his throwing ability. Bobby Hebert is back after taking a pay cut, and he also brings back some lofty numbers from last season: 2,978 yards passing and a career-high 24 touchdowns. The third-teamer here is Billy Joe Tolliver. Overall, the quarterback position should not be a problem for the Falcons.

RUNNING BACK

Erric Pegram enters his fourth year in the NFL as one of the league's bright young running backs. In '92 he gained 89 yards with no rushing touchdowns, but last year he exploded for over 1,000 yards. He hopes to do it again in 1994, and also hopes to get into the end zone more than his three visits of last year. Second-year man Tony Smith is the first back off the bench. A cast of dozens will be auditioning in training camp for a chance to make the roster of a team which again will use the passing game as the basis for the offense.

WIDE RECEIVER

Major changes are in store for what might have been the deepest crew of top-notch receivers in the NFL. Long-ball receiver Michael Haynes has moved to New Orleans. Restricted free agent Mike Pritchard has headed *way* west to the Denver Broncos. Andre Rison is a consistent FFL superstar. Though sometimes unpredictable off the field, on the gridiron there isn't a tougher receiver to guard in the NFL than "Bad Moon" Rison. In the last four years, Rison has scored an amazing 48 touchdowns!

The Birds have also signed Ricky Sanders away from Washington, where he scored four touchdowns with 601 yards receiving. However, Sanders failed his minicamp physical due to a rotator cuff problem, but he is expected to make the team. It should be fun to watch him in tandem with Rison. Even with Sanders and the steady Rison, depth is still a big problem at wide receiver, with the Falcons using four at a time. The draft and at least one other free agent signing look to be answers to that problem. When a tight end is used, third-year man Mitch Lyons will be in the lineup.

DEFENSE/SPECIAL TEAMS

In past years, if you were in an FFL league that used individual players on defense, the top pick on the "D" side was Deion Sanders. This year, though, the Falcons are in a quandary. Do they bring the thrilling Sanders back at big-time bucks, or do they take the money and put it to use elsewhere? The Atlanta Braves started the baseball season in fine fashion, and with Deion the starter in center field, he most likely won't hit a football field until late October. The smart money is on Deion taking a pay cut to play football in 1994; the team he will play for is, as of this writing, a big question mark. Tony Smith is a good return man, but he is no Deion Sanders.

KICKER

Norm Johnson is back after a good year in which he scored 140 FFL points. Always a good dome kicker, Johnson seems to have new life at the Georgia Dome. When looking for kickers, Norm Johnson is a pretty wise pick.

★☆★☆BUFFALO BILLS★☆★☆

by Larry Weisman
Sports Columnist
USA TODAY

Four times the Buffalo Bills went to the well and four times they failed to drink from that championship cup.

No NFL team had ever made it to the Super Bowl four years running, a feat monumental. And the few that had managed to lose four Super Bowls (Minnesota and Denver) at least had the good taste to spread those debacles over a couple of decades.

And so at last, Buffalo's run seems over. The team that stayed together despite its infighting finally came undone in the face of the salary cap, the aging of its mainstays, and the need to begin retooling.

Gone from the offensive line are ancient guard Jim Ritcher and promising tackle Howard Ballard, the former released and the latter lost to Seattle via free agency. Gone from the secondary: cornerbacks Nate Odomes, James Williams, Kirby Jackson, and safety Mark Kelso.

Another player rumored to be on his way out was running back Thurman Thomas, the mercurial star with three straight horrendous showings in the Super Bowl dogging him. Trade talk surrounded him in the offseason but he seems to have weathered it.

Can this aging, physically and mentally battered club make a fifth (and distinctly unwelcome) journey to the Super Bowl? Don't count on it. This party's over.

QUARTERBACK

Jim Kelly, at 35 and with creaky knees, can't get out of the pocket anymore and figures to have the worst protection of his career in Buffalo. He ranked eighth among QBs in FFL scoring, primarily on the strength of mid-range passing. His TD production slipped to 18 last year from 24 in 1992 and will slide further this year as the AFC East improves and the Bills decline.

Backup Frank Reich seems to play better coming off the bench and shows little interest in being a starter. He's capable if Kelly goes down but hasn't ever had to carry the team for a lengthy stretch. He's at his best when the Bills play a more conventional set and tempo than their quick-paced, three-wide-receiver game.

Depth behind these two amounts to journeyman Gale Gilbert, who is only on display during the preseason.

RUNNING BACK

Thurman Thomas, once so productive and explosive, scored six short rushing TDs in 1993 and did not catch a TD pass. Consider that fair warning. His TD total was half of the year before when he did serious damage in the 10-39 yard range.

Six heavy-duty seasons, complete with playoff slate, have worn Thomas down. Not that he'll never be any good again, but this could be the year that wear and tear catches up with him.

If you buy that scenario, think about spending a middle-round pick on Kenneth Davis. He's got better outside speed than Thomas, could wrest more playing time from Thomas, and also scored six rushing TDs last season, while having about one-third as many rushing attempts as Thomas. Davis is the goal-line go-to guy.

The Bills don't feed it much to Carwell Gardner and may look for depth here via free agency or in the draft.

50

WIDE RECEIVER

Gauge the problems in this area by the team's leading receiver--lead-footed TE Pete Metzelaars. Often the Bills found themselves dumping the ball short to the 6-foot 6-inch veteran, who made a career-high 68 catches (for a piddling 9.0 yard average and 4 TDs).

If your league uses a TE, Metzelaars isn't bad. But the Bills receivers, once a strength, look as if they need an overhaul. A pleasant surprise could be rookie TE Lonnie Johnson of Florida State, though he might figure more as an H-back. He had only 21 catches the last two years, though FSU's fast-break style didn't utilize the TE much.

Andre Reed's six TD catches seemed to come in bunches and he no longer has the downfield burst. The other starter, Bill Brooks, had a solid year as the possession receiver and scored five times. But neither guy is on the end of those 60-yard rainbows that rack up points.

The dude with the speed, Don Beebe, never gets to use it. He's almost always hurt. His 31 catches last season included 3 TDs, including one for 65 yards, but he cannot be counted on week-in and week-out due to his fragility.

Keep an eye on Russell Copeland, who could break into the lineup. The Bills are also high on rookie Bucky Brooks, their second draft selection. He's a bit of a project, though.

DEFENSE/SPECIAL TEAMS

The Bills did a great job in '93 of taking the ball away and giving themselves scoring opportunities. They scored five TDs on returns: three by the defense on INTs, one on a fumble and one by Copeland on a punt return.

That opportunism could easily wane. Odomes, who tied for the NFL lead in INTs with 9 (of the Bills' 23) departed as a free agent. In fact, the secondary likely will have three new starters, with only SS Henry Jones back.

The Bills also are soft on the run and need more bulk on the defensive line. They do a nice job getting after the QB, but most of that falls to DE Bruce Smith, who truly had a great, all-around '93 season which included 13.5 sacks. Top pick Jeff Burris figures at FS but might have to play the corner.

Copeland shows the potential for being a fine kick returner. The Bills' special teams are expertly coached by Bruce DeHaven and generally produce some big plays.

KICKER

Steve Christie ranked sixteenth among FFL kickers. True, he scored 124 points, but that was down 26 from the previous season in what was known as the year of the kicker. Though he made a 59-yard kick, his overall percentage declined slightly. He also had problems in the cold during the playoff game against the Los Angeles Raiders.

★☆★☆CHICAGO BEARS★☆★☆

by Larry Michael
NFL Play-by Play Announcer
Mutual Radio Network

Will the Chicago Bears be a better football team in their second year under head coach Dave Wannstedt? They finished the season losers of four straight, and an anemic offense was the reason. They averaged a depressing eight points a game during the final four weeks, and the changes you'll see in this team will mostly involve the offense. First the good news: the core of the defense remains intact despite the departure of Steve McMichael and Richard Dent. The bad news might really be good news in disguise, as the offense has had a major facelift. Last year's offense scored just 17 total touchdowns, so this year's crew doesn't exactly have a tough act to follow.

QUARTERBACK

Jim Harbaugh is out, and free agent signee Erik Kramer is in. Harbaugh threw just seven touchdowns in 15 starts last season, while Kramer started just five games but threw for eight scores. It looks like an improvement on paper for the Bears, but inevitably the success of Chicago's QB will once again hinge on the protection he'll receive from the offensive line, which will be looking for help in the draft. Former University of Florida star Shane Mathews will be one of the backups, while another free agent signing might take place to provide some experience.

RUNNING BACK

Just as was the case at QB, the Bears have some big changes in the backfield. Former Steeler Merril Hoge replaces Craig "Ironhead" Heyward at fullback, while former NY Giant Lewis Tillman lines up at tailback. Neither man did much scoring last year, but the 1993 stats won't mean much this season, and Tillman and Hoge will carry the load for Chicago. Tim Worley is the first backup. He's had his act together the last couple of years, and maybe his commitment will show dividends this season. Long-time Bears back Neal Anderson did not re-sign. The draft might bring some young depth, and the Bears signed free agent offensive lineman Andy Heck as a step towards re-establishing their ground game.

WIDE RECEIVER

It's tough to judge a wide receiving crew whose quarterback could only deliver seven touchdown passes last year, but the Bears do have some talent outside. Last year's top pick Curtis Conway developed slowly, but has the speed to get deep. Tom Waddle is steady though unspectacular. Depth is a problem, with help expected in the form of a high draft pick. The number one tight end is Chris Gedney, who didn't score a touchdown last year.

DEFENSE/SPECIAL TEAMS

Unsigned free agents could mean some big changes are in store for the Bears defense. Trace Armstrong and Mark Carrier will be back to lead defense, but the draft will have to yield a defensive lineman if Chicago is to improve. Richard Dent won't return, so who makes up for the loss of 12.5 sacks from Dent a year ago? Receiver Curtis Conway is also a dangerous return man.

KICKER

Returning for his tenth season in a Bears uniform, Kevin Butler is coming off another fine season, one in which he scored 143 FFL points. Butler's leg appears to be getting stronger with age, as he drilled five field goals from 50+ yards.

★☆★☆CINCINNATI BENGALS★☆★☆

By Dave Douglas
NFL Films

An 0 and 10 start. It doesn't get any worse than that. For David Shula, the NFL's youngest head coach, it was a trying season to be sure. Only once in 1993 did Cincinnati score more than 20 points but the Bengals managed to win three of their last six and Shula hopes the positive finish will make for a positive start in 1994. In this year's NFL draft, the Bengals made Ohio State defensive tackle Dan "Big Daddy" Wilkinson the first overall pick. Wilkinson will start and be a force for years to come. He's a tough run-stuffer and will be a pass-rushing monster on the inside.

QUARTERBACK

David Klingler was thrown into the fire in 1993. Behind a line that simply couldn't protect him, he spent the year running for his life on virtually every snap. The Bengals allowed a whopping 53 sacks and behind that porous front, Klingler rarely had time to find his targets. Klingler (190 of 343 for 1935 yds. and only 6 TDs) showed flashes of brilliance but since he had no time to scan the field, it was difficult for him to find his rhythm and post big numbers. He is not in the top echelon of fantasy passers, but he'd make a respectable backup for you. Jay Schroeder (78 of 159 for 832 and 5 TDs) will not be drafted by anyone.

56

RUNNING BACK

Veteran Seattle guard Darrick Brilz and New York Giant tackle Eric Moore were brought in to help shore up a line in need of overhauling. It doesn't seem like so long ago that Sam Wyche fielded one of the best front walls in the game, but now the Bengal line is a shadow of what it once was. That being said, the running game suffered in 1993. An unhappy Harold Green rushed for only 589 yards and never scored. Derrick Fenner was the go-to guy inside the 5-yard line but he scored only once.

Green gets the most carries, so of the two, he's the best bet in a backfield that really has no fantasy stars.

WIDE RECEIVER

Jeff Query (56 for 654 yds. and 4 TDs) was the Bengals' leading receiver and he will go undrafted. Rookie Tony McGee (44 for 525 yds. and 0 TDs) was a pleasant surprise and will be drafted in a year where solid tight ends are a precious commodity. The receiver you do want to take a good look at is youngster Carl Pickens. Pickens is Cris Carter-like. He makes big plays and he finds the end zone. Pickens caught just 43 balls, but he scored 6 touchdowns. He could explode this season to catch 60+ passes and 10 touchdowns. He'd be a late-round steal. Darnay Scott (WR, San Diego State) was the thirtieth pick in the draft and he's the burner that the Bengals needed.

DEFENSE/SPECIAL TEAMS

Larry Peccatiello has replaced Ron Lynn as defensive coordinator and he will change the Bengals to a 4-3 defense. He has the down linemen to do it in Daniel Stubbs, Alfred Williams, Tim Krumrie and John Copeland. "Big Daddy" makes the front four solid right now. Last season, Stubbs led the team with five sacks and he and Copeland will shine in the new alignment. Cornerback Mike Brim's three interceptions were good enough for the team lead. Peccatiello will take a team that totalled only 22 sacks and 12 picks and make them a much better unit almost immediately. Safety Louis Oliver was acquired from the Dolphins and he'll hit on every play. Free safety Darryl Williams is the hardest-hitting DB you never heard of.

Free agent Patrick Robinson handled nearly every punt return averaging 7.1 yards per attempt. Robinson and Eric Ball split time on kickoff returns. Lee Johnson was a busy man, punting 90 times for a 43.9 average, and he had none blocked.

KICKER

Rookie kicker Doug Pelfrey replaced Jim Breech and had a terrific season. He missed only 7 kicks and hit on 2 out of 3 from more than 50 yards out. He has the monster leg

★☆★☆CLEVELAND BROWNS★☆★☆

By Dave Douglas
NFL Films

After a hot division-leading start, head coach Bill Belichick had a parting of the ways with quarterback Bernie Kosar. Bernie packed up for Dallas, ultimately to collect his Super Bowl ring, while the Browns limped home at 7 and 9. They played hard yet couldn't keep pace with Pittsburgh and Houston. However, it looks like that could change in 1994. In Eric Metcalf and Michael Jackson they possess playmakers on offense. Defense is Belichick's strength. What they have to do is find a way to put it all together and play consistent football. The dog pound is ready and willing as always. Are the Browns? The drafting of cornerback Antonio Langham (Alabama) and receiver Derrick Alexander (Michigan) strengthens them on both sides of the ball immediately.

QUARTERBACK

It seemed Bernie Kosar would play for 20 years in Cleveland, be elected mayor, retire from public service, then die and have his ashes spread over Cleveland stadium. Alas, such was not to be, as the hometown hero is long gone. But something amazing happened after Bernie bolted. Vinnie Testaverde eventually took over and played interception-free football. Testaverde (130 of 230 for 1797 yards and 14 TDs) played the best football of his career down the stretch, and if he picks up where he left off, he'll be a top-fifteen fantasy quarterback.

In the spring, the Brownies picked up Mark Rypien, and he should be the main backup, bumping Todd Philcox to third-string clipboard duty. In 1993, Philcox performed in between Bernie and the Vin-Man and threw more interceptions than touchdowns. There is no place for Philcox on your FFL roster.

RUNNING BACK

Eric Metcalf is the most electrifying little back in the game. His pair of punt return touchdowns against the Steelers highlighted one of the greatest individual performances of the '93 season. Metcalf (611 rushing, 539 receiving for 3 TDs) is a versatile guy who fills out an FFL squad quite nicely. He's a threat to score from anywhere at anytime...anytime, that is, except inside the five-yard line. In the red zone, Tommy Vardell usually gets the call. "Touchdown Tommy" did so 4 times last year and he rushed for 644 yards. Which of the two do you pick first? Hmm...tough call. Keep in mind that Metcalf does a lot of his damage on special teams and Vardell got 42 more carries last year. Leroy Hoard tailed off after a super '92 campaign, rushing for only 227 yards.

WIDE RECEIVER

Michael Jackson enjoyed a great season by catching 41 passes for 756 yards and 8 touchdowns. Jackson scored more touchdowns than any other Brown and he is truly hitting his stride. He made circus grabs and averaged over 18 yards per catch. He's a bonus baby who can dial long distance and he's just a half-step behind the elite receivers in the NFL. Metcalf's 63 catches were tops on the team, but he's not a wideout or tight end. Mark Carrier was brought in from Tampa Bay and he hauled in 43 catches for 3 TDs, and also scored on a run and a return. Keenan McCardell caught 13 passes, but he scored on four of them, so see if he wins a starting job in the preseason. Tight end Brian Kinchen caught 29 passes and scored twice. He'll compete with Walter Reeves (from the Arizona Cardinals) for the starting spot. Rookie first-rounder Derrick Alexander could start at wideout.

DEFENSE/SPECIAL TEAMS

Ever heard of Anthony Pleasant or Rob Burnett? They combined for 20 sacks last season. Pleasant (11) and Burnett (9) provide a mighty one-two sack punch for Belichick, whose defense bagged the quarterback 48 times last season. Safety Eric Turner led the team with 5 interceptions, but as a team they only collected 13. Two free agent cornerbacks, Donald Frank (SD) and Don Griffin (SF), were signed to help in the coverage department. Clay Matthews is the oldest defensive player in the entire league. His 16th season will be like all the others...hard hitting.

Cleveland's special teams begin and end with Eric Metcalf. He handled nearly every punt return and scored twice while averaging 12.9 yards per return. He can single-handedly take over a game every time he handles a punt. Mark Carrier returned a punt for a touchdown as well. Metcalf shared the kickoff return job with Randy Baldwin. Brian Hanson averaged 44.3 yards per punt and he had two blocked.

KICKER

Matt Stover had a steady but unspectacular season by hitting on 16 of 22 field goals for 84 total points. He also boomed one from 53 yards.

★☆★☆DALLAS COWBOYS★☆★☆

by Larry Weisman
Sports Columnist
USA TODAY

They look like the Dallas Cowboys. But are they?

Are they the same dominating club with their offensive line shorn of depth, with their defense riddled by free agent defections and trades?

Most significantly, are they even the Cowboys we've come to know and love and hate without Jimmy Johnson?

No loss will be harder to overcome than that of Johnson, who departed in late March in a fit of pique after yet another blowup with owner Jerry Jones. Barry Switzer--an outlaw's outlaw when he coached at the University of Oklahoma--steps in for Johnson, but this is Johnson's coaching staff and Johnson's team, and who can guess how all will respond to a new hand on the reins?

True, the Cowboys won two consecutive Super Bowls. But these Cowboys? No. Johnson's Cowboys. How Jones and Switzer will fare and what sort of honeymoon they can expect from Dallas fans once again spoiled rotten by success ought to make for a wonderful autumn carnival.

QUARTERBACK

Troy Aikman might be the best in the NFL but that doesn't mean he's the best for fantasy players. And he isn't.

Though the Cowboys have great receivers, they don't throw for the end zone much. And when they're leading, which is most of the time, they feed the ball to Emmitt Smith and spin the clock.

So while it's great fun to watch Aikman hum those 20-yard rockets to Michael Irvin, there's not much in the way of points coming. When Aikman does connect big-time, however, there's value. He hit Alvin Harper for an 80-yard TD last year and Irvin for one of 61, so when Dallas wants to go downtown there's a great reward. It just doesn't happen enough.

With the loss of Bernie Kosar as a free agent to Miami, Dallas' backup situation looked unsettled. Jason Garrett can get the Cowboys out of trouble in relief but is not the answer as a stopgap starter. The Cowboys also tried and failed to sign Wade Wilson, who re-upped with New Orleans. So, in a fit of near desperation, the 'Pokes went out and signed ex-occasional Detroit Lion starter Rodney Peete. Peete scored 66 FFL points last year, and was good for a few touchdowns, but only grab him if your first two (or three) QBs go down.

RUNNING BACK

Emmitt Smith's holdout hurt his stats last year. His TD production fell by almost half to a total of 10, and 6 of his 9 rushing TDs were in the 1-to-9 yard area.

He's still a good choice because he generally has his hands on the ball and the offense is keyed around him. Remember that the Cowboys began spreading the ball around quite a bit near the goal line last year and Smith scored just 9 of their 20 rushing TDs.

FB Daryl Johnston may be the best at what he does, but that's not enough for the FFL. Blocking, unfortunately, doesn't count. Johnson caught 50 passes, more than twice his total number of rushes, and crashed the end zone a grand total of 5 times. When he scores by rushing, it's from the one. So don't go losing your head just because the Cowboys made him the highest-paid FB in the game. That was for Smith's sake.

The backups here--Derrick Lassic, Lincoln Coleman, Derrick Gainer--get too little playing time to even fool with. Lassic, a rookie last year, started when Smith held out. Lassic didn't play badly, but he's just not of that caliber.

WIDE RECEIVER

Irvin has caught 7 TD passes each of the last two seasons and that seems about where he'll always be. He's a great route runner but not the tremendous deep threat. Take him if you like him but don't expect Jerry Rice-type numbers.

Harper's the home-run guy, and though the Cowboys tried to trade him on draft day, they'll hang onto him for this season. Harper takes advantage of Irvin drawing double coverage and can beat man-to-man schemes, but he often gets lost in a zone. Still, a guy with 5 TD grabs in 36 catches and a 21.6 yards per catch average must be doing something right. Can this be the year he truly comes into his own? Are you man (or woman) enough to gamble?

TE Jay Novacek scored only one measly TD receiving last year and should have a better season. He's sneaky around the goal line and Aikman will look for him.

Sleeper: Kevin Williams. If Harper is gone, this second-year big-play guy jumps right into the lineup and makes things happen. He's not a bad choice as bench strength, though he really needs work on running his routes and knowing his reads.

Deep sleeper: Rookie Willie Jackson. Not a burner, but a guy who always seemed to come up big in Florida's big games.

The Cowboys could use some depth at TE, where the only backup to Novacek is Scott Galbreath.

DEFENSE/SPECIAL TEAMS

Johnson's focus was on big plays that could go for scores and that emphasis could be sorely missed. However, special teams coach Joe Avezzano also holds to that credo and he's still running this show.

Williams scored twice on punt returns as a rookie and is liable to do so again. Dallas' opportunistic defense only scored once, however, and needs to do more. Given the talent drain (DTs Jimmie Jones and Tony Casillas, SS Thomas Everett), that's not likely.

The strength of any play here would be special teams, though the 'Pokes did allow a 95-yard kickoff return for a TD last season.

KICKER

Mystery guest, please sign in. Steady Eddie Murray, aka Eddie Money, took the money (or Murray) from Philadelphia and departed as a free agent. At press time, he had not been replaced.

★☆★☆DENVER BRONCOS★☆★☆

By John Weiss
NFL Films

After contending for the AFC West title most of last season, the Broncos fizzled down the stretch, inexplicably losing at home to Tampa Bay, and then letting a heartbreaker get away in overtime against the Raiders. The loss to the Raiders in the season finale forced the 9-7 Broncos to play on the road in the AFC wildcard game, where they were burned in a rematch with the Raiders, 42-24.

It was still a pretty good start for Wade Phillips in his first season as head coach, especially considering that the Broncos fielded the NFL's youngest team. Denver's 53-man roster featured 27 new faces, including 15 rookies or first-year players.

What's in store for this young group in 1994? Well, if they can stay healthy and endure some more growing pains, the Broncos once again look like a solid playoff contender, and with a little Mile High magic, may even make another run at a division title.

QUARTERBACK

In 1993, no player benefited from a change of systems more than John Elway. Finally free from Dan Reeves' conservative playbook, Elway was given new life under first-year offensive coordinator Jim Fassel, who also coached Elway in the same capacity at Stanford.

Elway flourished in Fassel's new system and, statistically speaking, had the best season of his career. His impressive numbers included 348 completions (number one in the NFL); 4,030 yards (number one in the AFC) and 25 touchdown passes (number one in the AFC). His 92.8 quarterback rating and 63.2 completion percentage were also tops in the AFC.

Elway was always one of those quarterbacks who was much more valuable in the NFL than in the FFL. But those days are over. Elway's career has been reborn, and he now should be one of the top quarterback prospects on your FFL draft day.

RUNNING BACK

To help relieve some pressure on Elway, the Broncos need to improve their mediocre ground game of 1993. Rod Bernstine led the team in rushing last season with 816 yards (3.7-yard average) and 4 touchdowns before ending the year on injured reserve. He also had 44 catches for 372 yards. Bernstine once again will be the featured back as long as he stays healthy.

Robert Delpino was second on the team with 445 yards (3.4 average), and he was most effective at the goal line with a team-high eight rushing touchdowns. He added 26 catches for 195 yards.

Rookie Glyn Milburn had 231 yards rushing (4.4 average), and added 38 catches for 300 yards and 3 scores.

WIDE RECEIVER

There's an entirely new look to the Broncos' receiving corps in 1994, with the addition of former Chargers' All-Pro Anthony Miller and former Falcon Mike Pritchard.

Miller is fresh off a Pro Bowl season that included a career-high 84 catches for 1,162 yards and 7 touchdowns. His numbers could get even better as Elway's new featured deep threat. Pritchard is more of a possession receiver, having caught 74 passes for 736 yards and 7 touchdowns last year for Atlanta.

The upgrading of wide receivers may mean less opportunities for Pro Bowl H-back/tight end Shannon Sharpe. In 1993, Sharpe emerged as a true star, catching 81 passes for 995 yards and 9 touchdowns. Even with Elway now throwing to Miller and Pritchard, Sharpe should make enough plays to warrant high consideration on draft day.

Wide receiver Derek Russell had 44 catches for 719 yards and 3 touchdowns before suffering a sprained ankle in the seasons's thirteenth game. Arthur Marshall had 28 receptions for 360 yards and two scores, but was signed away from the Broncos in the offseason by the Giants. Longtime Elway target Vance Johnson signed with San Diego.

DEFENSE/SPECIAL TEAMS

The Broncos need to shore up a defense that ranked 19th in the NFL last season, 27th against the pass. To help in the secondary, the Broncos have added free agent cornerback Ray Crockett, who had two interceptions last season for the Lions, as well as defensive back Ben Smith, who was troubled with injuries in four seasons with the Eagles.

Hard-hitting safety Steve Atwater led the team with 141 total tackles (80 solo) and went to the Pro Bowl. Cornerback Tyrone Braxton was second with 111 (79 solo), and added 3 interceptions.

If there's one thing the Broncos know they can count on, it's the consistent pass rush of linebacker Simon Fletcher, who has led the team in sacks in each of the past six seasons. Fletcher had 13.5 sacks last year, and now has 43 over the past three seasons. To help up front, Denver traded for former 49er nose tackle Ted Washington, who had 3 sacks last season for San Francisco. Linebacker Mike Croel was third on the team with 110 tackles (79 solo). On special teams, Glyn Milburn returned 40 punts for a 10.6-yard average, fifth best in the AFC and eighth in the NFL. Derek Russell returned 18 kickoffs for a 20.8-yard average.

KICKER

Rookie Jason Elam had a pretty productive season in 1993, connecting on 26 of 35 field goals, including 4 of 6 from 50-plus yards, and 41 of 42 extra points. His 119 points ranked seventh in the NFL, and if the Broncos' offense is as productive as it was last year, Elam should once again be one of the top FFL kickers in 1994.

★☆★☆DETROIT LIONS★☆★☆

by Larry Michael
NFL Play-by Play Announcer
Mutual Radio Network

Head Coach Wayne Fontes couldn't settle on a quarterback last year, so this year the team cleaned house at that position. Scott Mitchell gets behind the wheel of the Lions' offense this year in the Motor City, and Fontes hopes to get more mileage out of Mitchell than he did from last year's revolving trio of Rodney Peete, Andre Ware and Erik Kramer. A healthy Barry Sanders is again the key to the offense, but despite two division titles in three years, Fontes' future just might ride on an improved defense and the performance of his new quarterback.

QUARTERBACK

Scott Mitchell, recovered from last year's shoulder injury in Miami, hopes to recharge the unique Detroit offense. Though he's never been a full-time starter in the NFL, Mitchell replaced the injured Dan Marino last year for the Dolphins, and in a limited period prior to his own injury, Mitchell fired 12 touchdown passes. It'll certainly be a new and different look for the left-hander in Detroit, however, as three good wide receivers, a tight end, and Barry Sanders will be the tools at his disposal. The back-up job is undecided at this time, though the Lions signed Dave Krieg away from the Chiefs.

RUNNING BACK

Barry Sanders is one of the elite backs in the NFL. Holder of almost all of Detroit's all-time rushing records, Sanders is expected to handle the football over 350 times this season as a runner and receiver. One hitch for FFL fans is the fact that going into last season Sanders averaged 14 touchdowns a year; last year he scored only 3. Sanders did miss some time with a knee injury, but that doesn't account for the drop in scoring. Derrick Moore is the main backup in the single back set, and last year he scored 4 touchdowns.

WIDE RECEIVER

Last year was a breakthrough season for four-year pro Herman Moore. A big target with tremendous leaping ability, Moore caught 61 balls last year, with 6 touchdowns (one went 93 yards!). Scott Mitchell will have a key resource in Moore running around the goal line, since there isn't a defensive back in the league able to out-jump Moore for the ball. Besides Moore, the Lions will deploy Willie Greene and Brett Perriman into their three wideout formations. The tight end position made a comeback in the Detroit offense last year, and this season free agent signee Ron Hall from Tampa Bay will be filling the spot.

DEFENSE/SPECIAL TEAMS

The Lions have added an impact FFL player in cornerback Robert Massey, formerly of the Cardinals. One of the most dangerous return men of all time, Mel Gray, who has been a mainstay for the Detroit team for the past five years, has not been re-signed. "Cap-a-nomics" might have claimed another specialization player in the form of Gray, but the possibility remains that Gray will return for less money.

KICKER

It's not often you hear a kicker referred to as a "stud," but the Lions' Jason Hanson fits the bill here. He made 28 of 28 PATs, and 34 field goals, with 7 attempts coming from outside 50 yards. This kid can kick. The third-rated kicker according to FFL statistics last year, Hanson has a strong leg and kicks in a domed stadium, a combination which just may make him the first kicker selected in FFL drafts everywhere this season.

★☆★☆GREEN BAY PACKERS★☆★☆

by Larry Michael
NFL Play-by Play Announcer
Mutual Radio Network

The rebuilding job began for Mike Holmgren in Green Bay in 1992. The hard work should begin to pay off in earnest this season if Green Bay can improve their running game; they have taken the first step with the signing of Tampa Bay's Reggie Cobb. Brett Favre to Sterling Sharpe will be a hot connection again in '94. Though the defense is in need of help at the linebacking position, the defensive line is scary with Reggie White and former Oiler Sean Jones at the ends. They had 13 sacks EACH last season, and you can already see the nervous look in the eyes of quarterbacks around the NFL. Hopes are high in Green Bay, as The Pack are coming off their first playoff appearance in a decade.

QUARTERBACK

Green Bay's General Manager Ron Wolf expects to ink Brett Favre to a new contract. Last season, Favre was number six overall in scoring in the FFL with 174 points, 19 total TD passes and one rushing TD. He's got mobility, a strong arm, and one of the best receivers in the NFL (Sterling Sharpe), so Favre will be a coveted FFL draft pick this season. The back-ups again this season are former Heisman Trophy winner Ty Detmer and second-year man Mark Brunell.

RUNNING BACK

The combination of backs Darrell Thompson and Edgar Bennett ended the season with both men being starters, but the Packers could use a back with breakaway speed. Bennett was solid as a rock with ten touchdowns, while Thompson contributed three scores. Drafting a running back is still a priority for the Packers, even though they signed free agent Reggie Cobb to a two-year deal. The Packers know they need to improve the backfield, and Cobb is a great addition.

WIDE RECEIVER

The Packers need to find a receiver to complement the incomparable Sterling Sharpe. Last year was another great one for Sharpe. Though he nursed an injured toe for part of the season, Sharpe broke his own record for most receptions in a year as he hauled in 112 balls. Eleven of those grabs were for touchdowns. Sharpe has recovered from the toe injury 100%, but if the Pack doesn't add a receiver, constant double coverage will certainly have impact on the Favre-to-Sharpe combination. Mark Clayton is gone, so last year's number-three receiver Robert Brooks should see more action. There is little depth at the wideout position, so another priority in the draft is finding a receiver who will allow Sharpe to keep his edge. The tight end is Jackie Harris, who scored four touchdowns last season.

DEFENSE/SPECIAL TEAMS

The sack masters Reggie White and Sean Jones will not only provide points for FFLers via the sack route, but will also rush quarterbacks into mistakes, which means more interceptions for the Green Bay secondary. The Packers have very good kick return teams, with Corey Harris and Robert Brooks returning. Brooks led the league in kickoff returns last year.

KICKER

The number one FFL point-producing kicker in 1993 was Green Bay's Chris Jacke. A very impressive accomplishment, since his home games are played on grass, often in below-freezing temperatures. Jacke racked up 182 points last year, with 6 field goals from the 50+ range. A tough pick in the FFL draft would be the first kicker selected--right now, it's an even toss-up between Jacke and the Lions' Jason Hanson.

★☆★☆HOUSTON OILERS★☆★☆

By Dave Douglas
NFL Films

The Oilers were 1 and 4. Warren Moon was benched. Houston was in deep trouble and Buddy Ryan hadn't even punched Kevin Gilbride yet. Then everything changed. Moon got hot. Gary Brown ran wild, and Buddy's defense was kickin' butt and takin' names. The Oilers went from last place to a division title fueled by 11 straight season-ending wins. What a ride it was. As usual, they folded in the playoffs as Joe Montana picked them apart in the Astrodome. The dust has settled, and Buddy has departed for Arizona and Moon has left for Minnesota. Now the Oilers must regroup once more under Jack Pardee.

QUARTERBACK

Warren Moon is long in the tooth but he could still put up some astronomical FFL numbers...in Minnesota. His 369-yard day versus Seattle and his 4-touchdown pass outing up in Cincy are the stats owners love to see...unless you're playing against Warren, of course. Last year Moon was hammered, benched and out of sync at times, but 303 completions for 3485 yards and a terrific 21 touchdown passes in 1993 make him a top flight draft pick for sure. He should prosper in Minnesota with Cris Carter to throw to. After eight seasons of waiting, Cody Carlson is finally Houston's starter. Last year in limited action he completed 51 passes for 2 touchdowns, but in a full season of the Run-and-Shoot he could be a very high draft pick...a top-fifteen QB for sure.

RUNNING BACK

Check out the math for Gary Brown: 1,002 yards rushing, 240 yards receiving. 8 touchdowns scored. Now factor in this: Brown only started the final *10* games. Over an entire season, Brown would have won the rushing title easily and blown up countless FFL calculators. He's right there with Emmitt, Thurman and the Barrys. Because of Brown, Lorenzo White rode the pines. If Brown goes down, however, White will do the "reversal of fortune," and it'll be his turn to replace Brown. No other Oiler backs are worth mentioning.

WIDE RECEIVER

You certainly will not find a draftable tight end in the Run-and-Shoot but there are a slew of wideouts. Last season, Webster Slaughter emerged as the best until an injury knocked him out of action. The injury may be serious, so see if Slaughter (77 for 904 and 5 TDs) performs in the preseason as hoped. Ernest Givins (68 for 887 and 4 TDs) and Haywood Jeffires (66 for 753 and 6 TDs) are two excellent receivers. I rate Jeffires higher because nagging injuries hampered him a bit and he'll return to form in 1994. Jeffires is split wide in the Run-and-Shoot while Givins is a slot guy, so Jeffires runs more bonus-point deep routes. Gary Wellman (31 for 430 and 1 TD) only saw action because of the Slaughter injury.

DEFENSE/SPECIAL TEAMS

Defensive coordinator Buddy Ryan may be gone but his replacement Jeff Fisher won't change a thing. Fisher worked with Buddy in Philly. He knows the 46 defense and the Oilers will be at their nasty best this season. Fifty-two sacks and 26 interceptions...those numbers will be hard to match. Sean Jones (13 sacks) is off to Green Bay while William Fuller (10 sacks) is now an Eagle. Ray Childress (9 sacks) returns, however. Draft pick Henry Ford (Arkansas) could start immediately at defensive end. Marcus Robertson (7), Cris Dishman (6) and Steve Jackson (5) helped Houston lead the league in interceptions.

Willie Drewrey returned every punt and averaged 6.7 yards. He's surehanded but doesn't possess blazing speed. Drewrey was the primary kick returner as well, averaging 19.5 per return. Punter Greg Montgomery has the strongest leg in the league, but for years he never punted enough to qualify for the Pro Bowl. Last season he did, and he boomed them nearly 47 yards every time to finally earn a trip to Hawaii.

KICKER

In 1993, Al Del Greco solved all of the kicking miseries that had plagued the Oilers of late. He was 29 of 34 including 4 of 7 from the 50 on out. Del Greco scored 126 points in a super year.

★☆★☆INDIANAPOLIS COLTS★☆★☆

By Dave Douglas
NFL Films

Last season, a troubled Colts club won only four games. Down the stretch, they lost eight of nine and in only three games in 1993 did they score more than 20 points. Ten times they were held to ten points or less. This is a club that needed enormous upgrading on offense. Head coach Ted Marchibroda took a long look at his prospects and decided that addition by subtraction was the way to go, so out went quarterback Jeff George and backup Jack Trudeau. Throughout his career, George had never finished anything he'd started. He was booed mercilessly by Colt fans and never found his game. Injuries plagued him as did his apparent lack of commitment. Trudeau was never really given an honest shot. The Colts were extremely active in the draft and traded up to get two of the first five picks. Instead of drafting a quarterback, however, they chose Marshall Faulk (RB, San Diego State) and Trev Alberts (LB, Nebraska).

QUARTERBACK

With Jeff George (234 of 407 for 2526 yds. and 8 TDs) off to Atlanta and Jack Trudeau (85 of 162 for 992 yds. and 2 TDs) released, Don Majkowski was the only rostered QB left. Majkowski's magic is an illusion...long left behind in Green Bay. George and Trudeau were replaced by former bear Jim Harbaugh. Harbaugh (200 of 325 for 2002 yds. and 7 TDs) will probably start and he's a bonus guy because he'll run for a few touchdowns as well. He's not a top-flight passer but would make a solid FFL backup. By acquiring Will Wolford and Kirk Lowdermilk in the

79

previous offseason, the Colts shored up a promising offensive line. Now they have to hope Harbaugh will find secondary receivers instead of running out of the pocket all the time.

RUNNING BACK

Last year, six rookie running backs led their teams in rushing, and that eye-opening stat held true to form in Indy. Roosevelt Potts rushed for 711 yards on 179 carries, and it appears he'll tote the ball even more in 1994. Potts is a no-nonsense punisher who doesn't fool anybody. He runs powerfully between the tackles and gets stronger as the game wears on. In fantasy football, you want a featured back who doesn't share carries, and although Potts didn't score last year, he should be considered a prime candidate as your second running back. Anthony Johnson and Rodney Culver, a pair of Notre Damers, rarely catch the ball and between them they scored five times. The real story here is Marshall Faulk. Faulk is the most explosive back to be drafted in years. He could be the next Barry Sanders. He'll go quickly, although he's untested. I believe he'll rush for 1,200 yards and be named Rookie of the Year.

WIDE RECEIVER

Reggie Langhorne was by far the Colts' best receiver in 1993. In a spectacular season, Langhorne caught 85 passes for 1038 yards. What did the Colts do with their big play target? They released him. Jessie Hester (64 for 835 yds. and 1 TD) remains but he is a lackluster fantasy receiver. Sean Dawkins is their play maker of the future. As a rookie last season, the Colts' number-one pick grabbed only 26 passes but he averaged nearly 17 yards per catch. Dawkins' role will be expanded in 1994, and if he's still there late in the draft, take a shot. Tight end Kerry Cash (43 for 402 yds. and 3 TDs) is a real sleeper. Marchibroda loves to use the tight end in his offensive game plan, so Cash fills the bill for the tight end spot in your draft.

DEFENSE/SPECIAL TEAMS

It is on offense where the most change is required. It is on defense where the most activity took place. Jon Hand and Eugene Daniel were re-signed. Linebacker Duane Bickett was released and replaced with former Packer Tony Bennett and rookie Trev Alberts. The future of once-dominant lineman Steve Emtman is uncertain. Two severe knee injuries have cast a shadow over a career that seemed limitless.

Linebackers Quentin Coryatt (150) and Jeff Herrod (142) were the leading tacklers, while free safety Ray Buchanan paced the team with 4 interceptions. NT Tony "The Goose" Siragusa plays the game with a passion; he is a wildman play-in and play-out. The Colts totalled only 21 sacks and if they hope to succeed this season, they'll have to heat up the pass pocket more often.

Clarence Verdin handled all the punt return chores and nearly every kickoff. He was released. A new returner will emerge in the preseason.

Punter Rohn Stark is a four-time Pro Bowler, and he averaged 43.3 yards per punt, sixth in the AFC.

KICKER

Kicker Dean Biasucci led the team in scoring with 93 points. He hit 26 of 31 field goals, and since the Colts have such difficulty in finding the end zone he's called on often. Biasucci is a reliable weapon who can hit from long distance and is always a solid fantasy kicker.

★☆★☆KANSAS CITY CHIEFS★☆★☆

By Dave Douglas
NFL Films

For the first time since 1971, the Kansas City Chiefs were division champions. They won 11 games in the regular season, then took care of Pittsburgh and Houston in the playoffs. In the AFC championship game, however, Thurman Thomas ran right through them and the Chiefs fell one victory short of an appearance in Super Bowl XXVIII. One can only wonder what Emmitt would have done to them down in Atlanta. The Chiefs have been a model of consistency under head coach Marty Schottenheimer. They have won 23 of their last 28 divisional games, and their 42 and 22 record since 1990 is the NFL's fourth-best.

QUARTERBACK

Joe Montana is the greatest quarterback in the history of pro football. Three Super Bowl MVP awards and four Super Bowl rings attest to that. It seems the only thing that can stop him are the proverbial ravages of time. Joe is 38 and last season he was only able to start 11 times. He will be drafted in your FFL league. When and where are the two key questions. Last season, Montana (181 of 298 for 2144 yds. and 13 TDs) was as precise as ever and if he can endure another season's beating, then he still must be considered a top-12 fantasy quarterback. Backup David Krieg signed with Detroit, so they brought in ex-'Niner Steve Bono.

RUNNING BACK

Christian Okoye is gone. Harvey Williams was waived. Look for Marcus Allen, Kimball Anders and Todd McNair to lead the attack in 1994. Allen was a huge surprise last season. He went undrafted in many fantasy leagues, but the owners who did add him later came away with some terrific production numbers (764 rushing, 238 receiving and 15 touchdowns). He still has the great vision, soft hands and uncanny nose for the end zone.

Allen will be neither a sleeper nor a first-rounder this year. See how the draft develops and squeeze him in during the middle rounds if you can. Anders rushed for 291 yards and caught passes for another 326, but he scored only once. His drop in the AFC championship was a stake in Marty's heart last year. Todd McNair is a third-down specialist, so don't draft him because he's simply not on the field enough. Keep your eye on draft pick Greg Hill (Texas A&M). He's got real size and speed and he could make an immediate impact.

WIDE RECEIVER

Willie Davis and J.J. Birden flourished by having that Montana guy throwing to them most of the season. Then again, who wouldn't? Davis (52 catches for 909 yards and 7 TDs) dropped some balls but he averaged nearly 18 yards per catch, so you take the good with the bad and ideally make him your third receiver. Birden (51 for 721 and 2 TDs) is one notch below Davis in ability and his draft position in the FFL. Tim Barnett had a quiet season and caught only 17 passes. Tight ends Jonathan Hayes and Keith Cash each caught 24 passes, but Cash is the better of the two and he won the touchdown battle over Hayes 4 to 1. Cash is the tight end of the future in Kansas City.

83

DEFENSE/SPECIAL TEAMS

The first priority for the Chiefs is to load up against the run. They're solid statistically but can't seem to stuff runners when they really have to. Their inability to stop the "Thurman-ator" up in Buffalo cost them a trip to the big dance. Lost are safety Kevin Ross (Atlanta), cornerback Albert Lewis (LA Raiders) and linebacker Lonnie Marts (Tampa Bay), but defensive tackle Joe Phillips has resigned and Tony Casillas was obtained from Dallas. Neil Smith led the NFL with 15 sacks and is now considered by many to be the best defensive end in the game. For the last five years, Derrick Thomas has been a Pro Bowl outside linebacker and the AFC's top vote-getter at OLB. Thomas logged a career-low 8 sacks but was asked to concentrate more on the run. Albert Lewis (6) and Charles Mincy (5) were the Chief's leaders in interceptions.

Kansas City's special teams are always solid and 1993 was no exception. They blocked 5 kicks and Lewis scored on a blocked punt. Dale Carter is one of the league's best punt returners when he wants to be. Kickoff returns were shared by many. Punter Bryan Barker's 42.6-yard gross average was the eighth-highest in the AFC.

KICKER

Ageless Nick Lowery made 23 of 29 field goal attempts and is the NFL's third all-time leading scorer behind Blanda and Stenerud. He is the most accurate kicker in league history, but plus-50-yarders may be a bit much to ask of him, as he is entering his 15th season.

★☆★☆LOS ANGELES RAIDERS★☆★☆

By John Weiss
NFL Films

The Raiders like to boast that they are the only team to reach the Super Bowl in the 1960s, '70s and '80s. And maybe this is the season they add the '90s to that list.

After finishing last season at 10-6 and coming within a game of the AFC championship, the Raiders appear ready to make a run at another Super Bowl in 1994. And even if they're not the best team in the conference, they're probably the most fun to watch. With their squadron of super-speed receivers, the Raiders should light up scoreboards across the league, and could provide you with several players to help you blast off in the FFL this season.

QUARTERBACK

What a difference a change of coasts--and systems--did for Jeff Hostetler. After putting up modest numbers in two years as a starter in the Giants' plodding run offense, Hostetler made the move West last year, shook the cobwebs from his right arm, and finally got a chance to play "Bombs Away" with a real air attack.

Hostetler let fly for 3,242 yards and 14 touchdowns, both career bests by far. He completed 236 of 419 passes for 56.2 percent, but also threw 10 interceptions, holding his quarterback rating down to 82.5. Hostetler's mobility also helped him run for 202 yards and 5 touchdowns.

As he gets more comfortable with the Raiders' system this season, Hostetler should connect for even bigger numbers, and he should be considered among your list of top-10 FFL quarterbacks on draft day. That's something you never would have dreamt of a couple years ago.

In limited duty last season, backup Vince Evans completed 45 of 76 for 640 yards, 3 touchdowns and 4 interceptions.

RUNNING BACK

The Raiders' big offensive problem last season was the lack of consistency in an injury-plagued running game, as they finished 26th in the league in rushing. Only Tampa Bay and Indianapolis were worse.

In his rookie season, Greg Robinson led the team in rushing with 591 yards (3.8 average), but scored only one touchdown. His year was cut short by a knee injury suffered in the 12th game. Robinson also caught 15 passes for 142 yards. If he stays healthy, Robinson is worth considering for your FFL backfield, but he's still too risky to put very high on your list.

Other than Robinson, the Raiders don't have much to offer in terms of big point producers. Nick Bell gained just 180 yards (2.7 average) and scored one touchdown. Fullback Steve Smith was limited by an ankle injury and finished with 156 yards (3.3 average) and no scores. Napoleon McCallum ran for 114 yards (3.1 average) and three touchdowns. The Raiders drafted Nebraska's Calvin Jones in the third round.

WIDE RECEIVER

Before last season, many wondered if this was supposed to be a receiving corps or a track club. Sure, they could leave defensive backs choking on their vapor trails, but could they catch the ball once they broke free? Well, we all found out that these Raider receivers have the soft hands to go with those blazing feet. And a few of these burners could help you race ahead in the FFL this season.

The best of the group is Tim Brown, the 1987 Heisman Trophy winner who finally blossomed into a star in 1993. Brown broke out with a career year--80 catches, an AFC-high 1,180 yards and 7 touchdowns--and he should produce similar numbers in 1994. Put him near the top of your receivers list on draft day.

Of the Raiders' other receivers, it's hard to tell which will put up the biggest numbers this season. Former Olympic sprinter James Jett led the AFC last year with a 23.4-yards-per-catch average, finishing with 33 receptions for 771 yards and 3 touchdowns.

Another speedster, Alexander Wright, had 27 catches for 462 yards and 4 touchdowns. And in his first NFL season, the Rocket--Raghib Ismail--blasted off with 26 catches for 353 yards and one score.

The Raiders lost last year's starting tight end, Ethan Horton, to free agency, and will now look to Andrew Glover to fill his spot. Bothered by a knee injury last season, Glover had just 4 catches for 55 yards and one score.

DEFENSE/SPECIAL TEAMS

With the emergence of a few young stars, and the addition of some old ones, the Raiders defense has slowly rebuilt itself to be one of the league's better units.

Last season, the defense ranked number three in the AFC, and the pass defense was the fifth-best in the NFL. One thing the team must improve on is creating turnovers, as its 23 takeaways were among the lowest totals in the league.

Howie Long is gone, but the Raiders still have a good group of pass rushers left to harass opposing quarterbacks. Defensive end Anthony Smith has developed into one of the league's top sack artists, finishing last season with a team-high 12.5. Greg Townsend was second with 7.5, and 310-pound defensive tackle Chester McGlockton was third with 7. McGlockton is coming off a broken leg suffered in the AFC wildcard game.

Outside linebacker Winston Moss led the team in tackles and anchored a solid linebacking corps. The Raiders looked to further enhance it by drafting Michigan State's Rob Fredrickson in the first round.

In the secondary, the Raiders' top performer is Pro Bowl cornerback Terry McDaniel, who led the team with five interceptions in 1993. The Raiders have also added free agent cornerback Albert Lewis, a perennial All-Pro with the Chiefs who led Kansas City with six interceptions last season.

On special teams, Raghib Ismail returned 25 kickoffs and led the AFC with a 24.2-yard average. Tim Brown had 40 punt returns and finished third in the conference with an 11.6-yard average.

KICKER

Based on last year's performance, Jeff Jaeger should certainly be among the top-five kickers on your FFL draft list.

Jaeger was the most productive kicker in the NFL in 1993, leading the league in scoring with 132 points, and tying a league record with 35 field goals. Jaeger connected on 35 of 44 attempts, including 4 of 7 from 50-plus yards.

★☆★☆LOS ANGELES RAMS★☆★☆

by Larry Michael
NFL Play-by Play Announcer
Mutual Radio Network

The Los Angeles Rams finished in last place in the NFC West last season, a fact which bothers hard-nosed veteran head coach Chuck Knox. The first two things Knox did to turn his team around were to get rid of a quarterback and to open his team's wallet. Jim Everett moved out of L.A., but stayed in the NFC West by signing with New Orleans. Coming in from division competitor Atlanta will be quarterback Chris Miller, who gets the big bucks as the Rams hope he stays healthy for a full season. The rest of the offensive weapons are there at the skill positions, but the draft is important to add depth to the offensive line. Help is also needed on defense as the Rams ranked 24th in the NFL last year in total defense.

QUARTERBACK

The tormented Jim Everett is gone, replaced by a healthy Chris Miller. Staying healthy is the biggest challenge for Miller, and the Rams have their fingers crossed. Last season he only played in three games for Atlanta, and he comes to a Rams team which will be looking for a young backup. T.J. Rubley, last year's surprise QB, is back. Rubley had 8 touchdown passes in 10 games last season, but make no mistake about it, Chuck Knox needs a new look at quarterback, so don't be surprised if Rubley's a third-stringer this season.

RUNNING BACK

The battering Ram Jerome Bettis is back after a tremendous rookie campaign. Bettis bulled his way for seven scores last year. More than just a short yardage back, Bettis has great speed for a man his size, and is capable of breaking a long run. With over 1,400 yards on the ground last year and 26 receptions, Bettis is headed for stardom. Cleveland Gary also returns to the Rams lineup, and even though he was primarily used as a receiver last season, Gary provides a good complement to Bettis. Tim Lester is a strong blocker, but won't carry the ball very much.

WIDE RECEIVER

Longtime Ram Henry Ellard is now a Washington Redskin. Speed man Willie Anderson hopes to be catching some bombs from Miller. Last season, two of Anderson's four touchdown catches went for 40+ yards. Look for Anderson's numbers to go up if Miller can stay healthy. Joining Anderson and the Rams will be Nate Lewis, acquired in a trade with San Diego. Lewis also had four touchdowns last season. The tight end is second-year man Troy Drayton. Drayton has good size and speed, last year receiving four touchdown passes. This is a good crew of pass catchers, and if Miller can get some protection, the Rams passing game should click nicely.

DEFENSE/SPECIAL TEAMS

Last year's leading sack-man, Sean Gilbert is back. Gilbert led the team with 10.5 sacks in '93. The defensive line has been strengthened by the acquisition of the Cowboys' Jimmy Jones. The much-traveled Clifford Hicks has also been added to the secondary, which looks for some help from the draft. The return man appears to be Nate Lewis, but that could certainly change as the start of the season approaches.

KICKER

Returning place kicker Tony Zendejas drilled 6 field goals from 50+ yards out last season, but that's about all there is to talk about. He didn't get very many opportunities as he hit 16 of 23 field goals. Once again, an overall improvement in the Rams offense should get Zendejas more chances in 1994.

★☆★☆MIAMI DOLPHINS★☆★☆

by Larry Weisman
Sports Columnist
USA TODAY

Let's see if we've got this straight...

The Miami Dolphins haven't won a Super Bowl since 1974 nor played in one since 1985. In Dan Marino's 11 seasons (encompassing 298 career TD passes), they've gone to one Super Bowl where they lost to San Francisco by more than three touchdowns.

They lost their last five games of the 1993 season, limping home with a five-and-six record after Marino suffered a season-ending Achilles' tendon injury. The club was sold in the offseason to H. Wayne Huizenga, the former trash magnate who now owns everything but the ozone layer.

Marino hadn't attempted a football-related activity through April. Shula is entering the final year of his contract and is 64 years old. Forget that he's now the all-time winningest coach in NFL history. Jimmy Johnson's lurking out there and would take Shula's job in a New York minute.

So, yeah, change is coming to the staid old Dolphins. They need to be thinking about a possible change of coaches (their last one was in 1970), and a new era coming at quarterback, with Marino's mortality established.

QUARTERBACK

Never had to discuss this issue in the plural much before. It was always Marino, front and center. The guy had started 145 consecutive games (discounting the strike replacement contests of

92

1987). Since the end of '83, his rookie season, he hadn't missed a single game except the three strike games played by fill-ins and wannabes.

Before the Achilles' tore against Cleveland last season, Marino ranked fifth in the NFL in passing efficiency. He had thrown 8 TD passes and 3 INTs in leading the Dolphins to a 3-1 start.

When he went down, Scott Mitchell relieved and won the Browns' game. However, he has departed as a free agent, and Steve DeBerg, older than the sands of time, probably won't be back. Bernie Kosar was signed as Marino's backup, but he's only good in quick fix situations.

So the issue is Marino. How quickly will he round into form? Problem is, he tends to round out of form and get a belly on him when he can't work out. However, there is no reason to believe his skills have diminished, and maybe the time off did the rest of his body some good.

RUNNING BACK

Terry Kirby had a stunning rookie year, mostly as a receiver. He caught 75 passes, including a four-game stretch late in the season when he made 31. His rushing average of 3.3 yards needs to come up, but he scored 6 TDs and really moves well in the open field when the Dolphins swing the ball out to him.

Kirby has replaced tough little Mark Higgs as the featured back. Higgie could see some goal line action but he's ill-suited to that role.

Keith Byars is a nice pick because he can put up points any number of ways. He accounted for seven TDs last year, including one passing, three rushing, and three receiving. He won't get many rushes, however.

Sleeper pick: Aaron Craver. He blew out his knee in preseason last year. The Dolphins had high hopes after his strong playoff performance the season before. If his speed returns, he could be the breakaway threat the team lacks.

WIDE RECEIVER

Hard to count them all up. Nearly everybody except TE Keith Jackson had excellent numbers, and he's likely to rebound from that sorry showing.

Irving Fryar put up the yards (1,010) and 5 TDs, including a 65-yarder. But it's hard not to like Mark Ingram (6 TDs), who blossomed when he got away from the New York Giants' stone-age attack.

With Tony Martin traded to San Diego, O.J. McDuffie, a number-one pick last year, figures to get more playing time in the multiple receiver sets. Try to steal him in the middle rounds.

Jackson's numbers (39 catches, 6 TDs) were held down by a nagging hamstring injury and Marino's absence. With Marino back feeding the ball to Jackson running down the seams of zones, happy days are here again.

DEFENSE/SPECIAL TEAMS

Nothing to get excited about here other than McDuffie, who returned two punts for TDs and put some life in the kickoff return team.

The defense isn't oriented toward takeaways, and the secondary is in flux with Louis Oliver gone and Jarvis Williams probably gone, which means that the starting safeties will probably be new pickups Michael Stewart (LA Rams) and Gene Atkins (New Orleans). Cornerback Troy Vincent, coming off a serious knee injury, may move inside.

When the club hit the skids last December, the defense was first to go. The Dolphins allowed 115 points and 1,230 yards in their last three games. The defensive line is extremely average and LB John Offerdahl can't stay healthy.

That's why the Fish spent six of their seven draft picks on defensive help. Rookie DT Tim Bowens is raw but powerful at 300 pounds, and OLB Aubrey Beavers will push for a starting job.

If it's possible to draft a single special teams player, think about McDuffie.

KICKER

Pete Stoyanovich is a fine kicker with great range. He has made 13 FGs of 50 yards or more in his five seasons, counting playoffs. For his career he is 23 of 34 from 40-49 yards, which is a remarkable 68 percent, and he's 11 of 21 from outside the 50.

He didn't get a lot of chances in 1993 to show off that leg but he's a consistent performer who can make the high-mileage boot. He turned down a huge free agent contract from New England and signed for less to stay with the Dolphins.

★☆★☆MINNESOTA VIKINGS★☆★☆

by Larry Michael
NFL Play-by Play Announcer
Mutual Radio Network

Dennis Green found a way to get the Vikings into the playoffs as a wild-card team, but the reality in Minnesota is that the team needs to do better offensively if they want to advance past the first round. The 17th-ranked offense in the NFL had injuries in the backfield as 1992 rushing leader Terry Allen missed the entire '93 season with a knee injury, and first-round draft pick Robert Smith went down. Allen is back in '94, while Smith will miss training camp, with hopes of being ready for the start of the season. The most dramatic change will come at quarterback where classy veteran Warren Moon has been brought in to replace the tandem of Jim McMahon and Sean Salisbury. Defensive stalwart Chris Doleman has been traded to Atlanta; for this team to improve this season, the changes on offense, especially at quarterback with Warren Moon, need to pay off.

QUARTERBACK

How many years does veteran Warren Moon have left ? His fate in Minnesota depends on an improved offensive line as well as an injury-free set of running backs. Minnesota uses a three wide receiver set, but leaving the Run-and-Shoot should do Moon some good. Last season he was the ninth-rated FFL scorer with 21 passing touchdowns, and one on the ground. If he equals those scoring totals this year, he will have had a very good season. The back-ups are inexperienced at best, with Gino Torretta and Brad Johnson. It is hard to imagine Denny Green going into the season without an experienced backup for Moon, who will celebrate his 38th birthday during the upcoming season.

RUNNING BACK

Two years ago Terry Allen was the third-rated FFL running back in the entire NFL. With 15 touchdowns, Allen was a star in the making, only to be cut down by a knee injury. How will he perform this season for the Vikings? How will last year's number-one pick Robert Smith perform this season? He's also trying to come back from knee surgery. These are question marks which won't be answered until the hitting starts. Last season's injuries opened the door for young Scottie Graham, who revitalized his career by taking advantage of the opportunity. In seven games, Graham gained close to 500 yards and scored three touchdowns. With four draft picks in the first two rounds, the Vikings will be looking to add another running back.

WIDE RECEIVER

The draft will be a factor as the Vikings need to add some youth to a fine, yet aging corps of receivers. Anthony and Cris Carter are back, Cris coming off what might have been his best year ever with 86 catches for 1076 yards and 9 touchdowns. Jake Reed returns along with veteran tight end Steve Jordan, who last year snagged just one touchdown pass. Qadry Ismail is part of the mix, but fresh face David Palmer, a second-round pick out of Alabama, is the wild-card in the Vikings receiving corps.

DEFENSE/SPECIAL TEAMS

One of the great pass rushers in the game, Chris Doleman, has moved on to Atlanta, but with the likes of John Randle returning, the Vikings defense should be in good shape. Kick returner Qadry "The Missile" Ismail came close to breaking several big plays last year, and maybe a year's experience will help get him into the end zone. Rookie David Palmer, along with Ismail, gives Minnesota a dangerous return crew. Underused Amp Lee comes over from San Francisco, and could be a threat on special teams, as well.

KICKER

Thirty-one year old Fuad Reveiz ranked 18th among FFL kickers last year, kicking 26 field goals, including one from 50+ yards. The controlled environment of the Metrodome provides Reveiz a good kicking venue, but he doesn't look to be a high FFL pick.

★☆★☆NEW ENGLAND PATRIOTS★☆★☆

By Dave Douglas
NFL Films

The New England Patriots won only five games and finished fourth in the AFC East, but Bill Parcells' team will make the playoffs this season. It's a bold prediction but not too ridiculous when you consider some important factors. Sure, they only won five times, but four of those wins were consecutive at the end of the season...something to build on. The Bills have lost some key players, Miami struggled last year, and the Colts and Jets are in transition, so perhaps Parcells' soft schedule will allow him to make his move and grab a wild-card spot. First-round pick defensive end Willie McGinest (USC) is the prototype Parcells defender...big and fast. The Cowboys coveted him and Parcells will unleash him right from the start.

QUARTERBACK

In 1993, Bill Parcells made Drew Bledsoe the first pick in the entire draft. What he got was a 6' 5" flamethrower who was as polished as any rookie passer ever to enter the league. Parcells used him conservatively at first then let him fire away toward the end of the year. Bledsoe (214 of 429 for 2494 yds. and 15 TDs) posted excellent numbers for a first-year quarterback. His 15 interceptions are not a concern because the Patriots were behind so often that he had to toss up some prayers against defenses primed for the pass. Bledsoe is a fantasy first-rounder, not so much because of his ability but because there's just not that many quality quarterbacks out there. He could easily have a 20+ touchdown pass season. Scott Secules was released (75 completions for 2 touchdowns in '93).

99

RUNNING BACK

No one loves to dominate more with the running game than Bill Parcells, but Bill will not play a straight smashmouth game in 1994. Bledsoe is the man he will ride.

Leonard Russell ripped off 1088 yards on an even 300 carries and scored 7 touchdowns. He's a top notch fantasy back and he will not last long. He'd be a perfect third-round pick. He caught 26 passes as well and he's the featured back, so don't let him get away. No other back had more than 50 carries for New England, so it's a one man show. Russell is clearly their work horse but keep your eye on Kevin Turner. Former Giant guard Bob Kratch was acquired to help make the ground game even more effective. Blair Thomas was acquired from the Jets, and Marion Butts (746 yds., 4 TDs) came over from San Diego, but Russell is still the key man.

WIDE RECEIVER

One guy carries...many catch. That's the problem when it comes to drafting a Patriot receiver. Tight end Ben Coates beat out Marv Cook (released) and led them all with 53 catches for 659 yards and 8 touchdowns. *Eight* touchdowns from a tight end? Remember Coates in your draft. Vincent Brisby was named to many all-rookie teams, and his 45 catches for 626 and 2 touchdowns will be improved upon in 1994. He's a true sleeper who'd make a great fourth receiver. Michael Timpson (42 for 654 and 2 TDs) put up virtually identical numbers but Brisby is the hot guy in their plans. Second-round pick Kevin Lee (Alabama) will compete for the starting job and just may win it.

DEFENSE/SPECIAL TEAMS

Thirty-four sacks and only 13 interceptions are numbers that Parcells will increase this season. Book it. Chris Slade (9) and

Andre Tippett (8.5) led the team in sacks while underrated linebacker Vincent Brown (158) led the team in tackles. McGinest will start and terrorize. Right corner Maurice Hurst paced them with four interceptions. The big news on defense is the acquisition of two former Giant veterans. Linebacker Steve Deossie and hard-hitting free safety Myron Guyton were brought in for their leadership ability, and Parcells will use them wisely. Last season, the young Patriot defense finished a respectable thirteenth in the league after only a year of molding.

Ronnie Harris and Ray Crittendon shared the punt and kick return duties last season, and while neither scored, both can flat-out fly. Former Cowboy Mike Saxon averaged 42.4 yards per punt, fourth-highest in team history.

KICKER

The kicking game was a real pain in the rear end for the Patriots last year, and after a failed bid to sign Pete Stoyanovich, New England is left to choose between Scott Sisson (a wretched 14 of 26) and veteran Matt Bahr (5 for 5 as a Patriot).

★☆★☆NEW ORLEANS SAINTS★☆★☆

by Larry Michael
NFL Play-by Play Announcer
Mutual Radio Network

After a 5-0 start last season, the Saints came marching in 3-8, to finish the season with a .500 record for the first time since 1990. The dip in the second half of the season, however, will not result in serious revamping of the roster. Last year's draft was a huge success with four rookies starting and three others making big contributions. Quarterback Jim Everett hopes to jump-start his career in New Orleans, with Wade Wilson back to battle for playing time. Plenty of talent in the backfield, as well as the signing of long-ball receiver Michael Haynes from Atlanta has head coach Jim Mora smiling. New Orleans has been on the doorstep of becoming a serious contender since the late '80s. Will this be the year New Orleans takes the next step?

QUARTERBACK

The much-maligned Jim Everett joins a returning Wade Wilson in a battle for the number-one quarterback job. The edge might go to Everett, but Coach Mora has shown an inclination in the past to go with the hot hand. Last year's relief QBs Mike Buck and Steve Walsh don't figure into the equation. The numbers on Everett and Wilson are adequate at best. Last year, Wilson delivered 12 touchdown passes to rank 20th in the FFL. Everett didn't even match Wilson's number. With the Rams, Everett threw for 8 touchdowns in 10 games. Neither man was the exclusive starter for his respective team in '93, so the outlook for the Saints is questionable. An improved ground game and increased speed at the

102

wide receiver position might do wonders for the FFL stats of the Saints' two signal callers.

RUNNING BACK

Last year's early-season rookie sensation Lorenzo Neal is back after a nasty ankle break. In his first two games he averaged 8.3 yards a carry, and this season a healthy Neal could go over the 1,000 yard mark. The multi-talented Brad Muster and Derek Brown will make major contributions, while the return of the injured Vaughn Dunbar gives the Saints plenty of depth in the backfield. If Neal and Dunbar are 100% this season, New Orleans should improve on the 10 rushing touchdowns the team tallied in '93. Added depth might come in the form of second-round draft pick Mario Bates.

WIDE RECEIVER

The move to New Orleans certainly gives Michael Haynes a chance to shine. The lightning-fast Haynes was the third choice at times behind Andre Rison and Mike Pritchard in Atlanta, but Haynes still caught 72 balls. He should surpass his total of four touchdowns from a year ago, and he has the speed to go all the way from any point on the field. Eric Martin (4 touchdowns in '93) and Quinn Early (6 TDs in '93) return, along with Torrance Small. Sure-handed '93 first-round pick Irv Smith is back at the tight end position, while longtime Saint Hoby Brenner has retired.

DEFENSE/SPECIAL TEAMS

Renaldo Turnbull leads the defense this season, after registering 13 sacks last year. Perennial Pro Bowler Rickey Jackson is unsigned, but there is a chance he could return for another year in

103

New Orleans if he accepts a pay cut. The team's leading interception man of a year ago, Gene Atkins (3 INTs) has moved on to Miami. The best all-around kick return man in the league plays for New Orleans--Tyrone Hughes led the NFL in punt returns, was second in kickoff returns, accounted for over 1,200 yards in kick returns, and scored three touchdowns via the return route.

KICKER

Record-breaker Morten Anderson is a favorite in the Big Easy. It's no wonder last season he again was one of the most consistent kickers in football, making 33 of 33 on extra points, 28 field goals, and a total of 146 FFL points. The Superdome is a factor for Anderson, who loves kicking indoors.

★☆★☆NEW YORK GIANTS★☆★☆

by Larry Weisman
Sports Columnist
USA TODAY

What a *marvelous* turnaround Dan Reeves sparked when he took over the New York Giants!

A team at war with itself and in need of new blood made bold personnel moves, reacted well to Reeves' disciplined style, and nearly won the NFC East. That late-season showdown with Dallas, lost 13-10 in overtime, was played out in classic dramatic style.

With Dan Reeves in control the Giants maintained the style that had won them Super Bowls under Bill Parcells. They led the NFL in rushing and they allowed fewer points than any other team. That's a great combination, especially for a cold-weather team.

Winning 11 games again, however, sounds like a tall order. Phil Simms, while coming off a terrific year, turns 39 in November and none of the backups seem even remotely ready to replace him. Lawrence Taylor is gone, and when will we ever see the likes of such a linebacker again? And will Mike Sherrard, recovering from a serious hip injury, so much as threaten the secondary?

Then there's free agency. Guard Bob Kratch and tackle Eric Moore, starters last season, departed. So did Lewis Tillman, the veteran back who so ably replaced Rodney Hampton, safety Myron Guyton, and cornerback Mark Collins.

The Giants will have a new look again, this time more in personnel than on the coaching staff.

QUARTERBACK

It's hard not to like Simms as a football player. Except if he's your key *fantasy* football player. The Giants' offense doesn't turn him loose except when the team is desperately behind, and his numbers reflect that. In what was widely regarded as a career year for Simms because of the team's play and his canny style, Simms threw 15 TD passes (of which an amazing *five* were nine yards or shorter). He doesn't run much and really doesn't dodge the pass rush so he really doesn't rack up the fantasy numbers. He has always been a great leader, but none of that counts in the fantasy game.

Behind him are Dave Brown and Kent Graham. That is better news for them than it is for you. They're unproven (and likely to stay that way so long as Simms draws breath).

RUNNING BACK

The equation really begins and ends with Hampton. The slashing tailback gets lots of carries but he put up only five TDs last year and his longest run of the season was 20 yards. He did have one breakaway TD run in the playoffs against Minnesota, but seemed last year to settle into that Giants bulldozer mode.

David Meggett, the little scatback everybody wants to copy, didn't puncture the end zone by rushing or receiving. If the Giants can't replace Tillman, Meggett could see more work. He ought to be doing the TD dance more often.

Fullback Jarrod Bunch, a big, plodding truck, should see more goal line action but he only scored two TDs in '93.

Remember, the Giants scored only 288 points last season, twelfth in the NFC. They're not wide-open, and they'd rather control the ball than score and give it up.

WIDE RECEIVER

After Sherrard's hip injury, the Giants lacked a go-to guy. Because Simms sees the field so well, he spreads the ball around. Good for the Giants, bad for you. Your best pick is TE Howard Cross, who keeps improving. Five of his 21 catches went for TDs, and the Giants really like to use the TE near the goal line.

Among the WRs, former Bronco Mark Jackson showed the most scoring punch. He scored four TDs on his 58 catches but had a late season slump, which is most troubling for a veteran.

Ed McCaffrey is a good number-three receiver. Chris Calloway lacks great speed, but the Giants like him and he had three TDs to spice his 35 grabs.

The intriguing guy is number-one pick Thomas Lewis, out of Indiana. He exploded up the charts in the weeks before the draft but caught many observers unaware. Though he didn't run well at the combine, he clocked 4.29 in the 40-yard dash on campus and 4.41 for the Giants. He *will* get playing time.

Still, the Giants don't throw a lot and they don't throw like they mean it. This is not the place to shop for the best in wide receivers.

DEFENSE/SPECIAL TEAMS

The Giants didn't allow any special teams scores and Meggett, hauling back kicks and punts, is usually good for at least one a year. And that's what he had in '93, one 75-yard punt return for a score.

New York likes to pay close attention to their special teams play, and kickoff specialist Brad Daluiso's lengthy kicks are usually difficult to return at all. Rookie CB Thomas Randolph comes with a reputation for blocking kicks.

The defense is sound more than it is opportunistic. The lone TD by return came from CB Mark Collins, who making tracks to

Kansas City in the offseason. He was also the top interceptor with four. If Randolph and fellow rookie Jason Sehorn are starting in the secondary, call the burn unit.

The Giants had 41 sacks. Their 28 takeaways rate as very average, but they had a plus-11 ratio in turnovers because they take such good care of the football.

KICKER

David Treadwell had a good year, riding in from Denver on Reeves' magic carpet to replace steady old Matt Bahr.

Treadwell hit 25 of 31, but was one of only three kickers not to try a 50-yard FG. When the long boot is called for, the Giants bring on Daluiso.

Don't go squandering any early picks on Treadwell, but don't be ashamed to take him after the top few kickers go.

★☆★☆NEW YORK JETS★☆★☆

by Larry Weisman
Sports Columnist
USA TODAY

Notable for their last-minute swoons and an offense that shone only between the 20s, the New York Jets made some radical but necessary changes in the offseason, not the least of which was dismissing head coach Bruce Coslet, who refused to accept an offensive coordinator and paid for his obstinacy with his job.

In his wake, he left a quarterback sniping at two key receivers and an offensive line in flux because of free agency.

Pete Carroll, the former defensive coordinator, steps into Coslet's job. He takes over an 8-8 team that could have been (and should have been) no worse than 10-6, a team that scored only 270 points (eleventh in the AFC). We wish him luck, because coaches saddled with underachieving teams need it.

QUARTERBACK

Plagued by a sore neck the second half of the season, Boomer Esaison played poorly. He had a great first half, but what is the fantasy league player to do when a club like the Jets can't even rest an injured starter, so bad is the backup?

Questions about Esaison's arm strength and durability, based on the latter portion of the '93 season, can't help but abound again. And his postseason rip jobs on WR Rob Moore and TE Johnny Mitchell ought to make for some interesting huddles.

Browning Nagle will not return as the backup but, honestly, who cares? He bombed as the starter in '92 and likely hasn't improved with so limited playing time. In the offseason, the Jets signed ex-Colt Jack Trudeau as a backup, but taking any Jets QB can be a dangerous play without much upside.

RUNNING BACK

It's hard not to like Johnny Johnson, who led the team in rushing *and* receiving. The Jets acquired him for just about nothing on draft day, and he relegated long-time do-nothing Blair Thomas to the ash heap.

Unfortunately, as productive as Johnson is between the 20s, he doesn't get it done at the goal line. He had three rushing TDs, and one receiving. Not good enough, unless there's a yardage bonus in your league.

The real player here is fullback Brad Baxter. He's the money man. He drove home seven rushing TDs in '93, but they were all shorties.

The guy with breakaway speed is Adrian Murrell, who had an interesting rookie year. He averaged 4.6 yards a carry, scored on a 37-yard run, and gave the team a different dimension. With Thomas gone as a free agent, Murrell might see more time and make you look smart if you grab him late for the heck of it.

WIDE RECEIVER

Rob Moore had that "go-to guy" look early in the season, then suffered an ankle injury. When he came back, the Jets wanted him running routes over the middle instead of deep and he didn't like it.

The upshot? The talented and acrobatic Moore had only one measly TD grab in his 64 receptions. He should be much more productive than that. As the Jets' transition player, he tried desperately to get a contract offer elsewhere but was unsigned by presstime. The Jets weren't going to let him get away, anyhow. You might want to.

110

Mitchell, the big, promising and still raw-as-red-meat tight end is the guy to grab. He had 6 TDs in 39 catches last year while slowed by a knee that he contended the club didn't treat properly. Esaison has always loved the play-fake and then going to the tight end down the seam, and Mitchell is made for that.

The Jets will be looking for depth at WR with Chris Burkett retired (perhaps temporarily). They picked Wyoming's Ryan Yarborough in the second round and like his size. He caught 153 passes for 28 TDs the last two seasons in wacky and pass-happy WAC, and he has great size and decent speed. He could start opposite Moore.

DEFENSE/SPECIAL TEAMS

Nothing special. Punter Louie Aguiar had the lowest gross average in the league and he is history, replaced by free agent Brian Hansen. The Jets had no special teams TDs, and only one return for a TD by the defense. Their kickoff return average of 14.7 yards was worst in the league and they were only middlin' taking back punts.

Sacks? A mere 29. Takeaways? Not bad with 37, but DE Jeff Lageman comes in off surgery again and FS Lonnie Young, a heady competitor, split for Cincinnati. A plus will be number-one pick Aaron Glenn. The Texas A&M cornerback gets after the ball well, and he's also a dynamic returner, leading the nation last year in punt returns with a 19.9 average. That's got to have the Jets excited. Watch this young man closely in training camp.

Defensively, with Carroll around, the Jets figure to remain solid. Special teams need a serious upgrade and a guy like Glenn can do wonders.

KICKER

Cary Blanchard had a rotten year. The Jets were 25th in the NFL in FG percentage (65.4), and Blanchard showed little accuracy in hand-grenade range.

He missed his only attmept from 50, was 5 of 10 from 40-49, and his long for the season was a mere 45 yards, with only one AFC kicker (New England's Scott "Missin" Sisson) having a shorter long for the year.

If he's not better, he's unemployed. Do you want that to happen on your watch? Look elsewhere, pilgrim.

★☆★☆PHILADELPHIA EAGLES★☆★☆

By Dave Douglas
NFL Films

Has anybody seen Ron Heller, Keith Jackson or Keith Byars? Oh, that's right, they were shipped off to Miami in 1993. How about the "Minister of Defense," Reggie White? He's now tending the flock in Green Bay. It seems the Eagles are in the midst of a clearance sale and the store never closes. Defensive end Clyde Simmons took off to join Buddy Ryan in Phoenix as did teammate Seth Joyner. In fact, Norman Braman sold the entire team to Hollywood producer Jeff Lurie. The Eagles blame the salary cap for their fire sale. In a new era where all 28 teams must put their "thinking caps" on, the Eagles seem to be placing their hopes on select free agents and draft picks. Getting young and cutting fat salaries is the order of the day in Philadelphia.

QUARTERBACK

How would the Dallas Cowboys have fared if they lost Troy Aikman and Michael Irvin for virtually the entire year? Well that's what happened to the Eagles when Randall Cunningham and Fred Barnett were injured in the fourth week and knocked out for the year.

Randall Cunningham is a quality first-round fantasy pick when he's healthy and happy. He says that his knee is fine, and he got married a year ago, so prospects for big numbers in 1994 for a healed and upbeat Randall are good. Randall has excellent receiving targets and he's a legitimate bonus baby by virtue of his unmatched ability to run for touchdowns. Watch his knees in the preseason. If the mobility is there, Randall should be one of the first

113

quarterbacks to go in your draft. Draft pick Bernard Williams (tackle, Georgia) had better not let Randall be blindsided.

Never before has the value of a quality backup been so high in the NFL and the FFL. Starters are banged up, yanked out, and replaced almost every week. In Philly, Bubby Brister proved himself a worthy replacement by leading the Eagles to a 4-2 finish after a shaky start. Brister was 181 of 309 and fired 14 touchdown passes in about 12 1/2 games. It seemed he would become a starter by signing with the Saints, but instead he returns as Randall's injury replacement. If you draft Cunningham, it might not be a bad idea to grab Brister in the late rounds as a fantasy insurance policy.

RUNNING BACK

Herschel Walker was a terrific all-around performer for the Birds last season. He earned the team's MVP award by running, receiving, blocking and volunteering for special teams duty. Unfortunately, just about all of his hard work was done between the 20-yard lines. He was their leading rusher (746 yards) and receiver (75 for 610) but only four times did he reach the end zone. Touchdowns are where it's at in the FFL, and Herschel just doesn't quite cut it in that department. If you need a third running back late in the draft, Walker might fit the bill. Heath Sherman (406 yards, 2 TDs), Vaughn Hebron (297 yards, 3 TDs) and James Joseph (140 yards, 1 TD) will more than likely fight it out to see who starts along with Walker. Rookie draft pick Charlie Garner (Tennessee) will vie for the starting spot in the preseason.

WIDE RECEIVER

The best by far is Fred Barnett and the knee injury he suffered against the Jets early in the '93 season is completely rehabilitated. He is Randall's main man. His combined numbers in '91 and '92 are a solid 129 catches for 2031 yards and 10

114

touchdowns. Barnett gets deep and he's a true leaper, so the long touchdown receptions that fantasy owners crave are certainly a possibility with "Downtown Freddie." Calvin Williams had to take his game to another level when Barnett went down, and he made great strides in 1993.

Williams was the possession receiver, and he caught 60 passes for 10 touchdowns, including one that went for 80 yards. He's a fourth-rounder. Barnett's a third. Ageless Mark Bavaro was an excellent acquisition at tight end for Rich Kotite. Bavaro caught 43 passes and scored 6 touchdowns.

DEFENSE/SPECIAL TEAMS

In the opinion of many, Bud Carson is the finest defensive coach in the game. He'll have his work cut out for him in 1994. Gone are the veteran all-pros who held offenses hostage for years. Last season, Tim Harris missed virtually the entire season. Keith Millard couldn't stay onsides and Reggie White's leadership was sorely missed. To make matters worse, Clyde Simmons and Seth Joyner had lackluster seasons. Still, Carson's defense did more than hold its own. The unit totalled 36 sacks, 20 interceptions and forced 22 fumbles. Andy Harmon led the team with 11.5 sacks. William Fuller (10 sacks) was signed to help offset the loss of Simmons and "the Fuller Rush man" is just what they needed up front. DE Burt Grossman (SD) is a great acquisition if his shoulder holds up. Safety Ben Smith is off to Denver. Second-round pick Bruce Walker (DT, UCLA) could split time with William "Fridge" Perry.

Eric Allen may be the best cornerback in the game and last season he picked off 6 and returned an amazing 4 of them for touchdowns. His 94-yard interception return journey against the Jets may have been the NFL's play of the year. Linebackers Seth Joyner and Byron Evans were the Eagles' leading tacklers.

Vai Sikahema wasn't nearly as explosive as he had been the previous year, as he failed to score on any of his team-leading 33 punt returns. Sikahema, Walker and Jeff Sydner shared the kickoff return duties, but Vai retired so it looks to be Sydner's job to lose. Last season punter Jeff Feagles averaged a perfect 40 yards per boot, but in the offseason ran West and joined Arizona, so the punting duty is, at presstime, vacant.

KICKER

Roger Ruzek was cut in favor of veteran Matt Bahr (8 of 13 field goals) and then brought back to replace Bahr. Now the Eagles have signed Cowboy kicker Eddie Murray to a two-year deal.

★☆★☆PITTSBURGH STEELERS★☆★☆

By Dave Douglas
NFL Films

Bill Cowher's Pittsburgh Steelers are on the verge of greatness in the opinion of many. They've spent the last two seasons battling their way into the playoffs before getting tossed out in their first playoff game. Last year, Pittsburgh won nine games in the regular season before dropping a 27-24 heartbreaker in OT against the Chiefs in the wild-card round. They just can't seem to get over the hump and get into the AFC championship game. Their defense is Super Bowl quality, and offensively they made great strides despite an injury to All-Pro running back Barry Foster. Cowher is tough but fair, a true player's coach, and in 1994 look for them to make their move. The drafting of Colorado receiver Charles Johnson was a solid first step.

QUARTERBACK

Neil O'Donnell improved significantly last season and emerged as a reliable field general. Despite a receiving corps that is average at best, he still managed to throw twice as many touchdown passes as interceptions. He operates behind one of the finest lines in football, perhaps the best in the AFC. While Cowher likes to establish the run first, O'Donnell still put the ball up 486 times, big numbers for an FFL quarterback. He completed 270 passes for 3,208 yards and 14 touchdowns. O'Donnell is not a Marino, Young, Aikman or Elway, but he'll be drafted in the second group of quarterbacks. Mike Tomczak started one game.

RUNNING BACK

When Barry Foster is healthy and into the game, he can dominate. Leon Searcy, John Jackson, Duval Love, Dermontti Dawson and Carlton Haselrig are powerful and mobile and behind that line Barry runs wild. Foster (711 yds. and 8 TDs) was injured for a chunk of last season but he was on a 1300-yard, 12-touchdown pace. His ankle injury is healed and he's expected to be the workhorse in 1994. When Foster went down against Buffalo on Monday night, Leroy Thompson stepped right in and the Steeler ground game never skipped a beat. Thompson (763 yds. and 3 TDs) is an excellent back, but if Foster's healthy, Thompson will not get enough fantasy carries to make him worth while. If Foster goes down, snatch him from the waiver wire immediately. Merril Hoge was picked up by the Bears but he was replaced with John L. Williams (SEA).

WIDE RECEIVER

The most productive was mammoth Eric Green. When he gets that 280 pounds turned upfield, he's unstoppable. He caught a team-leading 63 passes for 952 yards and scored 5 times. Green will be one of the first tight ends drafted. Jeff Graham (38 for 579 and 0 TDs) and Dwight Stone (41 for 587 and 2 TDs) put up similar numbers, and neither is a real impact FFL receiver. Free agent Yancey Thigpen turned only 9 catches into 3 touchdowns while Ernie Mills caught 29 balls and scored once. Tight end Adrian Cooper left for Minnesota. Top draft pick Charles Johnson has all the tools to be a superb player. He'll win the job and learn in his rookie year. He's one year away from stardom.

DEFENSE/SPECIAL TEAMS

The "New Steel Curtain" is young, lean and mean. In 1993 they punished opponents, collecting 42 sacks and a whopping 24 interceptions. Cornerback D.J. Johnson (ATL) and DE Donald Evans (NYJ) were lost to free agency, but the heart of the unit remains. Kevin Greene was a perfect fit when he came in from the Rams and led the team with 12.5 sacks. Linebacker Greg Lloyd topped the Steelers in tackles and added another 6 sacks. The leader of the defense is All-World Rod Woodson, perhaps the best defensive back in the NFL. Woodson picked off a team-leading 8 passes last season, the most by a Steeler since 1975. Carnell Lake and Darren Perry added 4 interceptions apiece. DE Ray Seals was acquired from Tampa Bay and he'll offset the loss of Evans. 1993 first round pick Deon Figures could fill in nicely for D.J. Johnson.

Rod Woodson returned every punt for an 8.2 yard average, and he shared the kickoff return assignments with Dwight Stone and rookie Andre Hastings. Punter Mark Royals averaged 42.5 yards per attempt and had none blocked.

KICKER

Gary Anderson was nearly perfect, hitting on 28 out of 30 field goals. He's made 9 straight postseason kicks, and last year he totalled 116 points.

★☆★☆SAN DIEGO CHARGERS★☆★☆

By John Weiss
NFL Films

You can't blame sports fans in San Diego for suffering from an identity crisis. One year after they had to endure the mass exodus of most of their Padres' stars, they watched as a number of big names from their Chargers also packed their bags and left town.

Among those gone via either trade or free agency are: last year's leading rusher Marion Butts; last year's leading receiver Anthony Miller; former first-round draft pick, defensive end Burt Grossman; longtime starting linebacker Gary Plummer; starting wide receiver Nate Lewis; and backup quarterback John Friesz.

Yes, Chargers fans will definitely need a program in 1994. And head coach Bobby Ross will need a lot of patience while reshuffling a team that finished 8-8 in an injury-plagued 1993 season. The Chargers need to stay healthy and fill in the right pieces to the puzzle to contend for the playoffs again.

QUARTERBACK

In 1993, a preseason shoulder injury bothered Stan Humphries throughout the year, and he and the Chargers' offense suffered. Humphries missed four games during the year, and finished with 1,981 yards passing, a 53.4 completion percentage, 12 touchdowns and 10 interceptions. To consider him on draft day you have to hope not only that he stays healthy, but that he adjusts to his new targets in 1994. He's a gamble, and you have to decide if you're willing to take the risk.

120

RUNNING BACK

With Marion Butts traded to New England, the stock of Natrone Means has skyrocketed since last season. As a rookie in 1993, Means finished second on the team behind Butts with 645 yards rushing (4.0-yard average) and also scored a team-high 8 touchdowns. He's definitely worth a look when it comes time to pick a running back.

Ronnie Harmon is still one of the league's most versatile players, finishing third among all NFL backs with 73 receptions in 1993. He also gained 216 yards rushing (4.7 average) and scored two touchdowns on the ground. Eric Bieniemy rushed for 135 yards (4.1 average) and one score.

WIDE RECEIVER

Without Anthony Miller and Nate Lewis, who do the Chargers turn to at receiver?

Well, they signed Vance Johnson away from Denver and traded for former Dolphin Tony Martin. Johnson had 36 catches for 517 yards and 5 touchdowns in 1993, before a season-ending ankle injury in the Broncos' 11th game. Martin missed four games last year after mid-season knee surgery, finishing with 20 receptions for 347 yards and three touchdowns.

The most promising of San Diego's holdovers is Shawn Jefferson, who had a career-high 30 catches for 391 yards and two touchdowns. H-back Alfred Pupunu started the final five games of last season and finished with 13 catches for 142 yards. Tight end Duane Young added six catches for 41 yards and two scores.

DEFENSE/SPECIAL TEAMS

Injuries to key starters Gil Byrd, Burt Grossman and Jerrol Williams decimated the Chargers' defense in 1993, as the unit slipped to number 18 in the league. San Diego's big problem was pass defense, which ranked dead-last in the NFL. The Chargers were number two in the league against the run.

Linebacker Junior Seau will once again be the heart of the defense, having led the team in tackles the past three seasons. Last year, Seau tallied 129 total tackles, 108 of which were solo, and also added two interceptions. The Chargers added linebacker help with the signing of Dennis Gibson, who ranked fifth on the Lions last season with 62 tackles (41 solo), and added one sack and one interception.

If you're looking for consistent sacks, it's hard to beat defensive end Leslie O'Neal, who once again led the Chargers in sacks with 12 in 1993. O'Neal now has 29 sacks over the past two seasons. Second-year defensive end Chris Mims added seven sacks and defensive tackle Shawn Lee had three. To help up front, the Chargers signed defensive lineman Reuben Davis, who had one sack last season with the Cardinals.

In the secondary, safety Darren Carrington led the team with a career-high seven interceptions, and was also third on the team with 79 tackles (67 solo). The Chargers added free agent corner-back Dwayne Harper, who had one interception last season for the Seahawks.

On special teams, Darrien Gordon finished as the NFL's third-leading punt returner with a 12.7-yard average on 31 returns.

KICKER

After showing off a red-hot foot to start last season, John Carney cooled his heels down the stretch, but he still finished fifth in the NFL in scoring with 124 points.

In two of the first three games, Carney accounted for all the Chargers' points with six field goals in each contest. But after that, Carney looked pretty average, hitting on just 18 of his last 27 attempts to finish at 31-of-40 for the year. He was 2-of-3 from 50-plus yards.

★☆★☆SAN FRANCISCO 49ERS★☆★☆

by Larry Weisman
Sports Columnist
USA TODAY

For fantasy league firepower, it's hard to match San Francisco.

The top-scoring quarterback. Top-scoring wide receiver. Second-ranked running back.

Better still, there's no reason to believe this group can't reproduce its feats of 1993.

Steve Young returns to run the offense, to fling the football to Jerry Rice or tuck it into Ricky Watters' gut. Or perhaps journey downfield with it himself. That's as good a trio as anywhere.

The 49ers concentrated their offseason moves on the defense, which hadn't been the thieving, conniving unit of old in some time and really let the team down against Dallas in the NFC championship team.

Ray Rhodes returns from Green Bay as defensive coordinator, and free agency has beefed up the defense. If the 49ers improve their kicking situation (and they hadn't at presstime), they will be even more of a smorgasbord from which to pluck FFL plums.

QUARTERBACK

No reason to believe Young won't be the first choice in most drafts. He accounted for 31 TDs last season and led the FFL in scoring with 273 points.

No QB threw more than Young's 13 TD passes in that all-important 10-39 yard range and his 5 TDs of 40 or more yards was second in the FFL. He also scampered in himself for a pair of TDs.

Given the weapons around him and the receivers, Young is bound to rack up huge numbers.

The backup situation remains unsettled. Apparently trying to restructure Steve Bono's salary didn't work, so the 49ers dealt Bono to the Chiefs.

Since he's gone, the chain of command then goes to Elvis Grbac, the former Michigan standout, and Bill Musgrave, a relatively immobile young guy with a good head. If the 49ers are forced to go to either, all bets are off, though Grbac has shown a flair for this offense in preseason action.

RUNNING BACK

Watters showed a great toughness around the goal line late last year and scored 10 rushing TDs, 8 in the 1-to-9 yard range. He is also improving as a pass receiver, which should increase his value. If he stays healthy for the entire season, there's reason to beleive he could produce 12-15 scores.

When fullback Tom Rathman went out early with a shoulder separation, veteran Marc Logan stepped in and performed very well. The 49ers seemed in no hurry to offer Rathman a new contract in the offseason and Logan figures as the reason. He rushed for 7 TDs and caught 32 passes, though none for TDs. The way the 49ers spread the ball around makes Logan an interesting sleeper pick.

Other 'Niners to watch include Rathman, who scored on 3 of his 18 carries last season, and Dexter Carter, who plays primarily on special teams but broke a 50-yard rush for a TD (though he had only 6 carries).

The new kid on the block is fullback William Floyd, the 49ers first-round draft choice. He's a truck who's dangerous around the goal line and could be the heir to Rathman's job.

WIDE RECEIVER

Rice is Young's go-to guy, and don't you forget it. He caught 15 of Young's 29 TD passes, while only six other players caught scoring passes.

Want to gamble? Make Rice your first pick. He so outperforms other players at his position that he can make up for waiting to take the QB. Rice also runs the end-around very well and scored a 43-yard TD on that play last year.

Explosive John Taylor had a down year in the point-production area, but should bounce back from a 4-TD showing.

Tight end Brent Jones, a consistent performer, put up 3 TDs last year among his 61 catches, and generally he is among the top guys in leagues that require a tight end.

There's little receiving depth beyond these guys that will matter to fantasy GMs. Rookie Cory Fleming might bear a look, but don't get too excited.

DEFENSE/SPECIAL TEAMS

Bad as the 49ers were on defense, they scored 5 TDs on returns. Rhodes will make them even more opportunistic and the addition by free agency of LBs Gary Plummer and Ken Norton surely will help. This makes the defense more attractive.

With Carter returning kicks, anything can happen, but not much happened last year. He hauled one punt back for a 72-yard TD but the 49ers ranked thirteenth (of 14) in the NFC in kickoff return yardage.

The 'Niners will be tougher against the run with number-one draft pick Bryant Young, a DT from Notre Dame, likely to get plenty of playing time.

KICKER

Mike Cofer must have pictures of 49ers' executives engaged in strange games to keep his job, kicking the way he does. He made 4 of 10 FGs from 40 yards and beyond, and didn't hit any from beyond 50. His long FG the last two seasons is 46 yards.

The only plus for him is that he gets lots of opportunities because the 49ers move the ball. But he only tried 26 FGs in '93, making 16, tying him with three others for least productive in the NFC.

Expect draftee Doug Brien of Cal, a number-three pick, to take Cofer's job. While he hasn't got a cannon for a leg either, at least he's been reasonably accurate (15 of 18 FGs for Cal last year).

★☆★☆SEATTLE SEAHAWKS★☆★☆

By John Weiss
NFL Films

The bad news for the Seahawks last year: they posted their fourth losing record in the past five seasons. The good news: they played about as well as anyone could have expected, and showed significant improvement over the year before.

After suffering through a 2-14 debacle in 1992, Seattle raised its record to 6-10 in 1993. What's more, the Seahawks doubled their point output from an anemic 140 to a respectable 280.

Tom Flores has this young team headed in the right direction, but the Seahawks are probably still a year or two away from seriously contending in the AFC West.

QUARTERBACK

The major difference in Seattle's offense last season was the spark added by rookie quarterback Rick Mirer, whose performance surpassed anyone's expectations.

Showing an incredible maturity, Mirer stepped right in and started all 16 games, the first rookie quarterback to start all of his team's games since 1973. In the process, he set NFL rookie records for most attempts (486), completions (274), and yards (2,833). He threw for 12 touchdowns and 17 interceptions, and also ran for 343 yards and three scores.

Most quarterbacks need two or three years in the league before they become productive. Mirer is way ahead of the game, and if he can once again stay healthy, his numbers (both NFL and FFL) will only get better in 1994. He's certainly among the top 10 or 12 quarterbacks you should consider on draft day.

RUNNING BACK

You would never have thought it, but the Seahawks had the AFC's number one rushing offense in 1993. That's especially surprising for a team playing catch-up much of the season.

The workhorse once again was Chris Warren, who posted his second straight 1,000-yard rushing season, despite missing the final two games with an abdominal injury. Warren finished with 1,072 yards (3.9-yard average) and 7 touchdowns. He added 15 catches for 99 yards. Warren has proven he's no fluke, and he's definitely one of the top FFL running back prospects for 1994.

In limited duty, Jon Vaughn ran for 153 yards (4.3 average). Longtime Seattle favorite John L. Williams signed as a free agent with Pittsburgh.

WIDE RECEIVER

The Seahawks had a couple of receivers put up pretty good numbers in 1993, and they have a chance to improve those stats as they continue to develop a rapport with Mirer.

Brian Blades came back strong from an injury-plagued 1992 season to post a team-record 80 catches for 945 yards and 3 touchdowns. The other starter, Kelvin Martin, had 57 receptions for a career-high 798 yards and a team-high 54 TDs.

Starting tight end Ferrell Edmunds had 24 catches for 239 yards and 2 touchdowns. Backup Paul Green added 23 receptions for 178 yards and one score.

DEFENSE/SPECIAL TEAMS

The Seattle defense slipped to number 23 in the league last season, number 26 against the pass.

To help in the secondary, the Seahawks signed Pro Bowl cornerback Nate Odomes away from the Bills, and he'll now join another Pro Bowler in safety Eugene Robinson. Odomes and Robinson tied for the NFL interception lead last season with nine apiece, and they now give Seattle two of the top ball hawks in the league. Over the last three seasons, Robinson has nabbed 21 interceptions while Odomes has 19. Robinson also led the Seahawks in tackles last season with 111 (84 solo), marking the fourth time in the last six years that he's led the team in that category. Cornerback Patrick Hunter was second on the team last season with four interceptions.

Defensive tackle Cortez Kennedy's numbers were down from his monster 1992 season, but he still made a big enough impact to go to the Pro Bowl. Kennedy fought his way through almost constant double-teaming to finish with 6.5 sacks and 77 tackles (60 solo). Second-year defensive end Michael Sinclair led the team with eight sacks despite playing in only the first nine games. To help take some pressure off Kennedy up front, the Seahawks drafted Texas A&M defensive end Sam Adams in the first round.

At linebacker, Terry Wooden was second on the team with 106 tackles (73 solo), and Rod Stephens third with 105 (75 solo). Pass-rush specialist Rufus Porter missed half of last season with a torn Achilles' tendon.

On special teams, Michael Bates averaged 20.1 yards on 30 kickoff returns, and Kelvin Martin averaged 8.4 yards while returning 32 punts.

KICKER

Accuracy wasn't the problem for John Kasay in 1993, but his lack of opportunities lowered his value as an FFL kicker.

Kasay connected on 23 of 28 field goals, including 3 of 5 from 50-plus yards, but finished with just 98 points for the season. That placed him only 19th in scoring among kickers. If you're looking at Kasay in 1994, you have to hope he gets more chances than he did a year ago.

★☆☆☆TAMPA BAY BUCCANEERS★☆☆☆

by Larry Michael
NFL Play-by Play Announcer
Mutual Radio Network

Sooner or later things are going to turn around for the Tampa Bay Bucs. This is a franchise that has been in double figures in losses for the last 11 straight years. Hard-working head coach Sam Wyche looks to turn around a Bucs team which finished 5-11 last year. The squad needs help on both sides of the ball, with the offense rated 25th in the NFL last year, and the defense ranked 22nd. Last year's leading rusher, Reggie Cobb, has moved on to Green Bay. The Bucs picked up a couple of key defensive players during the offseason, and the draft will help this team which longs for a winning season.

QUARTERBACK

Former University of Miami Quarterback Craig Erickson would have to be classified as a pleasant surprise last year. He threw more passes of 40+ yards for touchdowns (6) than any other quarterback in the NFL. His 171 FFL points put him ahead of such standouts as Warren Moon, Jim Kelly and Troy Aikman. When draft day for the FFL arrives, how many team owners will consider taking Craig Erickson ahead of the better-known quarterbacks? By FFL standards, Erickson is worth a top pick. The Bucs are in search of a veteran to back up Erickson, but their future might rest in the hands of number-one draft pick Trent Dilfer out of Fresno State.

RUNNING BACK

Tampa Bay is going to camp without Reggie Cobb, their leading rusher of a year ago. The Bucs are a team that scored just six total touchdowns on the ground all of last season, so there isn't much to talk about for FFL fans. If a draftee doesn't crack the starting lineup, it will be Vince Workman and Mazio Royster sharing most of the work. Last season they combined for 399 yards and three touchdowns. Draw your own conclusions. Second-round draft pick Erict Rhett of Florida has a chance to make an impact.

WIDE RECEIVER

The Bucs have one good one in Courtney Hawkins. He can go deep and over the middle, has good hands and fine speed. He should improve on his five touchdown receptions of a year ago, and key to his improvement will be who lines up on the other side. Lawrence Dawsey is fully recovered from a knee injury which sidelined him for all but four games last year, and Tyji Armstrong is also back. Horace Copeland goes into his second year as a good deep threat. Last year he averaged 21.3 yards a catch with four touchdowns, the longest going for 67 yards. Tight end is a question mark after the loss of free agent Ron Hall. Again, the draft could yield a receiver or tight end who would be a major contributor this season.

DEFENSE/SPECIAL TEAMS

Though top sack man Ray Seals has moved on, the Bucs defense will be better in '94 for a number of reasons. Even though he has some injury setbacks, last year's first-round pick Eric Curry was very productive at times; Santana Dotson heads into his third year with 15 sacks over the first two campaigns; Thomas Everett was acquired from Dallas; and Lonnie Marts was a pick-up from

Kansas City. There is no clear-cut lead return man, with Courtney Hawkins and Mazio Royster expected to carry some of the load returning kicks.

KICKER

The kicker again this year will be Michael Husted. Last season, Husted ranked 24th among kickers in the FFL with 102 total points. If the offense improves, Husted's numbers should also improve.

★☆★☆WASHINGTON REDSKINS★☆★☆

by Larry Weisman
Sports Columnist
USA TODAY

Just a little over two years ago the Washington Redskins were coming off one of the most dominating seasons they'd ever had.

A 14-2 record. A cruise through the playoffs. A drubbing of Buffalo in Super Bowl XXVI.

Now almost nothing remains from that season, from that championship.

Joe Gibbs? Gone two years now. Richie Petitbon? Fired after last year's 4-12 disaster. Super Bowl MVP Mark Rypien? Waived. The NFL's all-time leading receiver Art Monk? Offered a 50 percent paycut that he declined, ending his Redskins career after 14 years.

And that's just some of the bigger names. Jeff Bostic, Carl Banks, Charles Mann, Ricky Sanders. Outta here.

In comes Norv Turner, the former Dallas Cowboys offensive coordinator. In comes a new staff and new talent: John Friesz and rookie Heath Shuler to battle at quarterback, Ethan Horton at tight end, Ken Harvey at linebacker.

Can the Redskins regain even a hint of their former glory or has the rebuilding only begun? We're closer to the latter than the former, but every great journey begins with one step.

QUARTERBACK

Friesz is very much an average QB buffeted by coaching changes. And he's not been particularly durable.

Shuler, the number-three pick overall in the draft, has immense potential but is greener than your lawn. So which way do the Redskins go? And which way do you go?

Well, the Redskins likely will start Friesz as they try to sort out their offense. If someone has to get killed behind an offensive line getting reacquainted, it won't be the quarterback of the future. It'll be the quarterback of right now, and that's Friesz.

With targets like Horton, the disappointing Desmond Howard, and a slipping Henry Ellard, who signed as a free agent, don't expect much.

Shuler, Turner has said, will start as soon as he's able. That'll be a few weeks into the season, and if he's like every other rookie passer, will throw more picks than TDs.

RUNNING BACK

An area of some strength that figures to be better with LT Jim Lachey healthy again.

Reggie Brooks gained 1,063 yards as a rookie and scored three TDs, including an 85-yard breakaway. The coaching staff badly mishandled both him and Brian Mitchell, a free agent who only re-signed in late May, jerking them in and out of the lineup.

Bet on Brooks as the main man in a two-man backfield, with a ground game structured the way Dallas' was. Watch those preseason games carefully to see if Brooks gets work around the goal line. He'll be an interesting pick anyway, but if the 'Skins yank him in the deep red zone, hold off.

Fullback could fall to Frank Wycheck, a tight end and running back in college who impressed as a rookie. He'll catch some passes, but he's no sledge-hammer blocking.

Ricky Ervins and Earnest Byner don't seem to figure in Washington's plans.

WIDE RECEIVER

An area of uncharted waters. Ellard may be the best of this lot. He caught 61 passes for 945 yards but only 2 TDs for the LA Rams last year. The change of atmosphere ought to help him, but he has never been a big factor in the end zone.

Howard, the fourth pick in the draft two years ago, has been almost a total zero. He had 23 catches last year for a piddling 12.4 yard average, a long gain of 27, and no TDs. He had trouble learning Gibbs' offense, struggled with the changes in the passing game last year, and now starts over again. Ugh.

Horton had a down year for the L.A. Raiders, catching 43 passes, with one for a TD. He drops a lot of passes. Ugh. But Turner likes to use the tight end and Horton figures to be the guy. Feeling frisky? Take the long shot.

Rookie Tydus Winans out of Fresno State looks promising. Veteran holdovers Stephen Hobbs, Mark Stock and Greg Clifton won't add much to the mix.

DEFENSE/SPECIAL TEAMS

Washington punted very well last season and Reggie Roby gets the credit. And that's the highlight reel.

Mitchell, an exciting punt returner in previous years, slipped badly and the Redskins ranked thirteenth in the NFC in punt returns and didn't score. Nor did they score on kickoff returns. They'll be looking for someone to emerge here. In preseason, though, Turner has stated that Mitchell will be used as a back, a returner, and yes, even a quarterback for those tricky two-point conversion attempts.

The defense fell to 26th and had a middling 31 takeaways. But even in its doldrums the defense scored four TDs on returns and new defensive coordinator Ron Lynn will build on that.

This unit becomes a better FFL risk if a kick returner, be it Mitchell or someone else, comes to the fore.

KICKER

Chip Lohmiller had a terrible year. Holders changed, long snappers changed, and Lohmiller converted a meager 16 of 28 FGs. Worse, he lost his range. He was 1 of 4 from 40-49 yards, 1 of 6 from the 50 and out.

Taken the other way, he was 14 of 18 from 39 or less, which is passable.

He's better than he showed in Washington's all-around disaster of '93. He's a sneaky pick, but don't jump on him too early.

★5★

Quarterbacks

It's confession time: the QB is really the heart and soul of the team. Check out a team with a dippy quarterback and you've found a team that stinks. QBs are the guys who get most of the TV commercials. (Isn't that the most accurate scientific method for rating a player's value?) I mean, after all, when was the last time you saw McDonald's chase down a center or a pulling guard for a Big Mac commercial?

Quarterbacks can also play for a team for five years and never take a snap in a real game. Why? Because they are being groomed. Being a quarterback is like marrying the CEO's daughter and getting a really swell position with "Dad's" firm. No one can crack on you because one day you may be running the joint. Therefore, life is great!

DRAFTING STARTING QUARTERBACKS

In most fantasy leagues' scoring systems, quarterbacks generally are among the top producers. Therefore, I like the idea of selecting a solid quality quarterback for my first pick (unless Emmitt Smith is still on the board). The true art of drafting an upper-echelon quarterback may not be so simple if you pick near the end of the round. For example, if you have the tenth pick in a 12-team league, your prospects are looking dim. But let's just say somehow you were a bust in '93 and ended up with the third pick for the 1994 draft--hey, good news, you should have a shot at either John Elway, Steve Young, or the quite superb non-QB Emmitt Smith.

DRAFTING BACKUP QBs

I always stick to this adage: if you draft an explosive QB from an explosive, offensive-minded team, draft his backup as well. Last season I drove home the point that Steve Young would go bonkers with a solid season. I also stressed that those lucky enough to draft Young *must* also draft Steve Bono as his backup. Bono isn't Young, and isn't even in San Fran any more, but the proverbial San Francisco apple doesn't fall far from the tree! (In this case, the apple fell all the way to Kansas City, so now Bono will be the backup for Montana--*again!*)

This season I am excited over John Elway, Steve Young, Jeff George, Dan Marino and Troy Aikman--I expect a windfall from their offensive talents. Now, let's take a closer look at their backups.

STARTER	BACKUP	TEAM
John Elway	Tommy Maddox	Denver Broncos
Steve Young	Elvis Grbac	San Francisco 49ers
Jeff George	Bobby Hebert	Atlanta Falcons
Dan Marino	Bernie Kosar	Miami Dolphins
Troy Aikman	Rodney Peete	Dallas Cowboys

OK, this is where my backup theory gets put to test: if John Elway gets injured, do I really want Tommy Maddox leading my franchise? Hmmm, this is a gamble, but young Tommy Maddox is now entering his third season being tutored by John Elway; that in itself should be worth a draft selection.

Jeff George's backup is important because he has been known to get nicked up. Last season, the short-tossing Bobby Hebert had a good season stat-wise; but, despite being re-signed by the Birds, he will compete with Tolliver as a backup to George.

Dan Marino suffered the first injury of his career in '93; Scott Mitchell is no longer around as the backup, and that leaves the ancient warrior Steve Deberg or ex-Brown Bernie Kosar. Both are okay for a spot start or two, but not for a six- or seven-game stretch.

OTHER SOLID BACKUP QBs

QB

The best backup in the league may very well be Frank Reich of the Buffalo Bills. In fact, many experts believe that Reich (and not Kelly) would be Buffalo's best bet to win the big game--the Super Bowl. I think Reich is solid, but I disagree with the Kelly-bashing; after all, the only thing Jim Kelly has done is deliver his team to four straight Super Bowls!

With Joe Montana playing part-time in Kansas City, longtime Steve Young backup (and former Montana backup) Steve Bono is a good second FFL QB pick. Frankly, last season I was disappointed in David Krieg--I thought he would have worked well in tandem with Joe. Apparently, I wasn't the only one disappointed in him--in the offseason, he went to Detroit. Randall Cunningham (PHI) is no longer the indestructible player he once was--also, much of his former supporting cast (Keith Jackson and Keith Byars) have migrated to Miami. His backup is Bubby Brister. Sorry, folks, but I wouldn't want to place hopes of winning my FFL league championship on the shoulders of the

Bubster. In this case, I would attempt to draft a lower-echelon starting QB--a Scott Mitchell (DET) or John Friesz (WAS)--as my backup QB. Then, with my third QB pick, I would begrudgingly grab Brister.

1993 OFFICIAL TD BOMBERS (2 or more OVER 40 Yds.)

PLAYER	TEAM	NO.
Craig Erickson	Tampa Bay Buccaneers	6 TDs
Steve Young	San Francisco 49ers	5 TDs
Troy Aikman	Dallas Cowboys	4 TDs
Steve Beuerlein	Arizona Cardinals	4 TDs
Jim Everett	New Orleans Saints	4 TDs
Dan Marino	Miami Dolphins	3 TDs
Jeff Hostetler	Los Angeles Raiders	3 TDs
Bobby Hebert	Atlanta Falcons	3 TDs
Jim Kelly	Buffalo Bills	3 TDs
Scott Mitchell	Detroit Lions	3 TDs
John Elway	Denver Broncos	2 TDs
Brett Favre	Green Bay Packers	2 TDs
Warren Moon	Minnesota Vikings	2 TDs
Drew Bledsoe	New England Patriots	2 TDs
Phil Simms	New York Giants	2 TDs
V. Testaverde	Cleveland Browns	2 TDs
Stan Humphries	San Diego Chargers	2 TDs

THE DEAD ZONE...1993 DUBIOUS HONORS FOR MOST INTS

PLAYER	TEAM	INTS
Brett Favre	Green Bay Packers	24 INTs
Craig Erickson	Tampa Bay Buccaneers	21 INTs
Warren Moon	Minnesota Vikings	21 INTs
Jim Kelly	Buffalo Bills	18 INTs

PLAYER	TEAM	INTS
Rick Mirer	Seattle Seahawks	17 INTs
Bobby Hebert	Atlanta Falcons	17 INTs
Steve Beuerlein	Arizona Cardinals	17 INTs
Steve Young	San Francisco 49ers	16 INTs
Drew Bledsoe	New England Patriots	15 INTs
Wade Wilson	New Orleans Saints	15 INTs
Rodney Peete	Dallas Cowboys	14 INTs
Jim Everett	New Orleans Saints	12 INTs
Boomer Esiason	New York Jets	11 INTs
Jim Harbaugh	Indianapolis Colts	11 INTs
John Elway	Denver Broncos	10 INTs
Jeff Hostetler	Los Angeles Raiders	10 INTs
Steve DeBerg	Free Agent	10 INTs
Stan Humphries	San Diego Chargers	10 INTs
Mark Rypien	Cleveland Browns	10 INTs

QB

FAST FEET FEATS: 1993 QB RUSHING STATS

PLAYER	TEAM	YDS	AVG.	TDs
Steve Young	SF	407	5.9	2
David Klingler	CIN	282	6.9	0
Jim Harbaugh	IND	277	4.8	4
Brett Favre	GB	201	3.5	1
Jeff Hostetler	RAI	195	3.6	5
Rodney Peete	DAL	165	3.7	1
John Elway	DEN	153	3.5	0
Warren Moon	MIN	145	3.0	1
Troy Aikman	DAL	125	3.7	0
Boomer Esiason	NYJ	123	2.6	1
Neil O'Donnell	PIT	111	4.3	0
R.Cunningham	PHI	110	6.1	1
Jim Kelly	BUF	102	2.8	0
T.J.Rubley	RAM	102	3.5	0

PLAYER	TEAM	YDS	AVG.	TDs
Craig Erickson	TB	96	3.6	0
V.Testaverde	CLE	74	4.1	0
Joe Montana	KC	64	2.6	0
Bobby Hebert	ATL	49	2.0	0
Cody Carlson	HOU	41	2.9	2
Steve Bono	KC	14	1.0	1
Todd Philcox	CLE	2	1.5	1
Mark Rypien	CLE	9	.2	3

QUARTERBACK REVIEW

1. John Elway, Denver Broncos

Passing TDs	25
Rushing TDs	0
Total TDs	25
TDs over 40 Yds.	2
Total Passing Yds.	4,030
Interceptions	10

QB

Just leave him on the board when I draft! Elway is set up for an outstanding season--he now has a true quality receiver (Anthony Miller) to go with the young, talented receiving corps of Shannon Sharpe, Derek Russell and Mike Pritchard. Mark it down, Denver goes to the Super Bowl with gunslinging John Elway!

2. Steve Young, San Francisco 49ers

Passing TDs	29
Rushing TDs	2
Total TDs	31

TDs over 40 Yds.   5
Total Passing Yds.   4,023
Interceptions   16

I expect to hear the names Young and Elway all season. These are the two best QBs in the NFL. The difference is that the 49ers have done little to shore up their passing game. Jerry Rice is still the best, but John Taylor has dropped a bit, and who is being groomed? Still I like the 'Niners' chances with Steve Young running the team.

3. Jeff George, Atlanta Falcons

Passing TDs   8
Rushing TDs   0
Total TDs   8
TDs over 40 Yds.   0
Total Passing Yds.   2,526
Interceptions   6

This is where some people are going to say, "Jeff George #3?! What gives?" Crybaby George finally has an offense in which he can utilize his enormous talents. With George's cannon on that racetrack in Atlanta, throwing to Rison, Ricky Sanders and Deion, we could be talking about 30 TDs and 5,000 yards!

4. Dan Marino, Miami Dolphins

Passing TDs   8
Rushing TDs   1
Total TDs   9
TDs over 40 TDs   3
Total Passing Yds.   1,218

143

Interceptions   3

Marino will be chomping at the bit--he's back and ready to work with an improved receiving corps: Irving Fryar, Mark Ingram, Keith Jackson, Keith Byars, and the kiddies, O.J. McDuffie and Terry Kirby. Marino will make a run at the Super Bowl.

5. Troy Aikman, Dallas Cowboys

Passing TDs	15
Rushing TDs	0
Total TDs	15
TDs over 40 Yds.	4
Total Passing Yds.	3,100
Interceptions	6

QB

If Coach Barry and Owner Jerry allow Troy to sit back and continue to play football the way he has been, expect a great season. After all, he has Michael Irvin, Alvin Harper, Jay Novacek, Daryl Johnston, and my favorite sleeper, Kevin Williams, to toss to. Oh, and let's not forget Emmitt Smith. It appears that the only NFL team that can compete against the Cowboys is San Francisco. Aikman should step up his TD totals, and so should Irvin.

6. Brett Favre, Green Bay Packers

Passing TDs	19
Rushing TDs	1
Total TDs	20
TDs over 40 Yds.	2
Total Passing Yds.	3,303

Interceptions	24

I like Brett Favre. I especially like the fact that Favre has Sterling Sharpe to throw to. These two are developing the kind of second sense similar to Montana's and Rice's circa the mid-80's-- expect a huge season this year. Favre's only problem is a lack of *other* quality receivers, and his penchant for throwing into a crowd. This crowd-tossing got Favre picked off 24 times in '93-- that's got to cease!

7. Jeff Hostetler, Los Angeles Raiders

Passing TDs	14
Rushing TDs	5
Total TDs	19
TDs over 40 Yds.	3
Total Passing Yds.	3,242
Interceptions	10

Frankly, I didn't like Hostetler's chances in L.A. with the Raiders. Frankly, I was *wrong*. Hostetler proved to be a good quarterback on an average team. Hostetler can run and score, and he can fire off the bomb to what has to be the NFL's all-time fastest receiving corps: Tim Brown, James Jett, Alexander Wright and Raghib Ismail. (Whew, those names even make me *type* faster!) Look for major scoring from Hoss and the Raiders.

8. Scott Mitchell, Detroit Lions

Passing TDs	12
Rushing TDs	0
Total TDs	12
TDs over 40 Yds.	3

Total Passing Yds.   1,773
Interceptions   8

This is it for Detroit--win now or forget it. Barry Sanders is now hitting that prime time when an athlete's skills are at their peak, and the only way to go after peaking is down. Scott Mitchell can finally bring Detroit *one* starter. He has a future superstar in Herman Moore; believe me, Moore is one of the best receivers *now* in the NFL. It is Mitchell's job to get him the ball--expect it!

9. Cody Carlson, Houston Oilers

Passing TDs   2
Rushing TDs   2
Total TDs   4
TDs over 40 Yds.   0
Total Passing Yds.   605
Interceptions   4

With Warren Moon going way, way north to be a Viking, Commander Cody finally gets his shot to lead Houston's great receivers and strong running game. Expect a solid season for Carlson. The big concern over Carlson is whether he can play a full season without getting smashed and sidelined.

10. Randall Cunningham, Philadelphia Eagles

Passing TDs   5
Rushing TDs   1
Total TDs   6
TDs over 40 Yds.   2
Total Passing Yds.   850
Interceptions   5

QB

146

There once was a time when Randall was indestructible. No longer can that statement be made. This is a pivotal time in Cunningham's brilliant career, and this season will answer a great deal. Can he still cut it? Will his receivers (Fred Barnett in particular) remain healthy?

11. Warren Moon, Minnesota Vikings

Passing TDs	21
Rushing TDs	1
Total TDs	22
TDs over 40 Yds.	2
Total Passing Yds.	3,485
Interceptions	21

I like the idea of Warren Moon moving the Vikings--new surroundings, new success. The Vikes do not have the offense (especially the receivers) of the Oilers, but perhaps Moon can capture the magic the way Joe Montana did in 1993 with the Chiefs.

QB

12. Steve Beuerlein, Arizona Cardinals

Passing TDs	18
Rushing TDs	0
Total TDs	18
TDs over 40 Yds.	4
Total Passing Yds.	3,164
Interceptions	17

After having a season of working a system with receivers Gary Clark, Randal Hill and Ricky Proehl, you would expect Beuerlein to be ready for a solid '94 season. I still think he will, but it is hard to assess, because Joe Bugel's gone and Buddy Ryan is in. Watch for signs of life from Beuerlein during the preseason.

13. Jim Kelly, Buffalo Bills

Passing TDs	18
Rushing TDs	0
Total TDs	18
TDs over 40 Yds.	3
Total Passing Yds.	3,382
Interceptions	18

Although it's an impressive number for a second-tier starter, 18 TDs in 1993 is quite poor for a quarterback like Kelly. The Bills have made four straight Super Bowls with basically the same offensive lineup. Forget all the *stupid* comments about Kelly not winning the big one--at least he's *been* to four Super Bowls! Unfortunately, I think the Bills are beginning to fade and Kelly is getting too banged up to put up super numbers.

14. Neil O'Donnell, Pittsburgh Steelers

Passing TDs	14
Rushing TDs	0
Total TDs	14
TDs over 40 Yds.	1
Total Passing Yds.	3,208
Interceptions	7

O'Donnell is a solid quarterback, but I still think the Steelers need a major go-to wide receiver. Jeff Graham or Jeff Mills need to step up their game, and Eric Green needs to somehow play an *entire season!*

148

15. Drew Bledsoe, New England Patriots

Passing TDs	14
Rushing TDs	1
Total TDs	15
TDs over 40 Yds.	2
Total Passing Yds.	2,494
Interceptions	15

Along with fellow rookie QB Rick Mirer, Bledsoe had one of the finest seasons you could expect from a first-year starting QB. Although he took some king-sized hits, he battled back and had a stand-up year, and I expect great things from him this year as well. He has to watch his INTs, though. Bledsoe reads the field like a veteran, has a great arm, and is not afraid to run (or even catch) the ball for a score - I'd put him in the 12-14 TD range.

16. Erik Kramer, Chicago Bears

Passing TDs	8
Rushing TDs	0
Total TDs	8
TDs over 40 Yds.	1
Total Passing Yds.	1,002
Interceptions	3

Dave Wannstedt is putting together a nice little offense with the addition of Erik Kramer, Lewis Tillman and Merril Hoge. Kramer needs to get second-year receiver Curtis Conway pumping, and you just *know* he will hook up with the steady Tom Waddle.

17. Joe Montana, Kansas City Chiefs

Passing TDs	13
Rushing TDs	0
Total TDs	13
TDs over 40 Yds.	1
Total Passing Yds.	2,144
Interceptions	7

I still just don't know if Joe can take all of the pounding that goes with this position. It goes without saying that the Chiefs are only as good as Joe is. No Joe--No go! I think the Chiefs will be forced to use at least three QBs during this season (Montana, Matt Blundin and Steve Bono.)

18. Vinnie Testaverde, Cleveland Browns

Passing TDs	14
Rushing TDs	0
Total TDs	14
TDs over 40 Yds.	2
Total Passing Yds.	1,797
Interceptions	9

I never thought I would say this, but Vinnie Testaverde may *finally* be ready to reach the level of potential that he demonstrated in college. I like his receivers (Michael Jackson, Mark Carrier and Keenan McCardell). For now, though, the question remains: without Kosar around to steal his thunder, can the Vinster take charge and lead the Brownies? If not, a certain ex-Redskin will be anxious to step up and prove his steel.

KEEP AN EYE ON:

The development of Rick Mirer (SEA) and Drew Bledsoe (NE)--both could be top-twenty selections. Also, watch out for what happens with Mark Rypien. If the Vin-Man goes down, Ryp can start in a hurry.

I expect to see Erik Kramer (CHI) and Scott Mitchell (DET) demonstrate that they are quality QBs--both have the ability to throw 20-plus TDs. A lot of people will bypass these two due to their inexperience. It will be a mistake, since both are solid quarterbacks. Kramer will need Curtis Conway to push it up a major notch. Mitchell will find Herman Moore as his main hookup. Mitchell to Moore will get awfully redundant in 1994!

Cody Carlson (HOU) has waited patiently over the past several seasons for his opportunity--it's here *now!* Carlson is an excellent QB and he will fill Warren Moon's shoes nicely--look for a big season. A big question mark is whether last season's surprise star QB Craig Erickson will retain the starting job over the highly touted rookie Trent Dilfer. In Washington, the QB job is already rookie Heath Shuler's job going into camp.

QB

QUARTERBACK RATING

1. John Elway   Denver Broncos
2. Steve Young   San Francisco 49ers
3. Jeff George   Atlanta Falcons
4. Dan Marino   Miami Dolphins
5. Troy Aikman   Dallas Cowboys
6. Brett Favre   Green Bay Packers
7. Jeff Hostetler   Los Angeles Raiders
8. Scott Mitchell   Detroit Lions
9. Cody Carlson   Houston Oilers
10. Randall Cunningham   Philadelphia Eagles
11. Warren Moon   Minnesota Vikings

151

12.	Steve Beuerlein	Arizona Cardinals
13.	Jim Kelly	Buffalo Bills
14.	Neil O'Donnell	Pittsburgh Steelers
15.	Drew Bledsoe	New England Patriots
16.	Erik Kramer	Chicago Bears
17.	Joe Montana	Kansas City Chiefs
18.	Vinnie Testaverde	Cleveland Browns
19.	Chris Miller	Los Angeles Rams
20.	Rick Mirer	Seattle Seahawks
21.	Stan Humphries	San Diego Chargers
22.	Boomer Esiason	New York Jets
23.	Craig Erickson	Tampa Bay Buccaneers
24.	Phil Simms	New York Giants
25.	Heath Shuler	Washington Redskins
26.	Jim Everett	New Orleans Saints
27.	David Klingler	Cincinnati Bengals
28.	Jim Harbaugh	Indianapolis Colts
29.	Steve Bono	Kansas City Chiefs
30.	Trent Dilfer	Tampa Bay Buccaneers
31.	Rodney Peete	Dallas Cowboys
32.	Frank Reich	Buffalo Bills
33.	Mark Rypien	Cleveland Browns
34.	David Krieg	Detroit Lions
35.	John Friesz	Washington Redskins
36.	Tommy Maddox	Denver Broncos
37.	Chris Chandler	Los Angeles Rams
38.	Sean Salisbury	Minnesota Vikings
39.	Wade Wilson	New Orleans Saints
40.	Bernie Kosar	Miami Dolphins
41.	Bubby Brister	Philadelphia Eagles

QB

★6★

Running Backs

It used to be that running backs took several years to develop before they would get the opportunity to start in the NFL. Now, however, rookies seem to be starting and doing well. This position, though, has become the "burn-out" spot. With the major pounding that running backs take, it is difficult to gain any longevity and gray hair. For every Marcus Allen, there are 20 talented guys who limp out of the NFL after only four or five years.

Watching a stud like Emmitt Smith is a treat--but at his size, one must wonder how long he can take the ripping physical abuse that is aimed his way. Running backs deserve the big bucks. This position rarely sees players well into their 30s, whereas most other positions in football have veterans entering their tenth, eleventh and twelfth years.

Getting mileage out of your good running backs is one of the keys in winning at fantasy football. Since you get to start two players, you have additional scoring opportunities. You really need to get at least two scores per week from your running backs (in leagues that count only TD scores). If your league scores based on the performance (yardage and receptions) as well as TD scoring, then it is imperative that you draft and start productive players. If you end up playing a season by rotating ineffective running backs, you will be a first-class KNUCKLEHEAD, and lose.

Obviously, the best scoring and performance runners are Emmitt Smith, Ricky Watters, Barry Foster, Barry Sanders, Jerome Bettis, Rodney Hampton and Thurman Thomas. That's pretty much a no-brainer.

The *key* is to be aware during the exhibition season of any new developments or injuries. After all, the New Orleans Saints thought that Vaughn Dunbar was going to be a major player for their offense. He ended up blowing out a knee in exhibition season and missed the year. What I found to be amazing is that throughout the country, there were FFL'ers *still* drafting Dunbar-- what a waste!

As for developments, it was fairly obvious that the Bears were phasing out Neal Anderson. To draft a Neal Anderson (now a free agent) before a Rodney Hampton is not a good strategic move. You really need to be smart if you want to win. You also need to not be faked out by falling in love with a rookie who looks great in camp but is playing behind a solid star like Emmitt, Ricky or Barry. Amp Lee is a classic example of this, seeing only limited time behind both Watters and Marc Logan in SF.

If you draft a backup, draft him for just that--*as a backup*. If in '93 you had drafted Houston's Gary Brown as a backup for Lorenzo White, then you, my friend, are a certified genius! Someone out there was sharp enough to grab Brown as a security blanket for White--that's good strategy. Someone else probably drafted Ron Moore as a backup to Garrison Hearst (Cardinals). But what happens? Hearst blows out his knee, and enter Ron Moore for a very solid season.

You see, it is key to study up on the players--read all you can and watch out during exhibition season for trends, injuries, or player changes. Part of the fun and intrigue of playing fantasy football is following all the summer camps and the exhibition

RB

154

season, and keeping up with the cuts, injuries and changes. I can promise you that whoever won your league in 1993 was not some ill-advised, unprepared nudnik. I guarantee that *any* league winner was prepared, informed...*and a bit lucky!*

BONUS SCORING

In most FFL leagues, policy allows for bonus scoring. The bonus is based on distance scoring. The FFL suggests 40 yards as a distance barometer. Therefore, if a running back romps off for a 40-yard-plus TD run, he would receive double points. Another bonus comes when a running back catches a pass and scores a TD. If the yardage distance was 39 yards or under, the running back gets double points. If the pass play TD was 40 yards or more, the running back gets the famous "DOUBLE/DOUBLE!" The DOUBLE/DOUBLE is a rarity, but when it occurs...it is *sooo sweet*!

EXAMPLE POINT SYSTEM:

RB scores on a TD run 39 yards or less: 6 points
RB scores on a TD pass 39 yards or less: 12 points
RB scores on a TD run 40 yards or more: 12 points
RB scores on a TD pass 40 yards or more: 24 points

1993 TOP RECEIVING RBs

PLAYER	TEAM	REC.	REC. YDS.	TDs
Terry Kirby	Miami	75	874	3
Herschel Walker	Philadelphia	75	610	3
Ron Harmon	San Diego	73	671	2
Larry Centers	Arizona	66	603	3
Eric Metcalf	Cleveland	63	539	2

155

PLAYER	TEAM	REC.	REC. YDS.	TDs
Keith Byars	Miami	61	613	3
Edgar Bennett	Green Bay	59	457	1
J.L. Williams	Seattle	58	450	1
Emmitt Smith	Dallas	57	414	1
A. Johnson	Indianapolis	55	443	0
Vince Workman	Tampa Bay	54	411	2
Daryl Johnston	Dallas	50	372	1
Derrick Fenner	Cincinnati	48	427	0
T. Thomas	Buffalo	48	387	0
Rod Bernstine	Denver	44	372	0
Kimble Anders	Kansas City	40	326	1
Dalton Hilliard	New Orleans	40	296	1
Kevin Turner	New England	39	333	2
Dave Meggett	NY Giants	38	319	0
Glyn Milburn	Denver	38	300	3
Marc Logan	San Francisco	37	348	0
L. Thompson	Pittsburgh	38	259	0
Cleveland Gary	L.A. Rams	36	289	1
Marcus Allen	Kansas City	34	238	3
Merril Hoge	Chicago	33	247	4
Erric Pegram	Atlanta	33	302	3
Johnny Bailey	Arizona	32	243	0
Ricky Watters	San Francisco	31	326	1
Neal Anderson	Free Agent	31	160	0

RUNNING BACK REVIEW

1. Emmitt Smith, Dallas Cowboys

Rushing TDs   9
Receiving TDs   1

156

Total TDs	10
Rushing Yds.	1,486
Receiving Yds.	414

No question marks here. Emmitt wants to be the greatest running back of all time. Expect a 16-18 TD season.

2. Ricky Watters, San Francisco 49ers

Rushing TDs	10
Receiving TDs	1
Total TDs	11
Rushing Yds.	950
Receiving Yds.	326

Ricky Watters is now as crucial to the 49er offensive scheme as are Steve Young and Jerry Rice. Expect 14-15 TDs.

RB

3. Jerome Bettis, Los Angeles Rams

Rushing TDs	7
Receiving TDs	0
Total TDs	7
Rushing Yds.	1,429
Receiving Yds.	244

Bam Bam looks like he could potentially rush for 1,500 yards and score 15 TDs.

4. Barry Sanders, Detroit Lions

Rushing TDs	3

Receiving TDs	0
Total TDs	3
Rushing Yds.	1,115
Receiving Yds.	205

Peak time! I still believe that Barry has one *huge* season left in him--this is the year. Scott Mitchell will help take the load off Barry and give him a 12-TD season and 1,200-1,400 yards rushing.

5. Barry Foster, Pittsburgh Steelers

Rushing TDs	8
Receiving TDs	1
Total TDs	9
Rushing Yds.	711
Receiving Yds.	217

RB

'93 wasn't a typical Barry Foster season. The big question is will he be healthy for the full season? His style takes a ton of bashing....can he withstand the punishment? Look for 12-13 TDs.

6. Gary Brown, Houston Oilers

Rushing TDs	6
Receiving TDs	2
Total TDs	8
Rushing Yds.	1,002
Receiving Yds.	240

I really like this character and I fully expect to see him near or at the top in the AFC in rushing and scoring.

With a full-time opportunity, I expect 1,300 yards and 12 TDs.

7. Thurman Thomas, Buffalo Bills

Rushing TDs	6
Receiving TDs	0
Total TDs	6
Rushing Yds.	1,315
Receiving Yds.	387

Just like Barry Sanders, Thurman is at his peak. Still one of the most amazing receivers out of the backfield in NFL history. I like a 10-12 TD season and 1,300 yards rushing/400 yards receiving.

8. Natrone Means, San Diego Chargers

RB

Rushing TDs	8
Receiving TDs	0
Total TDs	8
Rushing Yds.	645
Receiving Yds.	59

The Chargers traded Marion Butts, and this completely opens the door for Natrone Means. Means scored 8 TDs in very limited playing time in 1993. I find it difficult to believe that Bobby Ross won't work Means into his offensive scheme as a *key* performer. Look for at least 12 TDs and 1,100 yards.

9. Terry Kirby, Miami Dolphins

Rushing TDs	3
Receiving TDs	3
Total TDs	6
Rushing Yds.	390
Receiving Yds.	874

Part of the new breed. Terry Kirby is exciting, and I think he will be a steal in this season's fantasy draft. Look at his receiving total--874 yards! Imagine him and a healthy Marino for an *entire* season! I look for Kirby to be the go-to runner/receiver for '94, with 10-12 TDs.

10. Rodney Hampton, New York Giants

Rushing TDs	5
Receiving TDs	0
Total TDs	5
Rushing Yds.	1,007
Receiving Yds.	210

RB

He was slowed by an injury in '93, and he *still* gained over 1,100 yards. I expect him to receive a heavy load in '94. I project 1,300 yards rushing and 10 TDs.

11. Reggie Brooks, Washington Redskins

Rushing TDs	3
Receiving TDs	0
Total TDs	3
Rushing Yds.	1,063
Receiving Yds.	186

Norv Turner will utilize Reggie Brooks similarly as he did with Emmitt Smith in Dallas. Expect Frank Wycheck to play the role of blocker and receiver (just like Daryl Johnston). Projection: 1,100 yards and 9-10 TDs.

12. Marcus Allen, Kansas City Chiefs

Rushing TDs	12
Receiving TDs	3
Total TDs	15
Rushing Yds.	764
Receiving Yds.	238

Marcus Allen had just a wonderful 1993 season, and who's to say that he can't duplicate those feats this season? Tell me--who in the NFL is better around the goal line? Once inside the five yard line, it becomes Marcus Allen territory.

RB

13. Reggie Cobb, Green Bay Packers

Rushing TDs	3
Receiving TDs	1
Total TDs	4
Rushing Yds.	658
Receiving Yds.	61

Signing Reggie Cobb could prove to be a heads-up move by Mike Holmgren. Cobb could easily have a sensational season in '94 with the Packers. Finally, Cobb is playing for a contender, and unlike the last decade of Packer RBs, Cobb can rush!

14. Ron Moore, Arizona Cardinals

Rushing TDs	9
Receiving TDs	0
Total TDs	9
Rushing Yds.	1,018
Receiving Yds.	16

Ron Moore proved to be a surprise as a replacement for the injured Garrison Hearst in 1993. Moore has the capabilities to score a dozen and rush for 1,200 yards, but he has to share the ball with Hearst (if he's healthy).

15. Lewis Tillman, Chicago Bears

Rushing TDs	3
Receiving TDs	0
Total TDs	3
Rushing Yds.	585
Receiving Yds.	21

In spelling for an injured Rodney Hampton, Lewis Tillman proved that he belonged in the NFL as a starter. He will get his chance and plenty of carries in Chicago. Projection: 1,000 yards rushing and 8-9 TDs.

16. Marshall Faulk, Indianapolis Colts

Rushing TDs	0
Receiving TDs	0
Total TDs	0
Rushing Yds.	0
Receiving Yds.	0

RB

Marshall Faulk has always struck me as a guy that was ready for the NFL straight out of high school. Well, now he's here, and expect him to be another coming of "Bam Bam" Bettis or Reggie Brooks. There's no doubt he will start, and I project 7-9 TDs in his inaugural season.

17. Chris Warren, Seattle Seahawks

Rushing TDs	7
Receiving TDs	0
Total TDs	7
Rushing Yds.	1,072
Receiving Yds.	99

Slowly the word is getting out on what a solid player Chris Warren is. I project 10 TDs and 1,100 yards rushing.

RB

18. Johnny Johnson, New York Jets

Rushing TDs	3
Receiving TDs	1
Total TDs	4
Rushing Yds.	821
Receiving Yds.	641

By the end of the 1993 season, Johnny Johnson was punishing tacklers. If Johnson *can start* the season just as ambitiously, I expect a solid season with 8-9 TDs and 1,000 yards rushing/600 receiving.

KEEP AN EYE ON:

Now, I realize that Gary Brown (HOU) was a fill-in for an injured Lorenzo White, but I can't help but be excited over his prospects. Brown is a quality runner, and he has that *look*. You know, that look that the great ones like Emmitt Smith display--the one that says, "I ain't going down." Who else has that *look?* How about Jerome Bettis (RAM)? Oh yeah, he has that scowl, and, like Gary Brown, arm tackling just isn't going to cut it.

Last season we saw plenty of terrific rookie runners who are running with the first team: Bettis (RAM), Reggie Brooks (WAS), Ron Moore (AZ), Natrone Means (SD), Terry Kirby (MIA), Derek Brown (NO) and Glyn Milburn (DEN). If Garrison Hearst (AZ) can come back from his knee injury, we will be watching a new young breed rushing the ball in the NFL.

Watch out for Erric Pegram (ATL), Chris Warren (SEA) and Leonard Russell (NE)--they should make the big leap into the top echelon of running backs for 1994.

RB

RB RATING

1.	Emmitt Smith	Dallas Cowboys
2.	Ricky Watters	San Francisco 49ers
3.	Jerome Bettis	Los Angeles Rams
4.	Barry Sanders	Detroit Lions
5.	Barry Foster	Pittsburgh Steelers
6.	Gary Brown	Houston Oilers
7.	Thurman Thomas	Buffalo Bills
8.	Natrone Means	San Diego Chargers
9.	Terry Kirby	Miami Dolphins
10.	Rodney Hampton	New York Giants
11.	Reggie Brooks	Washington Redskins
12.	Marcus Allen	Kansas City Chiefs
13.	Reggie Cobb	Green Bay Packers

14. Ron Moore	Arizona Cardinals
15. Lewis Tillman	Chicago Bears
16. Marshall Faulk	Indianapolis Colts
17. Chris Warren	Seattle Seahawks
18. Johnny Johnson	New York Jets
19. Leonard Russell	New England Patriots
20. Erric Pegram	Atlanta Falcons
21. Eric Metcalf	Cleveland Browns
22. Keith Byars	Miami Dolphins
23. Marion Butts	New England Patriots
24. Terry Allen	Minnesota Vikings
25. Rod Bernstine	Denver Broncos
26. Tommy Vardell	Cleveland Browns
27. Derek Brown	New Orleans Saints
28. Edgar Bennett	Green Bay Packers
29. Calvin Jones	Los Angeles Raiders
30. Erricht Rhett	Tampa Bay Buccaneers
31. Larry Centers	Arizona Cardinals
32. Ken Hill	Kansas City Chiefs
33. Harold Green	Cincinnati Bengals
34. Glyn Milburn	Denver Broncos
35. Herschel Walker	Philadelphia Eagles
36. Robert Smith	Minnesota Vikings
37. Tom Rathman	San Francisco 49ers
38. Lorenzo White	Houston Oilers
39. Robert Delpino	Denver Broncos
40. Scottie Graham	Minnesota Vikings
41. Heath Sherman	Philadelphia Eagles
42. Vince Workman	Tampa Bay Buccaneers
43. William Floyd	San Francisco 49ers
44. Garrison Hearst	Arizona Cardinals
45. Ken Davis	Buffalo Bills
46. Leroy Thompson	Pittsburgh Steelers
47. Mark Higgs	Miami Dolphins
48. Vaughn Dunbar	New Orleans Saints

RB

49. Ronnie Harmon — San Diego Chargers
50. Derrick Fenner — Cincinnati Bengals
51. Merril Hoge — Chicago Bears
52. Jarrod Bunch — New York Giants
53. Vaughn Hebron — Philadelphia Eagles
54. Daryl Johnston — Dallas Cowboys
55. Brian Mitchell — Washington Redskins
56. Derrick Moore — Detroit Lions
57. Carwell Gardner — Buffalo Bills
58. John L. Williams — Seattle Seahawks
59. Roosevelt Potts — Indianapolis Colts
60. Lincoln Coleman — Dallas Cowboys
61. David Meggett — New York Giants
62. Charlie Garner — Philadelphia Eagles
63. LeShon Johnson — Green Bay Packers
64. Steve Smith — Los Angeles Raiders
65. Lorenzo Neal — New Orleans Saints
66. Neal Anderson — Free Agent
67. Cleveland Gary — Los Angeles Rams

RB

68. Kimble Anders — Kansas City Chiefs
69. Earnest Byner — Cleveland Browns
70. Johnny Bailey — Arizona Cardinals
71. Leroy Hoard — Cleveland Browns
72. Harvey Williams — Los Angeles Raiders
73. Brad Muster — New Orleans Saints
74. Jon Vaughn — Seattle Seahawks
75. Nick Bell — Los Angeles Raiders
76. Aaron Craver — Miami Dolphins
77. Frank Wycheck — Washington Redskins
78. Adrian Murrell — New York Jets
79. Rodney Culver — Indianapolis Colts
80. David Lang — Los Angeles Rams
81. Eric Ball — Cincinnati Bengals
82. Darrell Thompson — Green Bay Packers
83. John Stephens — Kansas City Chiefs

84. Russell White	Los Angeles Rams
85. Dalton Hilliard	New Orleans Saints
86. Derrick Lassic	Dallas Cowboys
87. Reggie Rivers	Denver Broncos
88. Dexter Carter	San Francisco 49ers
89. Blair Thomas	New England Patriots
90. Marc Logan	San Francisco 49ers

RB

★7★

Wide Receivers

Wide receivers are the glamour boys. For example, if you wanted to borrow some cool threads, you wouldn't want to wear the hand-me-downs of, say, an offensive lineman, but you'd be slap-happy silly to grace the streets wearing a wide receiver's chic garb.

Wide receivers also always have hot-looking women riding in their Jaguars or Mercedes, whereas tight ends always leave the parking lot in wide-bodied pickup trucks. They also usually leave alone, or with a dog named Rusty or Shane. Big difference in rating cool, huh?

Wide receivers are also generally tight with the high-strung quarterbacks. Just look how long it took Jerry Rice to finally accept Steve Young as the San Francisco 49ers QB. Rice had a fierce loyalty to Joe Montana. QBs and WRs who find success hooking up for TDs have to build up a certain *feel* for one another. How many times have you seen Brett Favre looking for Sterling Sharpe when the game is on the line? Did you ever notice just how well Troy Aikman and Michael Irvin connect? It's as if they both share the same mind. How long do you think it will take

168

John Elway and Anthony Miller to hook up? How about Jeff George and Andre Rison? Is it any wonder that *both* Jeff Hostetler and Tim Brown had career seasons after Hoss joined the Raiders?

To me, there is something simply awesome about watching a quarterback and a wide receiver lock on and hook up for a 70-yard bomb. The bomb is football's answer to baseball's home run. It's exciting!

WIDE RECEIVER DRAFT STRATEGY

The wide receiver position is perhaps the most perplexing position to draft. You get to start three wide receivers in your FFL fantasy football lineup. The problem is selecting the potentially hot receivers. In leagues that count pass receptions as points, receiver selection is fairly easy. After all, in these leagues, a Curtis Duncan-type of possession receiver looks good. However, in a league that counts only TD scores as points, handy Curtis Duncan isn't much of a bargain because a TD is rare for Curtis D.

First, draft key team-leading receivers around the third round (second for Jerry Rice, Sterling Sharpe, Anthony Miller, Andre Rison and Michael Irvin). As a rule of thumb, I like to hook up my QB selection with a WR from the same team.

WR

QUARTERBACK	RECEIVER
Steve Young	Jerry Rice
John Elway	Anthony Miller
Jeff George	Andre Rison
Troy Aikman	Michael Irvin
Brett Favre	Sterling Sharpe
Jeff Hostetler	Tim Brown
Jim Kelly	Andre Reed
Dan Marino	Irving Fryar
Warren Moon	Cris Carter
Scott Mitchell	Herman Moore

QUARTERBACK	RECEIVER
Randall Cunningham	Calvin Williams
Joe Montana	Willie Davis
Vinnie Testaverde	Michael Jackson
Craig Erickson	Courtney Hawkins
Chris Miller	Flipper Anderson
Cody Carlson	Haywood Jeffires
Steve Beuerlein	Gary Clark
Jim Everett	Michael Haynes
Neil O'Donnell	Charles Johnson
Drew Bledsoe	Vince Brisby
Rick Mirer	Brian Blades
David Klinger	Carl Pickens

Another bit of strategy is to select the secondary receiver from a hot offensive team. Hot offensive teams are not necessarily the best NFL teams--but they are explosive scoring machines. Teams like Denver, San Francisco, Atlanta, Dallas, Miami, Buffalo and Houston have solid secondary receivers. Therefore, don't be hesitant about selecting a second banana such as:

WR

QUARTERBACK	NFL TEAM
Webster Slaughter	Houston Oilers
Ernest Givins	Houston Oilers
Derek Russell	Denver Broncos
Mike Pritchard	Denver Broncos
James Jett	L.A. Raiders
Alvin Harper	Dallas Cowboys
Kevin Williams	Dallas Cowboys
Mark Carrier	Cleveland Browns
John Taylor	San Franciso 49ers
Don Beebe	Buffalo Bills
Fred Barnett	Philadelphia Eagles
J.J. Birden	Kansas City Chiefs
Eric Martin	New Orleans Saints

170

QUARTERBACK	NFL TEAM
Nate Lewis	L.A. Rams
Desmond Howard	Washington Redskins
Randal Hill	Arizona Cardinals
Ricky Proehl	Arizona Cardinals
Kelvin Martin	Seattle Seahawks

WIDE RECEIVER REVIEW

1. Jerry Rice, San Francisco 49ers

Receptions	98
Touchdowns	15
TDs +40 Yds.	2
Total Rec. Yds.	1,503

Jerry Rice appears *so* fit that he will probably be playing well past the year 2000. This is an exciting season for receivers and Jerry Rice once again *has* to be the highest-rated wide receiver--*the greatest of all time, folks!*

WR

2. Sterling Sharpe, Green Bay Packers

Receptions	112
Touchdowns	11
TDs +40 Yds.	1
Total Rec. Yds.	1,274

Sometimes I wonder if this guy can be stopped. He is, to date, the *only* receiver in the Green Bay offense--I mean, the guy gets triple-teamed and he *still* catches 112 balls and 11 TDs! Incredible.

171

3. Andre Rison, Atlanta Falcons

Receptions	86
Touchdowns	15
TDs +40 Yds.	2
Total Rec. Yds.	1,242

If Andre Rison can grab 15 TDs from "Shag-Armed" Bobby Hebert, one wonders how many the fleet-footed Rison can catch from "Rocket-Armed" Jeff George. ESPN highlights should be hot this season!

4. Anthony Miller, Denver Broncos

Receptions	84
Touchdowns	7
TDs +40 Yds .	3
Total Rec. Yds.	1,162

Hoo-boy...I can't wait for this hookup...*Elway to Miller!* Stop it, this is the AFC Championship in gift wrapping! Can you hear the strategy now--*"OK...Anthony, go for the bomb." "I'll be at the goal post, John."*

5. Michael Irvin, Dallas Cowboys

Receptions	88
Touchdowns	7
TDs +40 Yds.	2
Total Rec. Yds.	1,330

Rating someone of Michael Irvin's talent fifth seems amazing, but that's just how solid the receiving troop is for 1994.

Irvin has snapped at new coach Barry Switzer, but I expect that that is Michael's way of saying, "Get me the ball in 1994 and all will be forgiven!"

6. Tim Brown, Los Angeles Raiders

Receptions	80
Touchdowns	7
TDs +40 Yds.	1
Total Rec. Yds.	1,180

Brown is *another* guy who could lead the receiving glamour boys in scoring for 1994! Tim Brown really developed as a premiere receiver last season, and he hooks up well with Jeff Hostetler. Brown is a quality receiver who was coveted by Raiders' conference rivals Denver and Kansas City this season.

7. Herman Moore, Detroit Lions

Receptions	61
Touchdowns	6
TDs +40 Yds.	1
Total Rec. Yds.	935

WR

Two Detroit baby-boomers will come of age and to prominence this season. Scott Mitchell at QB and Herman Moore will excite the Lion fans with their talent and results. Moore may soon be compared with Sterling Sharpe--not bad company!

8. Cris Carter, Minnesota Vikings

Receptions	86

173

Touchdowns	9
TDs +40 Yds.	0
Total Rec. Yds.	1,071

Cris Carter has finally proved to critics that he is a primary receiver and scorer. I am excited about the Warren Moon to Cris Carter matchup--Carter hasn't seen a QB of Moon's ability, and the two should click.

9. Mike Pritchard, Denver Broncos

Receptions	74
Touchdowns	7
TDs +40 Yds.	0
Total Rec. Yds.	736

With Michael Haynes moving on to New Orleans, it was assumed Mike Pritchard would have no problem stepping up and becoming "The Man" with Andre Rison in Atlanta. Well, now Pritchard is in Denver, competing with Anthony Miller for Elway's throws and continuing his rapid progress as a solid wide receiver. I still remember when Pritchard was called "the poor man's Rocket Ismail!" He is good as a mid-round draft pick, and good for eight or nine scores.

WR

10. Calvin Williams, Philadelphia Eagles

Receptions	60
Touchdowns	10
TDs +40 Yds.	1
Total Rec. Yds.	725

I have always thought that Calvin Williams was a good secondary receiver (behind Fred Barnett), but suddenly Calvin Williams is *The Man!* The key to Williams having a big season is the health of both Randall Cunningham and Freddy Barnett.

11. Webster Slaughter, Houston Oilers

Receptions	77
Touchdowns	5
TDs +40 Yds.	0
Total Rec. Yds.	904

After watching Webster Slaughter last season, it makes you wonder why the Browns let him go for zip, nada, nothing. Slaughter should be one of Cody Carlson's main targets (along with Haywood Jeffires, Ernest Givins and Curtis Duncan).

12. Michael Jackson, Cleveland Browns

Receptions	41
Touchdowns	8
TDs +40 Yds.	1
Total Rec. Yds.	756

WR

No longer a surprise, Michael Jackson has become a solid receiver. If Vinnie Testaverde can *finally* become the quarterback all the experts projected him as, Jackson will rise to the top.

13. Michael Haynes, New Orleans Saints

Receptions	72
Touchdowns	4

TDs +40 Yds.   1
Total Rec. Yds.   778

Michael Haynes surprised me by leaving Hot'Lanta for N'awlins, but his stats should be solid. The big question is if Jim Everett can shake off his last several L.A. Rams seasons and perform as he did five years ago. Haynes joining Eric Martin and Quinn Early will make for an interesting receiving corps--it's now up to Everett.

14. Andre Reed, Buffalo Bills

Receptions   52
Touchdowns   6
TDs +40 Yds.   2
Total Rec. Yds.   854

Andre Reed has not been able to get on track the way he was a couple of years ago; in fact, in his prime he once rivaled the likes of Rice and Sharpe. The inside skinny on him is that injuries are robbing Reed of his ability. The talent is still there.

WR

15. Haywood Jeffires, Houston Oilers

Receptions   66
Touchdowns   6
TDs +40 Yds.   1
Total Rec. Yds.   753

Haywood Jeffires is still a solid receiver who can snare 80-90 in a blink. Jeffires has never been a big touchdown receiver, but with his height and a new quarterback (Carlson), expect more end zone plays.

16. Willie Davis, Kansas City Chiefs

Receptions   52
Touchdowns   7
TDs +40 Yds.   1
Total Rec. Yds.   909

Davis is an exciting, quick receiver who has the knack of getting loose for the bomb. Once Davis was strictly a home run threat, but he now is developing into a solid receiver. Playing with Joe Montana will even make him better!

17. Gary Clark, Arizona Cardinals

Receptions   63
Touchdowns   4
TDs +40 Yds.   0
Total Rec. Yds.   818

Gary Clark missed a good portion of the season, but when he was healthy (if you can ever call Clark healthy with those two hamstring pulls...ouch!), Clark put up decent numbers. I would expect to see the fiery Clark back at the 1,000-yard mark and post 7-8 TDs.

WR

18. John Taylor, San Francisco 49ers

Receptions   56
Touchdowns   5
TDs +40 Yds.   2
Total Rec. Yds.   940

For the past several seasons John Taylor has been the ultimate secondary receiver on a team that features the greatest receiver of all time (Rice). Taylor has always been a dangerous receiver, but now he struggles to fight off injuries (and age.) Still, like Gary Clark, don't *ever* rule him out.

19. Fred Barnett, Philadelphia Eagles

Receptions	17
Touchdowns	0
TDs +40 Yds.	0
Total Rec. Yds.	170

I could almost repeat the sections on Gary Clark and John Taylor when discussing Fred Barnett. Freddy suffered knee damage early in '93. As with all injured players, just how well his knee responds to rehab will dictate his upcoming season.

20. Flipper Anderson, Los Angeles Rams

WR

Receptions	37
Touchdowns	4
TDs +40 Yds.	2
Total Rec. Yds.	552

I expected Flipper Anderson to be a top-five receiver by this stage of his career. Anderson has shown glimpses of greatness, and cracks of mediocrity. This is his chance. The arrival of Chris "IR" Miller should be welcomed by Flipper-- especially for the deep ball that Anderson prefers.

21. Courtney Hawkins, Tampa Bay Buccaneers

Receptions	62
Touchdowns	5
TDs +40 Yds.	1
Total Rec. Yds.	933

Hawkins is an up-and-coming receiver with huge talent. It's early in his career, but he could be ready to make a major jump and join the *Big Boys* soon!

22. Carl Pickens, Cincinnati Bengals

Receptions	43
Touchdowns	6
TDs +40 Yds.	0
Total Rec. Yds.	565

Ditto for Carl Pickens--on a team like Dallas, Denver, San Francisco, Miami or Atlanta, he'd be headed to the Pro Bowl. Pickens has the speed, hands, moves and ability to become a great player.

WR

23. Irving Fryar, Miami Dolphins

Receptions	64
Touchdowns	5
TDs +40 Yds.	2
Total Rec. Yds.	1,010

Always talented but never challenged--Irving Fryar is older, more mature and *now* hungry. If the Dolphins are going to make a challenge for a Super Bowl ring *now* is the time for both Miami and Fryar.

24. Rob Moore, New York Jets

Receptions	64
Touchdowns	1
TDs +40 Yds.	0
Total Rec. Yds.	843

Moore was entirely too nicked up in '93--Moore needs to play hurt and toughen up if he expects to develop into a Jerry Rice. The talent is there, but is the desire?

25. Alvin Harper, Dallas Cowboys

Receptions	36
Touchdowns	5
TDs +40 Yds.	2
Total Rec. Yds.	777

WR

Alvin Harper is a speedster and obviously very talented, but something is missing. Harper doesn't fight to get the ball; in fact he seems quite content to play second fiddle to Michael Irvin. If he doesn't watch out he will be playing third fiddle to Kevin Williams!

OTHERS WORTH DRAFTING

PLAYER	TEAM	REC.	YDS	TDs
Mark Carrier	Cleveland	43	746	3

PLAYER	TEAM	REC.	YDS	TDs
Ricky Sanders	Atlanta	58	638	4
Curtis Conway	Chicago	19	231	2
H. Copeland	Tampa Bay	30	633	4
R. Langhorne	Indianapolis	85	1,038	3
Tony Martin	Seattle	57	798	5
Eric Martin	New Orleans	66	950	3
Randal Hill	Arizona	35	519	4
Nate Lewis	Los Angeles	38	463	4
Brett Perriman	Detroit	49	496	2
Anthony Carter	Minnesota	60	774	6
Dwight Stone	Pittsburgh	41	587	2
Chris Calloway	New York	35	513	3
Arthur Marshall	New York	28	360	2
Vince Brisby	New England	45	626	2
J.J. Birden	Kansas City	51	721	2
Deion Sanders	Atlanta	6	106	1
Quinn Early	New Orleans	45	670	6
Victor Bailey	Philadelphia	41	545	1
Raghib Ismail	Los Angeles	26	353	1
Jeff Query	Cincinnati	56	654	4
Mike Timpson	New England	42	654	2
Gary Wellman	Houston	31	430	1
Curtis Duncan	Houston	41	456	3
Art Monk	Free Agent	41	398	2
Chris Burkett	New York	40	531	4
Jeff Graham	Pittsburgh	38	579	0
Gregory Clifton	Washington	2	15	0

WR

KEEP AN EYE ON:

I still like the chances of several young players to just explode upon the scene: Herman Moore (DET), Curtis Conway

(CHI), Kevin Williams (DAL), Horace Copeland (TB), Carl Pickens (CIN), O.J. McDuffie (MIA) and Derek Russell (DEN).

WR RATING

1.	Jerry Rice	San Francisco 49ers
2.	Sterling Sharpe	Green Bay Packers
3.	Andre Rison	Atlanta Falcons
4.	Anthony Miller	Denver Broncos
5.	Michael Irvin	Dallas Cowboys
6.	Tim Brown	Los Angeles Raiders
7.	Herman Moore	Detroit Lions
8.	Cris Carter	Minnesota Vikings
9.	Mike Pritchard	Denver Broncos
10.	Calvin Williams	Philadelphia Eagles
11.	Webster Slaughter	Houston Oilers
12.	Michael Jackson	Cleveland Browns
13.	Michael Haynes	New Orleans Saints
14.	Andre Reed	Buffalo Bills
15.	Haywood Jeffires	Houston Oilers
16.	Willie Davis	Kansas City Chiefs
17.	Gary Clark	Arizona Cardinals
18.	John Taylor	San Francisco 49ers
19.	Fred Barnett	Philadelphia Eagles
20.	Flipper Anderson	Los Angeles Rams
21.	Courtney Hawkins	Tampa Bay Buccaneers
22.	Carl Pickens	Cincinnati Bengals
23.	Irving Fryar	Miami Dolphins
24.	Rob Moore	New York Jets
25.	Alvin Harper	Dallas Cowboys
26.	James Jett	Los Angeles Raiders
27.	Ernest Givins	Houston Oilers
28.	Ricky Proehl	Arizona Cardinals
29.	Mark Ingram	Miami Dolphins

WR

30. Bill Brooks	Buffalo Bills
31. Desmond Howard	Washington Redskins
32. O.J. McDuffie	Miami Dolphins
33. Kevin Williams	Dallas Cowboys
34. Henry Ellard	Los Angeles Rams
35. Don Beebe	Buffalo Bills
36. Curtis Conway	Chicago Bears
37. Brian Blades	Seattle Seahawks
38. Mark Carrier	Cleveland Browns
39. Ricky Sanders	Atlanta Falcons
40. Horace Copeland	Tampa Bay Buccaneers
41. Chris Calloway	New York Giants
42. Nate Lewis	Los Angeles Rams
43. Eric Martin	New Orleans Saints
44. Art Monk	New York Jets
45. Randall Hill	Arizona Cardinals
46. Kelvin Martin	Seattle Seahawks
47. Ed McCaffrey	New York Giants
48. Brett Perriman	Detroit Lions
49. Vincent Brisby	New England Patriots
50. Charles Johnson	Pittsburgh Steelers
51. Arthur Marshall	New York Giants
52. Raghib Ismail	Los Angeles Raiders
53. J.J. Birden	Kansas City Chiefs
54. Terrance Mathis	Atlanta Falcons
55. Curtis Duncan	Houston Oilers
56. Thomas Lewis	New York Giants
57. Lamar Thomas	Tampa Bay Buccaneers
58. Michael Timpson	New England Patriots
59. Torrance Small	New Orleans Saints
60. Anthony Carter	Minnesota Vikings
61. Gary Wellman	Houston Oilers
62. Tom Waddle	Chicago Bears
63. Alexander Wright	Los Angeles Raiders
64. Chris Burkett	New York Jets

WR

183

65. Vance Johnson	San Diego Chargers
66. Johnny Morton	Detroit Lions
67. Floyd Turner	New Orleans Saints
68. Wendell Davis	Chicago Bears
69. Tim Barnett	Kansas City Chiefs
70. Qadry Ismail	Minnesota Vikings
71. Tony Martin	San Diego Chargers
72. Shawn Jefferson	San Diego Chargers
73. Robert Brooks	Green Bay Packers
74. Gregory Clifton	Washington Redskins

WR

★8★

Tight Ends

I can still remember the day that my son came home extremely discouraged because he was given the position of tight end on his 115-lb. football team. Even at his age, he knew that the quickest place to disappear on a football team was the tight end spot. In fact, I have a theory that Jimmy Hoffa is still alive and well. I am certain that he is a tight end for the Detroit Lions.

So you see, tight end is the most difficult offensive position to get pumped up over. Even the name is stupid...Tight End. Tight ends used to be the guys who were too big and slow to be wide receivers, and too small to be offensive linemen. So these 'tweeners find themselves mostly blocking against linebackers-- *Boring!*

Now what drives me batty is the penchant for offensive coordinators to get cute when their team is inside the ten-yard line. Instead of flipping a short pass to the tight end, they instruct the QB to lob the ball to a lumbering offensive lineman in what's known as a "tackle-eligible" play. This play *always* finds it's way onto ESPN's highlights--so coaches keep a-calling it.

But hope looks to be on the way! With the emergence of phenom Shannon Sharpe, I expect more and more offenses to

TE

follow suit and begin to throw to the tight end. In fact, I think we will see a record season for some tight ends, and maybe, just maybe, we can get rid of that tackle-eligible albatross.

TIGHT END REVIEW

1. Shannon Sharpe, Denver Broncos

Receptions	81
Touchdowns	9
Rec. Yds.	995

He has simply developed into a super player in his own right, has his own reputation, and doesn't have to live in the shadow of his superstar brother Sterling.

2. Ben Coates, New England Patriots

Receptions	53
Touchdowns	8
Rec. Yds.	659

TE

Don't be surprised to see Coates rated so high--he deserves it and he worked hard to master the tight end position. Solid player!

3. Keith Jackson, Miami Dolphins

Receptions	39
Touchdowns	6
Rec. Yds.	613

Here's a guy who has it all: size, decent speed, and hands like Fly Strips. Last year, he had a chance for a good season, but once Marino went down with his injury, so did Keith Jackson's stats. Therefore, a healthy Marino means a content Jackson!

4. Eric Green, Pittsburgh Steelers

Receptions	63
Touchdowns	5
Rec. Yds.	942

Green has so much talent, but he should take a lesson from Shannon Sharpe and Ben Coates...they hustle *all the time!*

5. Troy Drayton, Los Angeles Rams

Receptions	27
Touchdowns	4
Rec. Yds.	319

Another super-skilled young tight end who should lift the Rams offense and be a solid target for Chris Miller. Great potential!

TE

6. Johnny Mitchell, New York Jets

Receptions	39
Touchdowns	6
Rec. Yds.	630

Again, Green is an example of a super-talented end who can cruise after catching the ball. I would like to see him break his butt and hustle more, as do tight-end role models Sharpe and Coates. Mitchell could easily score in double-digits for '94.

7. Brent Jones, San Francisco 49ers

Receptions	68
Touchdowns	3
Rec. Yds.	735

Always a professional, always a solid performer. Expect numbers similar to last season, but more TDs.

8. Pete Metzelaars, Buffalo Bills

Receptions	68
Touchdowns	4
Rec. Yds.	609

Metzelaars continues to stun me--hey, this big lug was the Bills' leading receiver in '93! He's got pure hustle and a solid attitude to match!

TE

9. Ethan Horton, Washington Redskins

Receptions	43
Touchdowns	1
Rec. Yds.	467

Expect Horton to see plenty of action (since he is now in Norv Turner's "Use-the-Tight-End-like-Jay-Novacek" system). He could end up pulling a Metzelaars and leading the Redskins in receptions for '94!

10. Jay Novacek, Dallas Cowboys

Receptions	44
Touchdowns	1
Rec. Yds.	445

Jay was once one of the premiere tight ends, but lately he has suffered injuries and his production has dropped off. Still a solid pick.

11. Jackie Harris, Green Bay Packers

Receptions	42
Touchdowns	4
Rec. Yds.	604

When Brett Favre looks for a second receiver, it is generally tight end Jackie Harris. The guy is golden around the goal line and has great hands!

12. Tony McGee, Cincinnati Bengals

Receptions	44
Touchdowns	0
Rec. Yds.	525

TE

They are going to get confused in Cincinnati, because they now have Tim McGee (WR) and Tony McGee (TE)--hey, I'm already confused. (Geez, just wait for the stat nightmare on this one!) *This* McGee is a very solid young talent.

13. Ron Hall, Detroit Lions

Receptions   23
Touchdowns   1
Rec. Yds.   268

Hall is a good receiver, and now he's playing with Scott Mitchell in the 'Dome. Any guy on a team with Barry Sanders and Herman Moore is going to play third fiddle, but he could be used in short-yardage passing routes, or perhaps in the two-point conversion?!

14. Howard Cross, New York Giants

Receptions   21
Touchdowns   5
Rec. Yds.   272

When Cross first broke into the league, he couldn't catch a cold. But here is an example of another player with a great work ethic, and has it ever paid off! Very reliable in the end zone.

15. Steve Jordan, Minnesota Vikings

Receptions   56
Touchdowns   1
Rec. Yds.   542

A veteran who just refuses to be written off, Jordan is still a solid receiver. With Warren Moon aboard, he may see plenty of those one-two yard TD passes that will hopefully replace the tackle- eligible.

16. Keith Cash, Kansas City Chiefs

Receptions	24
Touchdowns	4
Rec. Yds.	242

Joe Montana digs this guy, and with good reason: he's a quality tight end.

17. Ferrell Edmunds, Seattle Seahawks

Receptions	24
Touchdowns	2
Rec. Yds.	239

To me, Edmunds is still a disappointment--I really felt he could have been a solid player.

18. Marv Cook, Chicago Bears

Receptions	22
Touchdowns	1
Rec. Yds.	154

TE

I expect a whole lot more from Cook in '94. Even though he does have to contend with the fact that he is primarily a blocking end, coach Dave Wannstedt cut his coaching teeth in a system that used the tight end as a scoring threat, so Cook should see some more action this season.

19. Mark Bavaro, Philadelphia Eagles

Receptions	44
Touchdowns	6
Rec. Yds.	498

Nearly written off by critics and fans alike, what does he do? Wham! He has a solid '93 season! Age and injuries have taken their toll on him, but as last season proved, you can't count Mark Bavaro out.

20. Kerry Cash, Indianapolis Colts

Receptions	43
Touchdowns	3
Rec. Yds.	402

Keith's brother is no slouch either! I look for him to maintain his current numbers, with Harbaugh at the helm in Indy.

KEEP AN EYE ON:

TE

Troy Drayton (RAM) received very little fanfare during his rookie season due to the emergence of Jerome Bettis. Please do not overlook this talented tight end. The big key to Drayton's season, though, hinges on the health of Chris "Red Cross" Miller.

Some people will be surprised at my selection of Ben Coates (NE) as the second-best tight end after Shannon Sharpe. Coates has won favor with Bill Parcells, and BP counts heavily on big, solid tight ends.

Johnny Mitchell (NYJ) has the talent, but he needs the burning desire. I feel Mitchell will explode in '94--he has sheer breakaway power and speed. This season, we will see the re-emergence of tight ends playing a more pivotal role. There are plenty of young, quality tight ends available to give the incumbent veteran stars (Novacek, Jackson, Green, Jordan, etc.) a real challenge: Sharpe, Drayton, Coates and Mitchell--watch 'em in '94!

TIGHT END RATING

1. Shannon Sharpe — Denver Broncos
2. Ben Coates — New England Patriots
3. Keith Jackson — Miami Dolphins
4. Eric Green — Pittsburgh Steelers
5. Troy Drayton — Los Angeles Rams
6. Johnny Mitchell — New York Jets
7. Brent Jones — San Francisco 49ers
8. Pete Metzelaars — Buffalo Bills
9. Ethan Horton — Washington Redskins
10. Jay Novacek — Dallas Cowboys
11. Jackie Harris — Green Bay Packers
12. Tony McGee — Cincinnati Bengals
13. Ron Hall — Detroit Lions
14. Howard Cross — New York Giants
15. Steve Jordan — Minnesota Vikings
16. Keith Cash — Kansas City Chiefs
17. Ferrell Edmunds — Seattle Seahawks
18. Marv Cook — New England Patriots
19. Mark Bavaro — Philadelphia Eagles
20. Kerry Cash — Indianapolis Colts
21. Derek Brown — New York Giants
22. Reggie Johnson — Denver Broncos
23. Frank Wycheck — Washington Redskins
24. Adrian Cooper — Free Agent
25. Maurice Johnson — Philadelphia Eagles
26. Rodney Holman — Cincinnati Bengals

TE

193

27. Derrick Walker	San Diego Chargers
28. Andrew Glover	Los Angeles Raiders
29. Ron Middleton	Washington Redskins
30. Keith McKeller	Buffalo Bills
31. Terry Orr	Washington Redskins
32. Jonathan Hayes	Kansas City Chiefs
33. Tyji Armstrong	Tampa Bay Buccaneers
34. Jamie Williams	San Francisco 49ers
35. Pat Carter	Los Angeles Rams
36. Rich Gedney	Chicago Bears
37. Walter Reeves	Arizona Cardinals
38. Alfred Pupunu	San Diego Chargers
39. Charles Arbuckle	Cleveland Browns
40. James Jenkins	Washington Redskins
41. Mike Dyal	Kansas City Chiefs
42. Travis McNeal	Los Angeles Rams
43. Derek Tennell	Minnesota Vikings

TE

★9★

Kickers and Punters

What is the problem with kickers? Last year the print, television and radio media treated kickers as if they were members of the Charles Manson clan trying to infiltrate and destroy the nation's sacred game of football.

Years ago, kickers were crazy sorts of guys who played soccer and somehow found their way to the football stadium purely because they could kick the ball through the uprights. These mudders were guys who spoke in broken language and looked pretty silly in an oversized uniform. Usually they were given the number 1, because they were so small. That generation of kickers replaced the lugs who use to play defensive tackle and could kick the ball a bit. These guys were as accurate as the local weather report; in other words, they missed the mark the majority of the time.

So please don't just blow past this chapter. In my humble opinion, the kicker is a very crucial part of a solid FFL franchise. Depending on your league's personal scoring system, generally I find that other than the quarterback position, the kicker position is a crucial component in building a winning franchise. Besides the

K/P

QB position, the kicker has the best opportunity to score every week--these points can save or make not only your week but seriously affect your entire season.

For the past few years I have pounced on those who treat the drafting of kickers as if they were washing William "Refrigerator" Perry's undergarments. Hey, WAKE UP! A hot kicker on a hot scoring offense is going to get mega-field goal and extra-point conversion opportunities (the two-pointer won't be used in a blowout of a game). Look at Eddie Murray last season in Dallas.

First Eddie "Money" was cut by the Tampa Bay Bucs. Then he was signed in Week Two to kick for Dallas, and kick *he certainly did*! Eddie Money got more opportunities to kick than Madonna has phone numbers. In fact, I theorize that Eddie had so many chances to kick that he must be tired...why else would he sign with the limping Eagles?

My tip to you would-be first-place wannabes is don't waffle on this pick and get stuck with some slug toiling for a team that finds itself behind and decides that the two-pointer is a necessary offensive weapon. Grab a hot kicker like Jason Elam, and "kick some major butt" in your league.

1993 FIELD GOAL LEADERS & 50-YARD BUSTERS

K/P

OK, take away my Junior 49er club pass...I'll fess up, I actually *do* get excited when a kicker attempts a 50-plus-yard field goal. I still get goosebumps watching replays of New Orleans kicker Tom Dempsey's 64-yarder against Detroit several decades ago. Since you have to draft a good field goal kicker, my advice is to grab an accurate blaster who plays on a good team. A team down 35-0 at halftime won't be bringing a sidewinder off the bench in the second half. Also, draft a player with legit leg strength to blast the 50-plus pops--o-o-o-h-h-h my, do those points add up!

PLAYER	TEAM	TOTAL FGs (20 or More)	50+
Jeff Jaeger	LA Raiders	35/44	4/7
Jason Hanson	Detroit	34/43	3/7
Chris Jacke	Green Bay	31/37	6/7
Al Del Greco	Houston	29/34	4/7
Eddie Murray	Philadelphia	28/33	3/5
Morten Andersen	New Orleans	28/35	1/5
Gary Anderson	Pittsburgh	28/30	0/0
Kevin Butler	Chicago	27/36	5/8
Jason Elam	Denver	26/35	4/6
Norm Johnson	Atlanta	26/27	2/2
Dean Biasucci	Indianapolis	26/31	1/2
Fuad Reveiz	Minnesota	26/35	1/6
David Treadwell	NY Giants	25/31	0/0
Pete Stoyanovich	Miami	24/34	2/2
Doug Pelfrey	Cincinnati	24/31	2/3
John Kasay	Seattle	23/28	3/5
Steve Christie	Buffalo	23/32	1/6
Nick Lowery	Kansas City	23/29	1/1
Greg Davis	Arizona	21/28	4/5

1993 EXTRA...EXTRA POINT GUYS

These are the guys who get the most opportunities for the extra banger due to heavy touchdown scoring. I don't expect the extra point to be suddenly dismissed due to the two-point conversion, so use this information for you draft preparation. Please don't over-rate Mike Cofer; he is <u>destined</u> to be replaced in San Francisco.

K/P

PLAYER	1994 TEAM	1993 EXTRA POINTS
Mike Cofer	San Francisco	59/61
Jason Elam	Denver	41/42

PLAYER	1994 TEAM	1993 EXTRA POINTS
Al Del Greco	Houston	39/40
Eddie Murray	Philadelphia	38/38
Pete Stoyanovich	Miami	37/37
Greg Davis	Arizona	37/37
Nick Lowery	Kansas City	37/37
Steve Christie	Buffalo	36/37
Matt Stover	Cleveland	36/36
Chris Jacke	Green Bay	35/35
Norm Johnson	Atlanta	34/34
Morten Andersen	New Orleans	33/33
Gary Anderson	Pittsburgh	32/32
Cary Blanchard	New York Jets	31/31
John Carney	San Diego	31/32

KICKER REVIEW

PLAYER	TEAM	THE INSIDE SKINNY/FAT
Jason Elam	DEN	Kicking what Elway can't scarf up
Pete Stoyanovich	MIA	Dan's back, so is offense
Chris Jacke	GB	Pack will attack big in '94
Norm Johnson	ATL	Points-a-plenty with Fleet Falcon's
Jason Hanson	DET	Improved offensive punch--DOME
Doug Brien	SF	Rookie or not--He's a nugget!
Jeff Jaeger	RAI	Too many opportunities not to like!
Steve Christie	BUF	Very solid and he gets plenty of shots
Morten Andersen	NO	If Everett fails, Andersen won't
Chip Lohmiller	WAS	Start-over time for once the best
Al Del Greco	HOU	Finally has job security
John Carney	SD	Solid season in '93 brings respect.
Tony Zendejas	RAM	Plenty of toe, few opportunities 'til '94

K/P

KEEP AN EYE ON:

Here is my concern about the kicking section--how does one get the *most bang for his kicker?* Chip Lohmiller (WAS) was great until he made that McDonald's commercial with Pete Stoyanovich. Well, maybe we can't blame that commercial, but how about going through his first year without the reliable ex-Redskin backup QB Jeff Rutledge (and, later in the season, without the injured Mark Rypien) holding for him? Or possibly the coldhearted fact that Washington's offense was so puny that just successfully calling a time-out nearly constituted a well-executed offensive play!

Whatever the case, the historically-winning Washington Redskins franchise took offensive football back into the leather-helmeted days of yore. If--(and this is a huge IF)--the Washington Redskins can move the ball down the field, Chip Lohmiller will once again be a solid FFL and NFL kicker. Therefore Lohmiller *could* be a steal, because franchises will shy away from him (particularly those that drafted him in '93!).

The hot kickers are going to come from teams that will move the ball and strike consistently on offensive: Denver, Green Bay, Atlanta, Miami, etc. will generate great kicking opportunities. I am curious about the kicking jobs in two NFL juggernauts: Dallas and San Francisco. Eddie Murray took his Super Bowl ring (and some extra money) to play in Philadelphia. The 49ers still have that weak-kicking Cofer choking their kicking game. Why a team as strong as San Francisco didn't upgrade their kicking game last season was a mystery. They will *never* win a Super Bowl with the irritable Cofer shanking field goals and extra points. It seems that the 49ers could be wising up--they drafted Doug Brien in the third round of this year's draft. Expect a no-fer for Cofer.

K/P

KICKER RATING

1. Jason Elam — Denver Broncos
2. Pete Stoyanovich — Miami Dolphins
3. Chris Jacke — Green Bay Packers
4. Norm Johnson — Atlanta Falcons
5. Jason Hanson — Detroit Lions
6. Doug Brien — San Francisco 49ers
7. Jeff Jaeger — Los Angeles Raiders
8. Steve Christie — Buffalo Bills
9. Morten Andersen — New Orleans Saints
10. Chip Lohmiller — Washington Redskins
11. Al Del Greco — Houston Oilers
12. John Carney — San Diego Chargers
13. Tony Zendejas — Los Angeles Rams
14. David Treadwell — New York Giants
15. Nick Lowery — Kansas City Chiefs
16. John Kasay — Seattle Seahawks
17. Greg Davis — Arizona Cardinals
18. Gary Anderson — Pittsburgh Steelers
19. Eddie Murray — Philadelphia Eagles
20. Matt Stover — Cleveland Browns
21. Cary Blanchard — New York Jets
22. Fuad Reveiz — Minnesota Vikings
23. Kevin Butler — Chicago Bears
24. Dean Biasucci — Indianapolis Colts
25. Michael Husted — Tampa Bay Buccaneers
26. Doug Pelfrey — Cincinnati Bengals
27. Matt Bahr — New England Patriots
28. Scott Sisson — New England Patriots
29. Mike Cofer — San Francisco 49ers

K/P

PUNTERS

If you think that kickers have it bad, how about the punter? Punters hang around with the kicker and the equipment guy. No one ever hangs up quotes from a punter in a locker room. Punters do draw the occassional "oohhhs and aahhhs" from the crowd, but they also hear the "boos" when they shank a punt in a close game.

Now I realize that no one drafts punters in the FFL or in the various leagues around the country (or around the world, since this game is global). So I'm not going to blow smoke at you and pretend that punters will make or break your upcoming FFL season--they won't. The reason I include punters is because a strong punter will help when choosing a defensive squad. How? Simply because a good punter is really a defensive manuever, since a deep, booming punt, or a precise inside-the-5-yard-liner can pin the opposition and force errors.

I am planning to start a scoring system for punters. How? Hey, why not give points for gross average, average (minus return yardage), or punts downed inside the 10-yard line? Why not penalize (subtract points) from a punter who gives up a return for a TD? Why not incorporate the punting game into the FFL?

PLAYER	TEAM	NO.	YDS.	INSIDE 20	GROSS AVG.	NET AVG.
Mike Horan	NYG	44	1,882	13	42.8	39.9
G. Montgomery	HOU	54	2,462	13	45.6	39.1
Rich Camarillo	AZ	73	3,189	23	43.7	37.8
John Jett	DAL	56	2,342	22	41.8	37.7
Harold Alexander	ATL	72	3,114	21	43.3	37.6
Tom Barnhardt	NO	77	3,356	26	43.6	37.5
Rich Tuten	SEA	90	4,007	21	44.5	37.3
Reggie Roby	WAS	60	3,447	25	44.2	37.2
Tom Rouen	DEN	67	3,017	17	45.0	37.1

K/P

PLAYER	TEAM	NO.	YDS.	INSIDE 20	GROSS AVG.	NET AVG.
Jim Arnold	MIA	72	3,229	15	44.5	36.8
Lee Johnson	CIN	90	3,954	24	43.9	36.6
Chris Gardocki	CHI	80	3,080	28	38.5	36.6
Chris Mohr	BUF	74	2,991	19	40.4	36.6
Bryan Wagner	GB	74	3,174	19	42.9	36.3
Rohn Stark	IND	83	3,954	18	43.3	35.9

★10★

Defense and Special Teams

When the FFL first came about, we would actually draft individual players on the defense. We would be allowed to start one linebacker and two defensive backs. In theory it looked like a winning idea, but in reality these players rarely scored. In fact, if you replayed the majority of TD returns by the defense, it's generally some unknown substitute who picks off an errant toss and returns it for a score.

Therefore, the FFL recommends drafting an entire defensive and special team unit, rather than individual defensive and special team players. This is done so that each franchise owner has a greater chance to score each week. This is especially true if your league counts interceptions, sacks and fumbles for points.

With all this in mind, here are my picks for the top defensive teams. These selections are made with the following criteria firmly in mind:

1. 1993's ranking
2. Offseason trades/acquisitions/player losses

DT/ST

203

3. Coaching changes/philosophy changes

4. Defensive team speed

5. Knack for lighting up the FFL scoreboard--lots of pick-offs, aggressive hitters (Buddy Ryan-types), kick returns, two-point safeties.

6. Attitude

THE SACKMEISTERS

Depending on your league, generally sacks are credited specifically to a *team*. Some leagues like to draft a defensive *player* and give points for sacks. So with that in mind, I will list the primo sackleaders from 1993--expect more of the same in '94.

PLAYER	TEAM	SACKS
Neil Smith	Kansas City Chiefs	15.0
Bruce Smith	Buffalo Bills	13.5
Simon Fletcher	Denver Broncos	13.5
Reggie White	Green Bay Packers	13.0
Sean Jones	Houston Oilers	13.0
R. Turnbull	New Orleans Saints	13.0
Richard Dent	Chicago Bears	12.5
Anthony Smith	LA Raiders	12.5
Kevin Green	Pittsburgh Steelers	12.5
Chris Doleman	Atlanta Falcons	12.5
John Randle	Minnesota Vikings	12.5
Leslie O'Neal	San Diego Chargers	12.0
Trace Armstrong	Chicago Bears	11.5
Keith Hamilton	New York Giants	11.5
Andy Harmon	Philadelphia Eagles	11.5
Anthony Pleasant	Cleveland Browns	11.0
Bryce Paup	Green Bay Packers	11.0
Sean Gilbert	Los Angeles Rams	10.5
Jeff Cross	Miami Dolphins	10.5

DT/ST

PLAYER	TEAM	SACKS
Dana Stubblefield	San Francisco 49ers	10.5
William Fuller	Houston Oilers	10.0

THE QUICK-HANDED INTERCEPTORS

I still maintain that the sweetest defensive score is when that defensive back zones in and reads the quarterback's darting eyes, rips off with a pass while in full gallop, and streaks down the sideline for a 65-yard TD intereception. In 1993 Eric Allen was incredible, with 4 of his swipes turning into touchdowns--4 TDS! So remember when choosing a defensive team, it is *really, really smart* to have Philadelphia because of Eric Allen. Teams like Philadelphia are maniacs when it comes to turning interceptions or fumble recoveries into touchdowns!

1993's LEADING INTERCEPTORS

PLAYER	TEAM	INTs	TDs
E. Robinson	Seattle Seahawks	9	0
Nate Odomes	Arizona Cardinals	9	0
Rod Woodson	Pittsburgh Steelers	8	1
Deion Sanders	Atlanta Falcons	7	0
Marcus Robertson	Houston Oilers	7	0
Darren Carrington	San Diego Chargers	7	0
Eric Allen	Philadelphia Eagles	6	4
Leroy Butler	Green Bay Packers	6	0
Kevin Smith	Dallas Cowboys	6	1
Tom Carter	Washington Redskins	6	0
Brian Washington	New York Jets	6	1
Chris Dishman	Houston Oilers	6	0
Albert Lewis	Los Angeles Raiders	6	0

DT/ST

PLAYER	TEAM	INTs	TDs
Michael McGruder	San Francisco 49ers	5	1
Vencie Glenn	Minnesota Vikings	5	0
Terry McDaniel	L.A. Raiders	5	1
Steve Jackson	Houston Oilers	5	1
JB Brown	Miami Dolphins	5	0
Charles Mincy	Kansas City Chiefs	5	0
Eric Turner	Cleveland Browns	5	0
Mark Carrier	Chicago Bears	4	1
Mark Collins	Kansas City Chiefs	4	1

DEFENSIVE TEAM TAKEAWAYS

When choosing a defensive team, be sure to use some panache and most of all *some sense*. Luck plays a major role in selecting the best defensive team, but common sense dictates that we should also be aware of the team's *takeaway* abilities. Teams that converge on the ball like an angry pitbull after a bone usually show that nasty streak of scoring potential. So, my advice to you would be to study the 1993 Takeaway list, and hopefully this information will help you *visualize* where your defensive scoring will come from.

DEFENSIVE TEAM	FUMBLE	INTs	TOTAL RECOVERIES
Buffalo Bills	24	23	47
Houston Oilers	17	26	43
Pittsburgh Steelers	14	24	38
Kansas City Chiefs	17	21	38
New York Jets	18	19	37
Seattle Seahawks	15	22	37
Detroit Lions	16	19	35
Philadelphia Eagles	15	20	35
San Diego Chargers	12	22	34
Minnesota Vikings	10	24	34
Green Bay Packers	15	18	33

DT/ST

DEFENSIVE TEAM	FUMBLE	INTs	TOTAL RECOVERIES
Denver Broncos	13	18	31
Washington Redskins	14	17	31
Chicago Bears	12	18	30
San Francisco 49ers	11	19	30
New Orleans Saints	20	10	30
New York Giants	10	18	28
Dallas Cowboys	14	14	28
Miami Dolphins	14	13	27
Arizona Cardinals	17	9	26
Cincinnati Bengals	14	12	26
Atlanta Falcons	11	13	24
Los Angeles Raiders	9	14	23
New England Patriots	9	13	22
Cleveland Browns	9	13	22
Tampa Bay Buccaneers	13	9	22
Indianapolis Colts	11	10	21
Los Angeles Rams	9	11	20

DEFENSIVE TEAMS' RUSH/PASS EFFICIENCY RATINGS

Many of the FFL leagues I talk with enjoy giving points for defensive teams' efficiency ratings. I would suggest that this standard of measure would also be quite useful when selecting a defensive team. You don't want to be stuck with some sludge-dragging defense that yields big yardage and plenty of touchdowns.

DEFENSIVE TEAM	RUSHING AVG	PASSING AVG	TOTAL AVG
Green Bay Packers	3.73	5.04	4.49
Chicago Bears	3.86	5.12	4.54
Cleveland Browns	3.67	5.30	4.59
New Orleans Saints	4.07	5.26	4.66
Minnesota Vikings	3.70	5.49	4.70
Kansas City Chiefs	3.56	5.63	4.71

DT/ST

DEFENSIVE TEAM	RUSHING AVG	PASSING AVG	TOTAL AVG
Pittsburgh Steelers	3.43	5.62	4.71
Dallas Cowboys	3.90	5.29	4.71
Detroit Lions	3.81	5.42	4.72
New England Patriots	3.86	5.60	4.73
L.A. Raiders	3.78	5.69	4.74
Miami Dolphins	3.62	5.80	4.85
Houston Oilers	3.45	5.68	4.86
Seattle Seahawks	3.67	5.77	4.90
New York Giants	3.92	5.61	4.91
San Francisco 49ers	4.46	5.26	4.94
Buffalo Bills	3.84	5.87	4.96
New York Jets	3.51	6.12	4.97
Cincinnati Bengals	4.26	5.84	5.02
San Diego Chargers	3.17	6.38	5.06
Denver Broncos	3.57	6.14	5.12
Tampa Bay Bucaneers	4.16	6.11	5.19
Philadelphia Eagles	4.45	5.89	5.20
Washington Redskins	4.12	6.59	5.35
Indianapolis Colts	4.38	6.56	5.37
Arizona Cardinals	4.30	6.25	5.37
L.A. Rams	3.86	6.81	5.39
Atlanta Falcons	4.26	6.84	5.70

DEFENSIVE TEAM RANKING

1. Philadelphia Eagles
2. Arizona Cardinals
3. Atlanta Falcons
4. Minnesota Vikings
5. Houston Oilers
6. Pittsburgh Steelers
7. New York Jets

DT/ST

208

8. Kansas City Chiefs
9. Buffalo Bills
10. San Diego Chargers
11. New England Patriots
12. Detroit Lions
13. Seattle Seahawks
14. Dallas Cowboys
15. Green Bay Packers
16. Denver Broncos
17. New Orleans Saints
18. San Francisco 49ers
19. Cleveland Browns
20. Washington Redskins
21. Chicago Bears
22. Miami Dolphins
23. New York Giants
24. Los Angeles Raiders
25. Cincinnati Bengals
26. Tampa Bay Buccaneers
27. Indianapolis Colts
28. Los Angeles Rams

SPECIAL TEAMS PLAYERS

Choosing a player or special team takes an equal mixture of research and luck, but, *WHOOMP,* if you hit it right--it's "Light Up the Scoreboard" time for your franchise. Tell me it's not exciting to watch highlights of a game and to witness your player or a player from your special teams streak into the open field and score! Oh yeah, baby, that's a big time pick-me-up!

DT/ST

1. When drafting a special team: If your league takes the approach of drafting a complete team, make sure it is a team with top-ranked return-men. The team concept gives

you the opportunity for multiple scores from multiple players.

2. When drafting a return specialist (individual players): Select a full-time kick or punt returner. It simply makes more sense (and points) to select a player who will get many opportunities to "touch" the ball. Also, as long as your returner is healthy, do not develop the bad habit of flip-flopping specialists. As a rule of thumb, you will get burned as the player you benched will seemingly always...*always score*!

3. Select a double-duty returner: A player like this has awesome value since he returns both kickoffs and punts--he becomes a double threat to score. Need I remind you gang: the more opportunities...the more scores.

4. Select a speedster: Sure, there are returners who lack burning speed and *do score*, but your best bet for a return is with a player who can flat-out speed by everyone--feets don't fail me now! Keep in mind that a kickoff or punt return for a touchdown is still a rarity. I still believe that the guy with the best shot to break the crease and leave would-be tacklers in his wake is the returner with lightning speed.

1993 PUNT RETURN STAT LEADERS
(At Least 15 Attempts)

PLAYER	TEAM	NO.	AVG. RET.	TDs
Tyrone Hughes	New Orleans	37	13.6	2
Eric Metcalf	Cleveland	36	12.9	2
Darrien Gordon	San Diego	31	12.7	0
Dexter Carter	San Francisco	34	12.1	1
Tim Brown	L.A. Raiders	40	11.6	1

210

PLAYER	TEAM	NO.	AVG. RET.	TDs
Kevin Williams	Dallas	38	10.6	2
O.J. McDuffie	Miami	40	10.6	2
Glyn Milburn	Denver	40	10.6	0
David Meggett	N.Y. Giants	32	10.3	1
Dale Carter	Kansas City	27	9.3	0
T. Brown	New England	25	9.0	0
Russell Copeland	Buffalo	31	8.8	1
Mel Gray	Detroit	23	8.6	0
Ronnie Harris	New England	23	8.6	0
Tony Martin	Seattle	32	8.4	0
Terry Obee	Chicago	35	8.3	0
Vai Sikahema	Philadelphia	33	8.3	0
Rod Woodson	Pittsburgh	41	8.2	0
Johnny Bailey	Arizona	35	8.0	1
Eric Guilford	Minnesota	29	7.3	0
Willie Drewrey	Houston	41	6.9	0
Brian Mitchell	Washington	29	6.7	0
Clarence Verdin	Indianapolis	30	5.8	0

1993 KICK RETURN LEADERS (At Least 20 Attempts)

PLAYER	TEAM	NO.	AVG. RET.	TDs
Robert Brooks	Green Bay	23	26.6	1
Tyrone Hughes	New Orleans	30	25.1	1
Tony Smith	Atlanta	38	25.0	1
Mel Gray	Detroit	28	24.6	1
Raghib Ismail	L.A. Raiders	25	24.2	0
O.J. McDuffie	Miami	32	23.6	0
Johnny Bailey	Arizona	31	22.6	0
Kevin Williams	Dallas	31	22.2	0
Eric Ball	Cincinnati	23	21.8	0
Qadry Ismail	Minnesota	42	21.5	0

DT/ST

PLAYER	TEAM	NO.	AVG. RET.	TDs
Curtis Conway	Chicago	21	21.4	0
Clarence Verdin	Indianapolis	50	21.0	0
Ray Crittenden	New England	23	20.8	0
Nate Lewis	L.A. Rams	33	20.7	0
Fred McAfee	New Orleans	28	20.7	0
Brian Mitchell	Washington	33	20.6	0
Michael Bates	Seattle	30	20.1	0
Dexter Carter	San Francisco	25	19.8	0
Robert Wilson	Tampa Bay	23	19.3	0
Desmond Howard	Washington	21	19.3	0
Patrick Robinson	Cincinnati	30	18.9	0
Randy Baldwin	Cleveland	24	18.5	0
Russell Copeland	Buffalo	24	18.2	0
David Meggett	NY Giants	24	16.8	0
Adrian Murrell	NY Jets	23	14.9	0

RETURN SPECIALIST RANKING

PLAYER	TEAM
1. Tyrone Hughes	New Orleans Saints
2. Eric Metcalf	Cleveland Browns
3. Kevin Williams	Dallas Cowboys
4. Dale Carter	Kansas City Chiefs
5. *Deion Sanders	Atlanta Falcons
6. *Tim Brown	Los Angeles Raiders
7. *Rod Woodson	Pittsburgh Steelers
8. O.J. McDuffie	Miami Dolphins
9. Darrien Gordon	San Diego Chargers
10. Mel Gray	Detroit Lions
11. Brian Mitchell	Washington Redskins
12. David Meggett	New York Giants

DT/ST

212

13. Glyn Milburn   Denver Broncos
14. Raghib Ismail   Los Angeles Raiders
15. Aaron Glenn   New York Jets
16. Russell Copeland   Buffalo Bills
17. Robert Brooks   Green Bay Packers
18. Qadry Ismail   Minnesota Vikings
19. Courtney Hawkins   Tampa Bay Buccaneers
20. Tony Smith   Atlanta Falcons
21. Clarence Verdin   Indianapolis Colts
22. Willie Drewery   Houston Oilers
23. Todd Kinchen   Los Angeles Rams
24. Terry Obee   Chicago Bears
25. Tony Martin   Seattle Seahawks
26. Corey Harris   Green Bay Packers
27. Desmond Howard   Washington Redskins
28. Curtis Conway   Chicago Bears
29. Eric Guilford   Minnesota Vikings
30. Nate Lewis   Los Angeles Rams
31. Patrick Robinson   Cincinnati Bengals
32. Terrell Buckley   Green Bay Packers
33. Jeff Sydner   Philadelphia Eagles
34. Amp Lee   Minnesota Vikings
35. Dexter Carter   San Francisco 49ers
36. Robert Wilson   Tampa Bay Buccaneers
37. Vincent Brown   New England Patriots
38. Fred McAfee   New Orleans Saints
39. Michael Bates   Seattle Seahawks
40. Eric Ball   Cincinnati Bengals
41. Randy Baldwin   Cleveland Browns
42. Russell White   Los Angeles Rams
43. Ray Crittenden   New England Patriots   **DT/ST**
44. Adrian Murrell   New York Jets

*Note: Please check during the exhibition season to ascertain if Deion Sanders, Tim Brown and Rod Woodson are still involved in the return game. These guys are locks to score, but they are also valuable cogs on offense (Brown and Sanders) and defense (Woodson and Sanders).

★11★

The Best of the New: The 1994 Rookie Freshman Class

The Rookie Class of 1993 was one of the best rookie group of players to not only enter the NFL, but to actually break into the starting lineups. Quarterbacks Rick Mirer and Drew Bledsoe jumped into the NFL as if they had held a clipboard on the sidelines for 3-4 years and had learned the intricacies of the complicated offensive schemes, as well as all of the defensive substitutions and looks.

Then bursting (or let's make that bustin') loose were Jerome Bettis, Reggie Brooks, Ron Moore, Natrone Means, Terry Kirby, etc. To my amazement--and to the chagrin of many veteran NFLers--rookies actually began to affect the NFL. As for fantasy football franchises, a rookie like Jerome Bettis was a gift from the FFL gods. Natrone Means turned out to be so good that San Diego didn't think twice about dealing Marion Butts to New England for a couple of chippy draft picks.

Are the days of ancient, backside-of-thirty running backs like MacArthur Lane, John Riggins and O.J. Anderson gone for good? Is Marcus Allen the *last* of this breed? Are rookies and second-year players going to dominate the league? I'd have to say that with the salary cap, the average life of a running back will be cut drastically. In fact, records set by Walter Payton may be safe, with the only true remaining competition coming from Emmitt Smith and Barry Sanders. In the NFL the word *longevity* will now just be another *long word*.

So keep an open mind when drafting rookies: there are some gems who will be impact players on their NFL teams for 1994. And remember, if you compare the 1993 stats of Jerome Bettis and Natrone Means with your two 1993 running backs, I'll guess that the rookie tandem outscored your veteran backfield. Who knows? With Bettis and Means, you possibly could have won (or placed higher) in 1993!

IMPACT ROOKIES

Impact means a player who *will* have an effect on his team in 1994. I like the chances of running back Marshall Faulk (IND). This team is geared to solely run the ball and toss the short passing game. There is little doubt in my mind that GM Bill Tobin wants to imitate the Dallas Cowboys. True, Jim Harbaugh is no Troy Aikman, but in truth Troy doesn't throw the ball 40 times a game--he hands off and tosses short to Emmitt Smith. Expect Indianapolis to do the same, and expect Marshall Faulk to explode.

Heath Shuler will be the starting quarterback in Washington unless he does something bizarre like run off with Tom and Roseanne Arnold and start a TV sitcom commune raising one-liners and punch-lines.

I fully expect Heath Shuler to be the second coming of ...*drumroll please*...Troy Aikman. It seems that everybody wants to be the Dallas Cowboys except Jimmy Johnson. Don't expect Shuler to chuck 20-25 TDs, but do expect a gradual learning curve

DT/ST

216

similar to the one experienced by Drew Bledsoe and Rick Mirer last season.

As for Trent Dilfer (TB), don't hand over the quarterback keys to the offense just yet. I still think that Craig Erickson is no slouch, and he could hang onto the job for 1994. Watch this one as it develops in summer camp and during exhibition season.

For excitement, I like the Minnesota selection of electrifying David Palmer as a wide receiver and return man. Second-year receiver Qadry Ismail and rookie Palmer are small but quick, and those are just the type of receivers that Warren Moon loves to throw to.

A rookie to watch for future bigtime development is fullback William Floyd in San Francisco. Floyd may cause job insecurity for Tom Rathman, and he definitely can get the job done around the goal line.

The rookie who should finish behind Marshall Faulk as the best rookie running back should be Kansas City selection Greg Hill. What a steal at the end (25th pick) of the first round! KC has to realize that Marcus Allen might not duplicate last year's incredible feats, so maybe Greg Hill will shoo away that miserable ex-number one pick Harvey Williams and get the majority of playing time.

A surprise to me was that running back LeShon Johnson was overlooked until the Green Bay Packers drafted him in the third round. Are you kidding me? Here is a guy who rushed for 1,976 yards in 1993 (leading the country in rushing), and 27 other teams passed him up until the third round? There were 12 other backs chosen before LeShon, but I think that other than Marshall Faulk and Greg Hill, LeShon Johnson may be the scoring and performance (yardage and receptions) type of player that the Packers have sorely missed. He does, however, meet the strong competition of veteran Reggie Cobb (traded fron the Bucs to the Pack). Check him out over the summer and see how he does--Is he a starter or second teamer to Cobb? Oh, and speaking of Cobb, don't overlook Tampa Bay rookie Errict Rhett. He may be the

217

lone running back star in Tampa now that Cobb is gone. Rhett could be a solid rookie and a good sleeper pick.

Receivers usually take time to develop and learn their routes, so I am generally cautious about fawning over rookie receivers, *but* two jump right out at me: Charles Johnson (PIT) and Johnny Morton (DET). Both should see starting jobs, and Johnson in particular is a much-needed acqusition for the anemic Steeler wide receiving corps.

Now the player who will lead *all the rookies in scoring* will most likely be Doug Brien. Yes, Doug Brien is a rookie kicker for the San Francisco 49ers. (By the way, for a team that always finishes at the top they did a superb job drafting.) Finally, that squibby-shank-choking-kicking Mike Cofer will be replaced and Doug Brien will score a zillion points. You see, kicking for San Francisco, Dallas, Denver, etc., will guarantee you zillions and zillions of kicking opportunities.

IMPACT ROOKIES

PLAYER	POS	TEAM	INSIDE SKINNY/FAT
Marshall Faulk	RB	IND	Has been ready for the pros for the past two seasons--Now it counts and so will his TDs!
Greg Hill	RB	KC	Needs to take the heat off Joe Montana--Hill is a 1,100 yard rusher and a 10-TD guy.
Errict Rhett	RB	TB	Who else will run in Tampa? Better breakaway threat than Reggie Cobb.

DT/ST

PLAYER	POS	TEAM	INSIDE SKINNY/FAT
Heath Shuler	QB	WAS	Second coming of Troy Aikman, but it is rebuilding time in the nation's capital.
Doug Brien	K	SF	Great pick--will score a zillion points. Looks like another Jason Elam.
William Floyd	RB	SF	A killer around the goal line, question is whether he gets the fulltime call over Tom Rathman.
Trent Dilfer	QB	TB	Still has to beat out incumbent Craig Erickson. If he does he will *initially* put up better numbers than Shuler.
Charles Johnson	WR	PIT	Finally a stud wide receiver in Steeltown--Great runner with the ball.
LeShon Johnson	RB	GB	A steal for Green Bay--But will he get the ball over Reggie Cobb and Edgar Bennett?
Johnny Morton	WR	DET	Should pair up well with Herman Moore and hook up well with Scott Mitchell--The Dome rocks in '94.
Charlie Garner	RB	PHI	Quick quiz: who besides Randall is successful rushing for big gains? Enter Charlie G.

DT/S

PLAYER	POS	TEAM	INSIDE SKINNY/FAT
David Palmer	WR	MIN	Overlooked by drafters until 2nd round--will shine in Minnesota.
Calvin Jones	RB	RAI	Scratch losers Nick Bell & Harvey Williams--Jones can fill the LA LA RB void.
D. Alexander	WR	CLE	So smooth and adds depth to the Browns corps of Michael Jackson and Mark Carrier.
Darnay Scott	WR	CIN	Joins flash Carl Pickens-- Suddenly Cincy has speed and hands.
Thomas Lewis	WR	NYG	Maybe a stretch, but he is better than what NY currently has.
Issac Bruce	WR	RAM	As long as Chris Miller stays healthy Bruce should stick some solid numbers.
Donnell Bennett	RB	KC	Would not be a surprise to see both Greg Hill and Bennett as a starting tandem.
Mario Bates	RB	NO	The Saints *always* draft great RBs-- now if someone could stay healthy.
Bert Emmanuel	WR	ATL	With Mike Pritchard going to Denver, Bert-E will see plenty of duty.

DT/ST

220

SEMI-IMPACT ROOKIES

Due to the salary cap structure, rookies will be guaranteed spots on their new teams. Most of these rookies will be played sparingly and developed as future projects. The quickest way to a starting role seems to be as a running back, so keep that in mind if you draft a semi-impact rookie.

PLAYER	**POS**	**TEAM**
James Bostic	RB	Los Angeles Rams
Bucky Brooks	WR	Buffalo Bills
Chuck Levy	RB	Arizona Cardinals
Kevin Lee	WR	New England Patriots
Gary Downs	RB	New York Giants
Malcolm Seabron	WR	Houston Oilers
Ryan Yarbough	WR	New York Jets
Byron "Bam" Morris	RB	Pittsburgh Steelers
Tydus Winans	WR	Washington Redskins
Jeff Cothran	RB	Cincinnati Bengals
Lonnie Johnson	TE	Buffalo Bills
Willie Jackson	WR	Dallas Cowboys
Corey Fleming	WR	San Francisco 49ers
Harrison Houston	WR	Atlanta Falcons
Kevin Knox	WR	Buffalo Bills
Brad Banta	TE	Indianapolis Colts
Lake Dawson	WR	Kansas City Chiefs
Chris Penn	WR	Kansas City Chiefs
Glenn Foley	QB	New York Jets
Sean Jackson	RB	Houston Oilers
Kurt Haws	TE	Washington Redskins
Jay Walker	QB	New England Patriots
Raymont Harris	RB	Chicago Bears
Terry Mickens	WR	Green Bay Packers
Butler By'note'	RB	Denver Broncos

DT/ST

221

PLAYER	POS	TEAM
Derrell Mitchell	WR	New Orleans Saints
Harold Bishop	TE	Seattle Seahawks
Lee Gissendaner	WR	Houston Oilers
Lloyd Hill	WR	Chicago Bears
Lamont Warren	RB	Indianapolis Colts
Doug Nussmeier	QB	New Orleans Saints
Steve Hawkins	WR	New England Patriots
A.J. Odofile	TE	Buffalo Bills
John Burke	TE	New England Patriots
Tony Vinson	RB	San Diego Chargers
Jay Kearney	WR	Green Bay Packers
Roiderick Lewis	TE	Houston Oilers
Orlando Parker	WR	New York Jets
Lamar Smith	RB	Seattle Seahawks
Perry Klein	QB	Atlanta Falcons
Robert Strait	RB	Cleveland Browns

DT/ST

★12★

Dick's Picks

Players are rated on the following criteria:

1. Projected team role: starter, scorer, major offensive force
2. Last year's scoring results
3. Is he a consistent solid producer or just a "Halley's Comet?"
4. FFL track record. Does player have solid stats or is he a one-year phenom?
5. Take injuries into consideration: did the player recover?
6. The individual player's NFL team. Is the team a force or a dead-dog offense?
7. The individual player's supporting cast (e.g., strong offensive line/offense injury-free?)
8. The individual player's team schedule (strong/weak)

I'M ON A ROLL NOW

Now this may seem easy to the casual observer/reader: simply look at all the other lists, line 'em all up, and number them.

The real trick is getting everything to slam into place and work. The other problem in rating players is that some leagues rate solely on scoring potential and other leagues use scoring and performance (yardage, etc.). With that in mind, I have rated players so that both groups--*scorers and performance*--will be able to utilize this list.

The main nemesis in rating players is that there is no way possible for one to predict the cursed injury bug. Look at Terry Allen (MIN) and Vaughn Dunbar (NO), who were prepared for solid seasons in 1993. Both suffered exhibition-season knee injuries. So you see, injuries make rating players a difficult task. The other problem in rating players is following all of the free agency moves. I'm sorry, but despite the belief of players and their agents, it takes a couple of seasons to mesh with another teams' offensive scheme and game plan. Players have to develop a *feel* for each other. Did you notice that no matter how good Steve Young was, it took him several years to hook up with Jerry Rice the way Joe Montana did? In fact, Rice even said it took him a while to get used to Young's spiral, as compared to Montana's. (After all, Young is left-handed.)

As I go to print with this book, I still have questions. For example, who will kick for Dallas? Whoever is fortunate enough to split those Dallas uprights will have a ton of points. I have questions concerning the quarterbacks in the NFL. Will we ever have a 40-TD guy (like Marino in '84 and '86)? Will all of the shifted, traded, released QBs (Jeff George, Warren Moon, Scott Mitchell, Erik Kramer, Chris Miller, Jim Everett, Mark Rypien, Jim Harbaugh, John Friesz, David Krieg, Jack Trudeau and Bernie Kosar, just to name a few) pick up their new systems quickly...or will they fail? What will be the status of last season's surprise QB, Craig Erickson? I would have rated him much higher this season, but with the Tampa Bay Bucaneers drafting the supposedly "can't miss rookie QB" Trent Dilfer, Erickson becomes questionable.

Will running backs (especially the young breed) continue to run amok and be successful? Last season, *so many* rookies jumped into the fray and stole the limelight from the veterans. Have offensive teams' rushing plays gotten so simple that rookies now crash-and-learn as opposed to crash-and-burn? Are these players that exceptional, or are the defenses just plain susceptible to the run? Does one rate the rookie running back crop for 1994 as potential starters in the NFL *now* or were the '93 rookies just a fluke? What about college phenom and number1 '93 draftee Garrison Hearst? Is he going to play in '94? Questions, questions, questions.

Keeping all of this in mind, I will give you perhaps the strongest list I have ever compiled. But please keep in mind that on paper everyone looks like a potential super scorer or yardage yahoo--the trick is getting these players off the paper and onto the playing field. The real trick is drafting players who score a ton and never get injured...that trick is *luck*. So to you, my friend...I wish you luck and a season of success!

TOP 150 SCORING AND PERFORMANCE PICKS

PLAYER	POS	TEAM
1. John Elway	QB	Denver Broncos
2. Steve Young	QB	San Francisco 49ers
3. Emmitt Smith	RB	Dallas Cowboys
4. Jeff George	QB	Atlanta Falcons
5. Dan Marino	QB	Miami Dolphins
6. Ricky Watters	RB	San Francisco 49ers
7. Jerome Bettis	RB	Los Angeles Rams
8. Jerry Rice	WR	San Francisco 49ers
9. Sterling Sharpe	WR	Green Bay Packers
10. Andre Rison	WR	Atlanta Falcons

225

DICK'S PICKS

11.	Barry Sanders	RB	Detroit Lions
12.	Troy Aikman	QB	Dallas Cowboys
13.	Jason Elam	K	Denver Broncos
14.	Brett Favre	QB	Green Bay Packers
15.	Barry Foster	RB	Pittsburgh Steelers
16.	Anthony Miller	WR	Denver Broncos
17.	Michael Irvin	WR	Dallas Cowboys
18.	Gary Brown	RB	Houston Oilers
19.	Tim Brown	WR	Los Angeles Raiders
20.	Natrone Means	RB	San Diego Chargers
21.	Jeff Hostetler	QB	Los Angeles Raiders
22.	Scott Mitchell	QB	Detroit Lions
23.	Thurman Thomas	RB	Buffalo Bills
24.	Terry Kirby	RB	Miami Dolphins
25.	Pete Stoyanovich	K	Miami Dolphins
26.	Herman Moore	WR	Detroit Lions
27.	Cody Carlson	QB	Houston Oilers
28.	Randall Cunningham	QB	Philadelphia Eagles
29.	Rodney Hampton	RB	New York Giants
30.	Reggie Brooks	RB	Washington Redskins
31.	Chris Jacke	K	Green Bay Packers
32.	Marcus Allen	RB	Kansas City Chiefs
33.	Warren Moon	QB	Minnesota Vikings
34.	Cris Carter	QB	Minnesota Vikings
35.	Jim Kelly	QB	Buffalo Bills
36.	Mike Pritchard	WR	Denver Broncos
37.	Ron Moore	RB	Arizona Cardinals
38.	Reggie Cobb	RB	Green Bay Packers
39.	Chris Warren	RB	Seattle Seahawks
40.	Steve Beuerlein	QB	Arizona Cardinals
41.	Calvin Williams	WR	Philadelphia Eagles
42.	Norm Johnson	K	Atlanta Falcons
43.	Neil O'Donnell	QB	Pittsburgh Steelers
44.	Erik Kramer	QB	Chicago Bears
45.	Jason Hanson	K	Detroit Lions

226

46. Doug Brien	K	San Francisco 49ers
47. Jeff Jaeger	K	Los Angeles Raiders
48. Shannon Sharpe	TE	Denver Broncos
49. Chris Miller	QB	Los Angeles Rams
50. Marshall Faulk	RB	Indianapolis Colts
51. Webster Slaughter	WR	Houston Oilers
52. Michael Jackson	WR	Cleveland Browns
53. Drew Bledsoe	QB	New England Patriots
54. Leonard Russell	RB	New England Patriots
55. Michael Haynes	WR	New Orleans Saints
56. Ben Coates	TE	New England Patriots
57. Johnny Johnson	RB	New York Jets
58. Andre Reed	WR	Buffalo Bills
59. Haywood Jeffires	WR	Houston Oilers
60. Keith Jackson	TE	Miami Dolphins
61. Joe Montana	QB	Kansas City Chiefs
62. Erric Pegram	RB	Atlanta Falcons
63. Willie Davis	WR	Kansas City Chiefs
64. Steve Christie	K	Buffalo Bills
65. Eric Metcalf	RB	Cleveland Browns
66. Gary Clark	WR	Arizona Cardinals
67. John Taylor	WR	San Francisco 49ers
68. Morten Andersen	K	New Orleans Saints
69. Vinny Testaverde	QB	Cleveland Browns
70. Fred Barnett	WR	Philadelphia Eagles
71. Troy Drayton	TE	Los Angeles Rams
72. Johnny Mitchell	TE	New York Jets
73. Marion Butts	RB	New England Patriots
74. Chip Lohmiller	K	Washington Redskins
75. Flipper Anderson	WR	Los Angeles Rams
76. Al Del Greco	K	Houston Oilers
77. Courtney Hawkins	WR	Tampa Bay Buccneers
78. Rick Mirer	QB	Seattle Seahawks
79. Steve Bono	QB	Kansas City Chiefs
80. Stan Humphries	QB	San Diego Chargers

227

81. Keith Byars	RB	Miami Dolphins
82. Boomer Esiason	QB	New York Jets
83. John Carney	K	San Diego Chargers
84. Terry Allen	RB	Minnesota Vikings
85. Rod Bernstine	RB	Denver Broncos
86. Carl Pickens	WR	Cincinnati Bengals
87. Irving Fryar	WR	Miami Dolphins
88. Brent Jones	TE	San Francisco 49ers
89. Rob Moore	WR	New York Jets
90. Alvin Harper	WR	Dallas Cowboys
91. Eric Green	TE	Pittsburgh Steelers
92. Tony Zendejas	K	Los Angeles Rams
93. James Jett	WR	Los Angeles Raiders
94. Tommy Vardell	RB	Cleveland Browns
95. Derek Brown	RB	New Orleans Saints
96. Craig Erickson	QB	Tampa Bay Buccaneers
97. Trent Dilfer	QB	Tampa Bay Buccaneers
98. Ricky Sanders	WR	Atlanta Falcons
99. Derek Russell	WR	Denver Broncos
100. Edgar Bennett	RB	Green Bay Packers
101. Ernest Givins	WR	Houston Oilers
102. Ricky Proehl	WR	Arizona Cardinals
103. Brian Blades	WR	Seattle Seahawks
104. Mark Ingram	WR	Miami Dolphins
105. Bill Brooks	WR	Buffalo Bills
106. Desmond Howard	WR	Washington Redskins
107. O.J. McDuffie	WR	Miami Dolphins
108. Pete Metzelaars	TE	Buffalo Bills
109. Ethan Horton	TE	Washington Redskins
110. Kevin Williams	WR	Dallas Cowboys
111. Henry Ellard	WR	Washington Redskins
112. Horace Copeland	WR	Tampa Bay Buccaneers
113. Tony Zendejas	K	Los Angeles Rams
114. Chris Calloway	WR	New York Giants
115. Nick Lowery	K	Kansas City Chiefs

228

116. Nate Lewis	WR	Los Angeles Rams
117. Calvin Jones	RB	Los Angeles Raiders
118. Heath Shuler	QB	Washington Redskins
119. Larry Centers	RB	Arizona Cardinals
120. Jim Everett	QB	New Orleans Saints
121. Errict Rhett	RB	Tampa Bay Bucaneers
122. Harold Green	RB	Cincinnati Bengals
123. Lawrence Dawsey	WR	Tampa Bay Buccaneers
124. Ken Hill	RB	Kansas City Chiefs
125. Eric Martin	WR	New Orleans Saints
126. Glyn Milburn	RB	Denver Broncos
127. Herschel Walker	RB	Philadelphia Eagles
128. Robert Delpino	RB	Denver Broncos
129. Curtis Conway	WR	Chicago Bears
130. Randal Hill	WR	Arizona Cardinals
131. Don Beebe	WR	Buffalo Bills
132. David Klingler	QB	Cincinnati Bengals
133. Tom Rathman	RB	San Francisco 49ers
134. Lorenzo White	RB	Houston Oilers
135. Mark Carrier	WR	Cleveland Browns
136. Garrison Hearst	RB	Arizona Cardinals
137. Sean Dawkins	WR	Indianapolis Colts
138. Vaughn Hebron	RB	Philadelphia Eagles
139. Vince Workman	RB	Tampa Bay Buccaneers
140. Vincent Brisby	WR	New England Patriots
141. Charles Johnson	WR	Pittsburgh Steelers
142. Vic Bailey	WR	Philadelphia Eagles
143. Greg Davis	K	Arizona Cardinals
144. Phil Simms	QB	New York Giants
145. Gary Andersen	K	Pittsburgh Steelers
146. Eddie Murray	K	Philadelphia Eagles
147. Matt Stover	K	Cleveland Browns
148. William Floyd	RB	San Francisco 49ers
149. Cary Blanchard	K	New York Jets
150. Fuad Reveiz	K	Minnesota Vikings

229

★13★

About the 1994 FFL Software

by David C. Dewenter
Director
FFL Software Development

1994 FFL Fantasy Football Software

Programmed by	David C. Yager
	Michael B. Hughes
Tested by	David Dewenter
	Bill Kelly

Franchise Football League
P.O. Box 9805
McLean, Virginia   22102

Order Processing: 1-800-872-0335
Technical Support: 1-703-893-4861

Monday-Friday (10am - 6pm EST)

Prodigy Service ID# GDXS68F

T he first thing your league will want to do is to elect or designate a Commissioner from your pool of franchise owners. The Commissioner is responsible for conducting league business, arbitrating league disputes, recording all draft information, team line-ups and trades, and providing weekly scoring and standings reports to franchise owners. The Commissioner should have easy access to a computer to fulfill these duties efficiently throughout this season. Throughout this manual when **FFL** is used it refers to the **Fantasy Football** software program.

To help your league get started, the FFL has provided your league with this simple, easy-to-use software that:

- organizes your league's NFL draft using current NFL rosters
- charts the weekly starting lineups for each franchise owner (up to 16 franchises)
- executes trades
- tracks released/waived and injured reserve players
- tracks all essential statistics on NFL players each week
- automatically tabulates FFL scoring, based upon your league's system, to determine weekly winners and year-to-date leaders
- prints franchise owner mailing labels
- allows you to edit and track head-to-head schedules with playoffs
- automatically updates your league's NFL rosters with new players through the weekly scoring update services
- creates unlimited number of play-types for your league to use, in addition to the 40-plus categories already included through any of the stat services
- new "reset season" option lets owners test their scoring

231

system before season starts and save franchise info and rosters

The following instructions are for computer operation only. For game rules and scoring, see the chapter on League Setup. If you would like more information on drafting strategies and complete 1993 NFL Statistics, see earlier sections of this book.

WHAT DOES MY COMPUTER NEED TO GET STARTED?

This new version of the FFL software is very "user friendly" and is easier to use than ever before. No matter what your level of computer experience, you can operate the program with ease. In fact, it's so simple that you should only need to read these directions once. After that, you will have the computer commands on the bottom of your computer screen and the **[F1] Help** key is available any time to guide you through the FFL program. Remember, your league's Commissioner is the only player who needs access to an IBM-compatible computer.

Here's what you need to play the FFL:
- 386SX/20Mhz or compatible computer (**386DX Recommended**)
- Monochrome Monitor & Graphics Card or better
- 3.5" 720K floppy disk drive
- Hard Disk drive (**10-20MB** available for complete program and season's worth of statistics)
- At least 640K RAM
- Printer can be standard IBM/Epson dot matrix or HP LaserJet Series or compatible
- Mouse optional

- Your ***CONFIG.SYS*** file, located in the root directory of your computer's hard drive, must have a minimum of **Files=50** and **Buffers=30** set up before the FFL program can run properly. *Consult your computer's operating system manual* on how to edit this file.

NOTE:

Please read the following installation instructions carefully so that you can properly set up your computer for the FFL program to operate smoothly.

INSTALLING THE FANTASY PROGRAM

To install the FFL program on your computer system, please follow these instructions carefully. A limited knowledge of the DOS operating system can be helpful; however, the commands that you will need to install the FFL program are provided below, so that even a computer beginner should be able to complete the installation easily.

The instructions for each step appear in **bold** print and on a separate line. These instructions assume that the computer has been started ("booted up") and you now see the DOS prompt of C: (or the letter of the hard drive on which you are going to install the game). These instructions also assume that this computer is not running on a network, because this may cause memory conflicts and the FFL program may not run properly.

If you have a menu system on your computer, it is necessary for you to exit out of it so that you are at the DOS prompt before you begin the installation. (See *Software Troubleshooting* for further help.)

1. Create a directory on your hard drive by typing at the C: or D: prompt

MD\FFL then press **[ENTER]**

2. Now get into this directory by typing again at the C: or D: prompt

CD\FFL [ENTER]

3. Place the FFL program diskette in the A: or B: drive and type from your C:\FFL prompt
if disk is in A: **A:install [ENTER]**   or
if disk is in B: **B:install [ENTER]**

You will now see a number of files appear on your screen as the program copies them into the FFL directory.

SIGNING IN WITH THE FFL

To start the program after installation, type at the C:\FFL prompt

STARTFFL [ENTER]

To start the program after booting up your computer, type
C: [ENTER]
CD\FFL [ENTER]
STARTFFL [ENTER]

> ## *IMPORTANT*:
> You *cannot* run the 1994 FFL program from any menu system, such as DOS Shell or Windows, because this will cause the program to crash and you may lose important data. Be sure to exit any of these menu systems before starting the program. It also may not run properly on a network because of memory conflicts, so we advise running the FFL program on a stand alone computer that is not running on a network.

You may want to also read the **README.TXT** file when you get a chance to find out about any changes made since this manual was printed. This file can be loaded into any common text editor, such as DOS EDIT or EDLIN.

Important Keystrokes, Commands, and Terminology: most of these keys will appear on the screen when they are available.

- **Arrow keys**: press these keys to move the highlight bar up and down or to move it back and forth from the left/right windows while drafting, trading, or selecting starting players.
- **[Enter]**: place the highlight bar on the menu selection, player, play-type, or other item you want, press **[Enter]** to make that selection.
- **Menu Lettering**: type the letter that appears in front of the menu selection you wish to make, or move the highlight bar to that selection.
- **Mouse functions:** moving the mouse forward or backward will move the **highlight bar** through the list of selections that appear. In many of the windows you will see the ↑ and ↓ **arrows** appear on the right side. By placing the cursor on one of them and pressing the **left mouse button**, you will

scroll down the list or report that you are viewing. The **left button** acts as the **[Enter]** key and the **right button** acts as the **[Esc]** key.

- **[End]**: saves what you have been working on. It works when you are entering/editing scoring plays in **Update Weekly Scoring**, player information in **Draft Night**, or point assignment ranges in **Player Point Assignments**.

- **[Delete]**: will erase entire entries in the **Player Point Assignments** and **Update Weekly Scoring** sections, as well as erase players from the program's database in the **Draft Night** section. You will be prompted to make sure that this is what you want to do.

- **[Insert]**: to add a new player, scoring play, or point assignment range, press **[Insert]** while the highlight bar is in the designated window.

- **[ESC]**: pressing the Escape key in any selection, menu, or report will back you out to the previous menu.

- **[F1]**: placing the highlight bar on the selection or entry blank you want and pressing **[F1]** will display a **Help** screen with further information on that topic.

- **Quick Jump**: inside any window of players that is sorted by name, you may simply type the player's name you are looking for exactly as it appears. That means last name first and in ALL CAPS, followed by a comma and a space, then the first name with only the first letter capitalized.

- **[F2]**: use this function key to change the current week from the **Main Menu**.

- **[F3]**: while viewing reports (not **Screen Reports**) you may press **[F3]** and enter the name of a specific player you wish to search for in that report, and then press **[Enter]**.

- **[F4]**: while in **Draft Night**, you may quickly look up the players who have been drafted to that point by pressing the **[F4]** key.

- **[F5]**: allows you, only in **Draft Night,** to edit an existing player's information, (for example, the NFL team of which

he is a member). To save what you have entered, press
[End]. To exit without making any changes, press **[ESC]**.

- **[F6]**: While in any of the player transaction windows (**Draft
  Night**, **Select Starting Players**, **Release a Player**, **Trades**
  or **Injured Reserve**) you may use this key to view a
  franchise's current roster status.

- **[F8]**: while the highlight bar is in one of the entry screens
  and you wish to delete one of the fields that may have been
  entered incorrectly, press **[F8]** and the entire field will be
  deleted. This will save you time by not having to continually
  press the **[Delete]** key to clear the field.

- **[F9]**: allows you to sort a list of players (by name, position,
  or NFL team) in the **Draft Night**, **Select Starting Players**,
  Trades, **Waivers**, and **Injured Reserve** sections, or when
  manually entering scoring plays in the **Update Weekly
  Scoring** section.

- **[F10]**: depending upon how the list of players is sorted (see
  [F9] above), you may quickly jump to players grouped by
  their positions or jump to a specific player by typing in his
  last name.
  Note: This can also be done using the **Quick Jump** feature
  described on the previous page.

- **Select**: indicates that you should choose a menu selection,
  player, or other topic either by moving the **highlight bar**
  using the **arrow** keys by typing the **letter** immediately
  preceding the topic, or by moving the **mouse** forward or
  backward. When the highlight bar is on the selection you
  want to make, press the **[Enter]** key or the **left mouse
  button** to execute that selection.

This section will discuss the main body of the new FFL program, and is organized by the exact menu titles from which you can choose throughout the program. To make it easier to look for help should you need it, the letters in the table of contents correspond to the same choices you have from menu to menu. Throughout the program a feature has been included to help you with the new FFL program. You may press the **[F1]** key to pull up a **Help** screen for any particular section on which you are working.

How to read the 1994 FFL title bar layout:

Mon Aug 29, 1994 - is today's date, which is read from your computer's own internal clock.

Week: 1 of 1 - displays the **Current Week** (the **first** number) you are working in and the **Latest Week** (the **second** number) you can access. The Latest Week is the next week you are able to update.

LEAGUE NOT SET UP - is where the name of your league will appear.

V7.0 - is the version number of the FFL program you are working in. This number is important to know should you need to call for technical support.

A. LEAGUE SETUP

Once you have installed the FFL program, you must now configure your league to the way you and your franchise owners would like the FFL season to run. This is the first set of steps toward getting ready to kick off your Fantasy Football season.

From the **Main Menu** select **League Setup** by using the **arrow** keys to place the highlight bar, or by typing the corresponding menu letter and then pressing **[ENTER]**.

a. Enter League Name

Here is where you will name your Fantasy Football League. It can be from 1-25 letters and can be changed at any time during the season. Press **[ENTER]** to return to the **League Setup** menu.

b. Set Up Franchises

Now enter up to 16 franchise names that will be competing in your league this year. These names may be up to 20 letters in length.

NOTE:

It is important to note that once you have drafted players onto a franchise, you may change the name of that franchise, but you <u>may not</u> change the order in which the franchises are listed. The players' names are assigned to the particular franchise number location on the list.

If you are going to **Draft By Round** (entering the draft picks as they are being made), you must enter the franchise names in the order in which they will be drafting. If you are going to **Draft By Franchise** (entering all the draft picks after they have been made), you may enter the franchises in any order you wish. When you are finished entering your league's franchise names, press **[ESC]** to exit to the **League Setup** menu.

Here, as well as in the **Reports and Graphs** section, you have the option to print mailing labels for each franchise, should you need to mail out weekly stats. These labels are formatted for either laser or dot-matrix printers. For lasers, you will need to use **Avery® Labels #5161**, and for dot-matrix, you will need to use **Avery® Labels #4145**.

c. Set Warning Messages

This feature enables the program to warn you if you are going beyond the limits you have set up in the **Set Up Player Positions** section, i.e., too many players being drafted or started for a particular position on a franchise. Use the **arrow** keys to select the option you want, press **[ENTER]**, and you will be returned to the **League Setup** menu.

d. Set Draft Order

Here is where you will tell the program what method your league will use to enter your draft selections. If you are entering the draft picks as the franchise owners make them, this will allow you to choose from two automatic drafting orders on **Draft Night**. Select the method you wish to use, then press **[ENTER]**, and you will be returned to the **League Setup** menu.

 • Method #1 -- a straight 1-16, 1-16, 1-16 drafting order. This means every franchise owner picks in the same order throughout the draft. Franchise #1 will pick first and Franchise #16 will pick last in every round of the draft.

 • Method #2 -- an alternating order of 1-16, 16-1, 1-16. This means that the drafting order will reverse after each round. In the first round, and all odd-numbered rounds thereafter, Franchise #1 will pick first and Franchise #16 will pick last. In the second round, and all even-numbered rounds thereafter, Franchise #16 will pick first and Franchise #1 will pick last.

*If your league uses some other form of determining the order from round to round you may also enter the owners' draft picks after completing the draft. You would enter them in the **Draft by Franchise** method in the **Draft Night** Menu Option.

e. Set Current Week

This option will allow you to go to any week of the 17-week season for which you have already updated the weekly scores, so you may double-check the starting lineups, the scoring plays, releases and trades, etc. If you make any changes, be sure to run the **Update Weekly Scoring** again so that your changes can take effect. Remember that any changes to starting lineups will only be changed *for that week* and will not be passed to the next week. After you have finished working in that week, be sure to **Set Current Week** to the week you originally came from so you can continue your season.

f. Set Player Positions

Here is where you will define how many players can be drafted and started per franchise. This is already set up to comply with the recommended totals as defined by the FFL (see below for recommended FFL setup).

Code	Position	#Draft	#Start
QB	Quarterbacks	4	1
RB	Running Backs	6	2
WR	Wide Receivers	6	3
TE	Tight Ends	2	1
K	Kickers	2	1
DT	Defensive/Special Team Units	2	1
LB	Linebackers		
DB	Defensive Backs		
DL	Defensive Linemen		
OL	Offensive Linemen		
	Total Draft Picks	**22**	**9**

Select **Set Player Positions** from the **League Setup** menu and press **[ENTER]**.

Select either **Add a Position**, **Display/Edit Positions** or **Print Positions** from this menu. You may create additional player positions such as **Head Coach** with a position code of **HC**. You may also set the total number of players to be drafted and started at each position. These numbers are not set in stone and the program will let you exceed these limits, but it will display a warning message.

To change information about an existing player position select **Display/Edit Positions** and then select the position you wish to edit. You can get a printout of these positions in the **Reports and Graphs** section of the program. When you have finished with this section, use the **[ESC]** key to return to the **League Setup** menu.

g. Set Up Play Types

In this section you will be able to create your own **Play Types**
for your league to use to award points in addition to the standard
FFL scoring system. Select **Set Up Play Types** from the
League Setup menu and press **[ENTER]**.

You can either **Add Play Types**, **Display Play Types, or Print
Play Types**. If you select **Add Play Types**, you will be given
the next available slot to add a play type.

When you select **Display Play Types**, you will now see the
standard **FFL Play Types** already set up for you and the **User
Defined Play Types** can be set up in any of the available slots.
These are some of the more popular types of plays used today.
You may use these and/or create additional play types in the
spaces provided.

Even if you subscribe to any of the **FFL Service Updates**, you
will need to manually enter plays for the play types that you
created to be awarded points in the **Update Weekly Scoring**
section each week. The weekly scoring services provide only
the scoring plays defined on the screen, or **System Defined**.
However, you will be able to set up the point ranges for both
System Defined and **User Defined Play Types** so that when
these plays are entered into the update section, the points for
that play will automatically be awarded. You can get a printout
of both play types in the **Reports and Graphs** section of the
program. These point ranges are set up in the following section
called **Set Up Player Point Assignments**. When you are
finished defining your new plays, press the **[ESC]** key to return
to the **League Setup** menu.

h. Set Player Point Assignments

This section will allow you to add or modify any point play

range you want. Based on the **FFL Distance Scoring Ranges** and **FFL Performance Scoring Increments**, you can set up point ranges to account for any scoring system, and the specific number of times a player performs a task or commits an error.

After selecting **Set Player Point Assignments** from the **League Setup** menu, you may select either **FFL Distance Scoring Ranges** or **FFL Performance Scoring Increments**. **Ranges** are for those point assignments that your league wants to award a specific number of points for a play that falls in a range (i.e., *Touchdowns* or *Field Goals*). **Increments** are for when your leagues wants to award points for each time a play happens (i.e., *Rushing Yardage*, *Interceptions*, or *Passing Completions*).

In the **FFL Distance Scoring Ranges** module, the fields are described as follows:

Position:	Lower Range:	Points:
Play Type:	Upper Range:	

Lower and upper ranges refer to yards a play may cover or the number of times a certain play may occur. For example, a player point assignment such as this will appear for a *Quarterback* throwing a touchdown *pass* between *10* and *39* yards resulting in *9* points:

Position: **QB**	Lower Range: **10**	Points: **9**
Play Type: **Pass / TD**	Upper Range: **39**	

To modify an existing range, move the highlight bar down using the **arrow** keys or the **[Page Down]** key until you see the range you want. Press **[ENTER]** on that range and it will appear in the entry box on top. Move the highlight to the place you want to change and type in the value you desire. Press **[ENTER]** and then press **[End]** to save the change.

To add a new play range, press the **[Insert]** key to take you to the Play Range Entry box. Press **[ENTER]** to bring up the selections for the position or group for which you would like to have this range be credited. Move the highlight bar to the position you desire and press **[ENTER]**. Then press **[ENTER]** again to bring up the list containing the play types. When you have highlighted the play type for which you wish to set up a range, press **[ENTER]**.

Here, in the **FFL Performance Scoring Increments** module, player point assignments may be created for performance related stats, such as rushing yardage, passing yardage, receiving yardage, sacks, interceptions, fumbles, or any other category your league might wish to award or penalize points.

Position:	Start:	Points:
Play Type:	End:	Qty:

For example, if you wanted to reward *10* points to a *Running Back* for *rushing* at least *100* yards in a game, then you would want to set up a point assignment like this:

Position: **RB**	Start: **100**	Points: **10**
Play Type: **Rushing Yards**	End: **100**	Qty: **1**

Then, let's reward the same *Running Back* another *1* point for every additional *10* yards he *rushes* in that game.

Position: **RB**	Start: **101**	Points: **1**
Play Type: **Rushing Yards**	End: **999**	Qty: **10**

So if he rushes 98 yards in a game, he will get 0 points, but if he rushes 159, he will get 15 points. He gets 10 points for reaching 100 yards and another 5 points for the additional 59 yards rushed.

To delete any number of ranges, press the **[F5]** key to enter the

245

mass delete mode. You may now press **[F2]** to select individual lines you wish to delete, or you can press **[F5]** to delete the entire listing of Player Point Assignments and set up all your own assignments. When you are ready to delete your selections, press **[F3]**. You can now press **[ESC]** to return to the main **Player Point Assignment** screen.

NOTE:

Deleted point assignments are unrecoverable **and if you accidentally delete any of these ranges** *you must reenter them manually.* **Before making any changes you should copy all "POINTS" files to diskette as a backup copy just in case. For example, type from the C:\FFL prompt:**

Copy points.* A: [ENTER]

---

i. Set Monitor Type

If you are having trouble with the display, choose from either the **Color** (CGA, EGA, MCGA, VGA or Mono VGA) or **Monochrome** (Hercules) setting.

j. Divisions

If you select **System Defined Divisions**, the program will automatically set up the divisions based on how many franchises you have. If you have 8 or 10 franchises, you will have two divisions; if you have 12 or 14 franchises, you will have three divisions; and a 16-franchise league will have four divisions.

You will now see the divisions as the FFL program has defined them for you. You may change the titles of each division on the screen by typing over the names already listed. When you are done, press **[ESC]** and another box will appear asking which method of playoffs your league would like to use. A choice of

No Playoffs will simply calculate the rankings based on regular season wins/losses.

If you select **Custom Divisions**, you can select the number of divisions your league will be divided into and specify which teams belong in each divison. You may customize your divisions and still use the **System Defined Schedules**, but depending upon how much you alter the division layout, you may affect the balance of head-to-head matchups. Use the **NFL and FFL Schedules Reports** and the **Division Set Up Report** in the **Reports and Graphs** section to help you edit the divisions and schedules properly.

> ### Note:
> If you select Custom Divisions, you *must* manually pair the franchises in the Playoff Schedule in Custom Schedules.

---

k. Schedules

You can either have the program set up the head-to-head schedules for you by selecting **System Defined Schedules**, or you can modify any individual week or the entire season and playoffs by selecting **Custom Schedules**. When editing schedules, you should have already mapped-out your league's schedule on paper so that you can more easily keep track of which teams have already played and how many times.

- *System Defined Schedules* are already set up for you for leagues of 2 - 16 franchises that match franchises head-to-head as evenly as possible. The weeks of playoffs are the weeks at the end of the regular season. For example, 3 weeks of playoffs would be weeks 15, 16 and 17 of the NFL season.

- *Custom Schedules* will allow you to set the number of weeks in the complete season, the number of weeks in your league's regular season, and the number of weeks in your playoffs.

Note: Before doing any editing, it is always good to make a backup copy of the "DEFINE.DAT" file, which the program uses to save the schedules, as well as other information vital to your league.

When editing schedules, you should have already mapped out your league's schedule on paper so that as you edit each week's matchups you can easily keep track of which teams have already played and how many times.

After doing this, you can set or modify the **Regular Season** weekly head-to-head schedules or the **Playoff Schedules**. The playoffs are usually not set until the your regular season has ended.

Regular Season Schedules can be modified on a week-by-week basis or for the entire season. First, select the week you want to edit by moving the highlight bar and pressing **[Enter]**. You will now see the **System Defined Schedule** for that week.

Playoff Schedules can be modified as well on a week-by-week basis. The first week will display the **System Defined** matchups based upon current win-loss records. A new feature this year allows franchises to have "**Byes**" during the playoffs, but these must be set up by the Commissioner for that week. Use function keys at the bottom of the screen to edit these schedules. To save what you have done, press **[F2]**.

If you feel you have really messed up the entire schedule and you want to start all over again, you can use the **[F3]** key to **Reset Schedule** back to the **System Defined Schedule**.

Note: Use the **Franchise Schedules Reports** and the **Division Set Up Report** in the **Reports and Graphs** section to help you edit the divisions and schedules properly.

l. Set Up Printer Options

This will initially set up your printer options, but you will be prompted again each time you enter the Reports and Graphs section.

Select Defaults

Here you can select a default setting of whether you wish to print reports to a printer, screen, or diskette.

Printer Codes

If you are having a compatibility problem between our program and your printer, in the FFL program you can select what are known as "escape codes" for your printer. These should be listed in your printer manual. If you make a mistake and want to delete or reset these settings, use the **[F3]** and **[F4]** keys.

Note:

If you do not have your printer's manual, call your printer's manufacturer's technical support department to get these codes (for NORMAL and condensed print). (Do *not* call our Technical Support Department to receive these codes because the technical support representatives do not have printer manuals in stock.)

m. Set Up Roster Transactions

This section will allow you to set up fees for any player transactions your league owners make during the season. These is also a separate report in **Reports and Graphs** to print these out.

Set Up Fees

You can set up separate fees for each roster move a league owner makes throughout the season. For example, your league may charge $1 for every player pickup or release and $2 for each trade. These can easily be tracked for you here.

Delete Transactions

If during the season the Commissioner has made a mistake in a transaction, here you can delete any transaction from any week during the season so that owners will be charged the correct amount for transactions at the end of the season.

n. Program Maintenance

This is a very important section for those Commissioners who like to test their league's scoring system before the season starts or who are very conscious of limited hard drive space.

Purge Play Files

This is a very important new automatic/manual feature that will allow you to save valuable hard drive space throughout the football season. The program will delete all the **"Play01.I∗∗"** index files for **Week #1**, for example, and recreate the **"FFLPLAY.1"** file that you uncompressed from the file downloaded from **FSPI** or **PRODIGY**, and it will include any changes you have made. This can **save** almost **50%** of the **hard disk space** that would be normally used to store these index files. Once you have completed a week of updating there is no further need for these files, but if you back up to this week and enter the **Update Weekly Scoring** module, the program will regenerate these files to let you view, edit, or re-update that week's scores.

Reset Season

This is a new feature for the 1994 FFL software. This will allow you to test your league's scoring system before the season starts. You can run a few updates and get several weeks into your test season and then have the program reset itself back to the beginning without losing any team info or rosters. This feature will, however, clear out all scoring plays and points from the master play file so that all franchises are back to zero points in Week #1. You can even reset the entire program without saving the franchise info, so that the program will start over in Week #1 with no franchise info or rosters.

In all cases, any play types, point assignments or other rules you have set up will be saved. **Only the franchise info, roster, plays and current week status are changed.**

B. DRAFT NIGHT

Tonight's the night you and your fellow franchise owners begin to put together your dream teams for the season. Distributing copies of the existing **1994 NFL Roster** to your fellow franchise owners can make conducting the draft much easier.

The **NFL Roster** can be printed from the **Reports and Graphs** section in the Main Menu or by pressing the **[F4]** key under **League Setup**. Franchise owners may draft NFL players who are not on this list. (Although the **Draft Night** section allows for the addition of players not listed, the weekly stat files will automatically update and add new players to the player database) If your league is not entering the draft picks directly into the computer during the draft, the **Draft Night Player List** is a helpful report for the Commissioner to use. This report prints out the same **NFL Roster** list, but with space available to record the franchise that drafts the player. This makes it much easier for the Commissioner to enter the draft picks later.

From the **Main Menu**, select **Draft Night** and you will then be asked to Select Draft Method:

Method 1 - Draft by Round:
This should be used by leagues that have access to a computer during the draft. This method tracks draft selection order by round and allows one pick per franchise for each round, similar to an actual NFL draft. It rotates from franchise to franchise based on the order in which you entered the franchise names during the **League Setup** portion of the **Main Menu**.

Set up the computer in a central location so that each franchise owner has access to it during the draft. The Commissioner may want to operate the program or assist other owners. The left window will display those players available to draft. The right window will display the name of the franchise and its selected players. The current round and pick will be displayed above the two windows.

When Franchise #1 picks the player it wants to draft, the Commissioner or franchise owner should scroll through the list of players, using the **arrow** keys or the **[F10]** key, to locate the player's name with the highlight bar and press **[ENTER]**. This moves the player from the **Available NFL Players** window (left) and places him in the Franchise window (right) and onto that franchise's team. At this point you may either press **[F1]** to record the pick and move on to the next selection, or **[F2]** to reverse the pick and allow you to select another player. At any point during the draft, franchise owners may take a break simply by pressing the **[ESC]** key twice to return to the **Main Menu**. The FFL program records all draft choices through that round, and your league can continue the draft at any time.

252

If the wrong player is drafted, press **[ESC]** to get to the options menu: **Draft by Round** or **Draft by Franchise**. Select **Draft by Franchise**; when the box of franchises appears, select the franchise that drafted the wrong player. Using the **right arrow** key, move the highlight bar over to the franchise window and onto the wrong player selected, press **[ENTER]** and the player will be moved back to the **Available NFL Players** list. Now use the **left arrow** key to move the highlight bar back to the **Available NFL Players** list, select the player the franchise wants, and press **[ENTER]** again to move the player onto that franchise. After that, press **[ESC]** twice to go back to the options menu and re-select **Draft by Round**. You will return to the current round and current pick.

It is important that when you remove one player from a franchise, you put one back on that franchise. Otherwise, the round-pick sequence will be incorrect and will be re-set to round 1, pick 1, (but you will not lose any of the previous picks).

Method 2 - Draft by Franchise:

This should be used by leagues that do not have access to a computer during the draft and by the Commissioner to make adjustments throughout the season. This method makes it easy for the Commissioner to enter each franchise's picks after the draft. **It allows the Commissioner to input all drafted players for each franchise at the same time, rather than one pick per franchise**. This method can be used by **all leagues** to make adjustments, such as adding players, correcting errors, drafting players released by other franchises, or for leagues that have a supplemental draft.

Use the appropriate menu options from the Main Menu to execute those transactions. This will allow the FFL program to remember any points that may have been scored by these players in previous weeks. If you do try to delete a player from a franchise that has scored points, you will receive an error message.

After you select **Draft by Franchise**, a window will appear listing the franchises. Select a franchise by using the **arrow** keys to move the highlight bar and press **[ENTER]**. Now, two windows will appear. The left **Available NFL Players** window contains a list of the available 1994 NFL Players. The right window displays the franchise name that is drafting. Have each franchise's list of drafted players handy.

Scroll through the list of players in the left window to locate the player, place the highlight bar on the name and press **[ENTER]**. This moves the player off the **Available NFL Players** list and into the franchise window. The highlight bar will automatically move back to the **Available NFL Players** window. Simply select the next player to be drafted and press **[ENTER]**. When all the players for that franchise have been drafted, press **[ESC]**. Repeat this procedure for the next franchise to draft.

To **remove** a player from a franchise, use the right **arrow** key to move the highlight bar to the franchise window. Place the bar on that player, press **[ENTER],** and the player's name will appear in the **Available NFL Players** window.

At any time during the draft, the Commissioner can take a break by simply pressing the **[ESC]** key twice to return to the **Main**

Menu. The FFL Program records all draft choices, and the Commissioner can continue the draft at any time.

Both Method 1 and Method 2 Users:
After the draft has been completed, it's a good idea to print **Franchise Rosters** and **Starting Lineup Worksheets**. Return to the **Main Menu** and select **Reports and Graphs**. Make sure your printer is **ON**. Select **Print Franchise Rosters** from the **Player Information** menu. Then select **Starting Lineup Worksheets** from the **Weekly Reports** menu and distribute the reports to each franchise owner to track weekly starting lineups.

Important Keys to Make Your Draft Easier:
There are a number of special features that can be used during the draft to aid Commissioners or franchise owners in picking players for their teams.

- **Searching** for a player's name can be done by simply typing (in **CAPS**) the player's last name. As you type each letter you will see the list of players scroll closer to the player you are looking for. If you make a mistake in typing, just press any of the arrow keys to reset the search mode. You can start typing the name again. This can be used in any window that contains player information sorted by **Player's Name**.
- **Arrow Keys Up & Down:** Moves the highlight bar vertically to scroll through the list of available and drafted players in both windows.
- **Arrow Keys Right & Left:** Moves the highlight bar from the **Available NFL Players** window to the **Franchise** window and back.
- **[F1]:** Help window available throughout FFL program.
- **[F4]:** Lists all NFL players who have been drafted to that point. To access this option, press **[F4]**. A window will appear on the screen. To return to player windows, press **[ESC]**.
- **[F6]:** This function will show the status of the current

franchise's drafted players, started players, and players on IR.

- **[F9]:** Changes the order in which players are displayed, both in the **Available NFL Players** window and the **Franchise** window. Players can be displayed alphabetically, by position, or by NFL team. Players are initially displayed in alphabetical order. To access this option, press **[F9]**. A window will appear on the screen. Select the desired display order, then press **[ENTER]**. Players are immediately listed in selected order. To return to player window, press **[ESC]**.

- **[F10]:** Quickly locates specific player by name, position, or team.

  If players are displayed alphabetically, the **[F10]** key will quickly locate a specific player by typing in his last name in **CAPS**. If the players are displayed by position, the **[F10]** key will quickly locate a specific group of player positions. If players are displayed by NFL team, the **[F10]** key will quickly locate a specific NFL team. To access this option, press **[F10]**. A list of players, positions, or teams will appear. Select the appropriate option, press **[ENTER]**. To return to player window, press **[ESC]**.

  Note: All entries must be typed exactly as they appear. Last names in UPPER case and first names in upper and lower case (i.e., SANDERS, Barry).

- **To Edit a Player:** The **[F5]** key allows you to edit a player in either the **Available NFL Players** window or the **Franchise** window. Using the **arrow** keys, scroll through the list until you find the player you want to edit, then press **[F5]**. Now using the **arrow** keys, move the highlight bar to where you want to edit. When you are done, press **[End]** to save the change or **[ESC]** to cancel the change. You may only edit a player's name and the NFL team he plays for, but **not his position**. To do this you must delete him and reenter his complete information. If you do change his name or position the update service may not update his stats properly.

- **To Delete a Player from the NFL Roster:** Place the highlight bar on the player to be deleted and press **[Del]**. One last window will appear asking for confirmation before deleting the player.
- **To Insert a New Player's Name:** The FFL provides a comprehensive up-to-date **1994 NFL Roster**; additionally, if you subscribe to any of the stat update services, the program will update and add new players throughout the season when you import each weekly stat file.

If a franchise wants to draft a player whose name does not appear in the **Available NFL Players** (left) window, select this option by pressing **[Insert]**, while in the left-hand side window, to enter a new player's information. A window will appear allowing the Commissioner/franchise owner to type in the player's last name and first name, and to select the player's position and NFL team name. (If you decide not to add this player to the list after the window has appeared on the screen, simply press **[ESC]**.) Press **[End]** to record new player's information.

C. Select Starting Lineups

Every week, the Commissioner records each franchise's starting lineup using the FFL program.

Choose **Select Starting Lineups** from the **Main Menu**. A window will appear listing the names of each franchise in the league. Use the highlight bar to select the desired franchise and press **[ENTER]**. Now, two windows will appear.

The left window displays the franchise's **Non-Starting Players**. The right window displays the franchise's **Starting Players**. To move the highlight bar from window to window, use the right and left **arrow** keys.

To select a starting player, place the highlight bar on the desired player in the left window and press **[ENTER]**. This automatically moves the player's name from the left **Non-Starters** window and places it in the right **Starters** window. Select each starting player using the same process until there are the appropriate number of starting players on each franchise. When complete, press **[ESC]** to select the next franchise.

To bench or delete a player from the starting lineup of a franchise, place the highlight bar on the desired player in the right window and press **[ENTER]**. The player's name automatically moves from the right window of **Starting Players** to the left window of **Non-Starting Players**.

When the starting lineups for each franchise in the league have been recorded, press **[ESC]** twice to end and return to the **Main Menu**.

The starting lineups are automatically carried over to the next week after you run the **Update Weekly Scoring**. Once you have processed the scoring plays, a window will appear asking to "**Reset Current Week?**" If you are confident you are finished with this week's updating, you should select **Yes**, because the FFL program will automatically set up the next week's starting lineups based on the present week's lineups. You will still be able to make changes to the starting lineups in the **Select Starting Lineups** section.

D. MAKE TRADES

The Commissioner records all trades using the FFL program. Select **Make Trades** from the **Main Menu**. After the window appears, use the highlight bar to select "Franchise #1" involved in the trade, and then press **[ENTER]**. Now a second window will appear. Again using the highlight bar, select "Franchise #2" involved in the trade and press **[ENTER]**.

Two windows will appear on the screen. The left window displays the roster of all players on the first franchise and the right window displays the roster of the second franchise. To make a trade, select the player to be traded from Franchise #1 by placing the highlight bar on his name, and press **[ENTER]**. The player's name will automatically move from the left window to the right window.

Trade players from Franchise #2 to Franchise #1 using the same procedure. If you are making a 2-for-1 or 3-for-2 trade, use the right and left **arrow** keys to change windows and select players.

To reverse a trade, follow the same steps as above, using the highlight bar and **[ENTER]** key. If you make a mistake, simply go to the other franchise and highlight the player placed there in error. Press **[ENTER]** to move the player back to the original team, then re-select the correct player. No harm is done if a trade is reversed in the same week, and when a player has not scored in that or successive weeks. If you reverse a trade in a later week and the player has scored points (starting lineup or non-starting lineup), you will see the player twice on **Player Scoring Reports** for a short time; this is normal and will subside. Press **[ESC]** twice to end the trading and return to the **Main Menu**.

E. RELEASE A PLAYER

If a player seems no longer useful to your team and you wish to draft or pick another available player, then you must first release or take the unwanted player off your team. Select **Release a Player** from the **Main Menu**. Select the franchise with the highlight bar and press **[ENTER]**. Two windows will appear; on the left is the franchise roster and on the right is the Released Players list. Select the player to be released by moving the highlight bar with the **arrow** keys and press **[ENTER]**. The player will automatically be moved onto the Released Players list and off the franchise roster. To put a player back on a franchise's roster, or if an error was made, re-enter the **Draft Night** section using **Method 2, Draft by Franchise,** and then add a player to the roster following the same directions you used to enter the draft picks. *Note:* Players become eligible to be drafted again by other franchises after being released.

F. Injured Reserve

If, during the season, NFL players become injured or sent down to the minor leagues, they can be placed on **Injured Reserve** by their NFL teams. This means they are not available to play, and are not available for other teams to pick up. If a player is unable to play in the NFL for a couple of weeks, an FFL franchise owner may place the player on Injured Reserve in order to hold on to him, but only if the NFL team does that as well. In the FFL, owners are limited to four such transactions during the season to prevent stockpiling of talent.

Select **Injured Reserve** from the **Main Menu**. Select the franchise with the highlight bar and press **[ENTER]**. Two windows will appear; on the left is the franchise roster and on the right is the **Injured Reserve**. Select the player to be placed on the **Injured Reserve** and press **[ENTER]**. The player will automatically move onto the **Injured Reserve**. To put a player back on a team's roster or if an error was made, use the right **arrow** key to get into the right window, place the highlight bar on the player's name, and press **[ENTER]**. To exit, press **[ESC]** twice to return to **Main Menu**.

G. Update Weekly Scoring

Here is where you will update your league's fantasy points every week. If you are using either of the update services (i.e., **The PRODIGY Service** or **Fantasy Sports BBS**), be sure that you have downloaded the weekly file (i.e., **FFLPLAY.1**) and have executed it from the **C:\FFL** prompt to extract that week's stat file before you enter this section on the **Main Menu**. These instructions are explained in the **Subscribing To Weekly Scoring Updates** section of this manual.

If the program detects the stat file for the week you have selected, it will import and assign your league's fantasy points to the plays stored in it. If the program was unable to match any of the plays to the players in your master roster file, you will be prompted to edit these plays if you wish to at this time. This mismatch may be caused by either a player name being misspelled in the stat/roster files, or by plays in the stat file for a new player not stored in the master roster file.

At this time, you can manually update these plays with the correct player name by highlighting the player's name and pressing **[ENTER]**. You may now press **[F10]** to bring up the current master roster of players. The program will attempt to match the closest name, but you may need to scroll up and down to be sure. If you cannot find the correct match, then this player might be a new player to be added to your league. (In almost all cases these players will be new players.) If you do find the player's correct name, highlight him and press **[ENTER]** then **[End]** to save him in the play file. His name should now disappear from the list of unmatched names.

After you have corrected all the names you can, press **[Esc]** to proceed to the main update menu. Now you may automatically add these new players by selecting **Update Rosters**.

You can also edit/enter any of that week's plays or go straight to **Updating This Week's Plays**.

Once the update process has been completed, you will be prompted to reset the week and pass your league's lineups forward. If you feel that you have made a roster lineup or point assignment error, choose **NO**, otherwise choose **YES** and the program will set up your league's lineups for next week. You may still back up and make changes, but you may need to run the update process again. If you back up and just make a starting roster change, then you won't need to run through the update process again.

Note:
Responding YES to resetting the lineups is the only way to get into the next week of the season.

H. REPORTS AND GRAPHS

From these menu selections you can either print or view these reports:

a. Weekly Reports

A. User-Defined Reports

> Can be configured to print combination of reports each week.

B. Weekly Winning Report

> Prints total starting and non-starting points for each franchise for that week and year-to-date.

C. Weekly League Summary Report

> Will print league standings with current results and next week's matchups. At the end of your league's regular

season you will have the option to have the matchups reflect the playoffs.

D. Player Scoring Report

Prints total starting and non-starting points for each player on each franchise for that week. At the end of your league's regular season you will have the option to have the matchups reflect the playoffs.

E. Scoring Plays Report

Prints all the scoring plays awarded to each player on a franchise, both starting and non-starting, for that week. At the end of your league's regular season you will have the option to have the matchups reflect the playoffs.

F. Starting Lineups Worksheets

Prints all the players, listed by franchise, and whether they were started the previous week, with additional space for franchise owners to indicate whether they want the player to start this week.

G. Pre-Game Roster Report

Prints the upcoming week's games, with each head-to-head matchup on a separate page. Includes both starting and non-starting rosters with year-to-date points. At the end of your league's regular season you will have the option to have the matchups reflect the playoffs.

H. Starting Roster Report

Prints just the starting roster results for the entire league.

I. Customize Weekly Reports

Here is where you can customize the "A. User-Defined Reports" discussed earlier. You can select all the reports your league wants to see on a weekly basis and print them all by just choosing one report.

b. League Setup Reports

A. Player Point Assignments

Prints the current scoring play ranges that the program uses for assigning point values to the play file in the **Update Weekly Scoring** section.

B. Player Positions

Prints both pre-defined and user-defined player positions used to credit **Player Point Assignments**.

C. Play Types

Prints both pre-defined and user-defined play types used to create scoring plays for Quarterbacks, Wide Receivers, and any other positions your league may have created.

D. Division Setup

Prints your league's divisional setup to hand out to league members before the start of the season.

E. Mailing Labels

Print mailing labels for up to two owners per franchise. For dot-matrix printers use **Avery Labels #4145**, and for laser printers use **Avery Labels #5161**.

c. Franchise Standings

A. Graph of Season Scoring

Prints a graph of the year-to-date scoring totals for each franchise.

B. Graph of Points For / Against

Prints a graph of the year-to-date starting roster points scored and allowed by each franchise

C. Season Standings

Prints each franchise's record, winning percentage, and total points scored and allowed.

D. Division Standings

Prints your league's overall and divisional breakdown of wins-losses-ties and points for/allowed. Also includes previous head-to-head results and next week's matchups.

d. Player Information

A. NFL Roster Report

Prints the current database of NFL players available for drafting, listed by position or NFL Team. This report is a very good handout for franchise owners on **Draft Night**.

B. Franchise Roster Report

Prints each franchise's roster of players.

C. Draft Night Players List

Prints the same list of players as **NFL Roster Report**, but also provides space for entering the franchise name that drafts that player. Very helpful report for Commissioners who are not entering the draft picks as they are made on **Draft Night**.

D. Non-Drafted Scoring Players

Prints a year-to-date scoring report for all non-drafted players, with scoring listed by the week. Very useful report for franchise owners to locate a productive player not yet on a team.

E. Top-40 Point Leaders

Prints the top-40 players, by position, based on their year-to-date fantasy point scoring.

F. Released Players

Prints all players released by week.

G. Injured Reserve

Prints a history of all players placed on Injured Reserve.

H. Roster Transactions

Prints all player roster moves on a week-by-week basis. This includes moves such as trades, releases, and newly drafted players.

I. Roster Transaction Fees

This new report will print a franchise-by-franchise listing of all transaction fees charged throughout the season, if the fees were set up in the **League Set Up** section.

e. NFL & FFL Schedules

A. Schedules By Week

This will print your league's entire season schedule. It can print the entire 17-week schedule or just your league's regular season schedule based upon what is set up in the **Divisions/Schedules** section of **League Set Up**.

B. Schedules By Franchise

This will print each franchise's regular season schedule and which franchise they play from week to week. This can also can be set to reflect playoffs.

C. Schedules With Playoffs Report

This will appear to be the same report as Schedules By Week, but this report will also include your league's playoff format. Depending upon which week you generate this report, the program will attempt to match up which franchises in the playoffs, based on the records that week.

D. NFL Schedules

Prints entire 1994 NFL schedule or a single week. Single weeks are also printed in the **Weekly League Summary Report**.

f. Stat Reports

A. Drafted Stat Detail

Shows comprehensive major league stats for all current players on each franchise. These are total year-to-date stats for each player, whether he was on this franchise or not in the past.

B. Non-Drafted Stat Detail

Shows comprehensive NFL stats for all non-drafted players in your league. These are total year-to-date stats for each player, whether he was on this franchise or not in the past.

C. Season Franchise Stat History

Shows comprehensive NFL stats for all current and former players while they played for each franchise.

D. Top-40 Stat Leaders

Shows the top-40 players for each of the NFL stat categories included in the weekly stat update file or manually entered.

E. Season Scoring Summary Report

Prints a spreadsheet-like report, similar to the one in the back of the *FFL Journal*, which displays all Distance scoring (NFL point scoring plays) information for each player with his year-to-date fantasy points. Can be sorted by player name, position or ranking.

F. Box Score Report

This new report prints a weekly box score report similar to those found in the sports section of your newspaper. Breaks down distance scoring plays based on time and quarter info from actual NFL games (if you get stats via update service). Also breaks down most other statistical info from players on either franchise for that week.

g. Screen Reports

This is a very handy tool for the Commissioner to quickly look up information on a specific franchise's performance while on the phone with a franchise owner.

When you select this option, a window appears containing the year-to-date total points for starting/non-starting players for each franchise. Move the highlight bar to a specific franchise, press **[ENTER],** and you will now see the season broken down by weeks for that franchise. Move the highlight bar to any week, press **[ENTER],** and you will see each player's points scored that week, whether starting or non-starting. Now move the highlight bar to a specific player, and press **[ENTER]** to see the plays for which the player was awarded points that week. Move the highlight bar to the specific play you want to see, press **[ENTER]**, and a more detailed description will appear.

f. All Reports

Here you have quick access to all the reports the 1994 FFL program has to offer, without having to go through multiple menus.

I. FILE INDEXING

From time to time during the season, it may become necessary to re-align the master files the program uses. This simply helps the program to run more smoothly if errors occur. Errors may be caused by the repeated adding, editing, or deleting of information in those files.

NOTE:

File Indexing does not reset the FFL program to the beginning of the season, but rather it re-aligns certain index markers that allow the program to work with that particular data file.

The files to be concerned about are:

- **Point file** - works in tandem with the file Player Point Assignments works.
- **Player file** - NFL Player Rosters (This file will become quite large; unless you have a lot of time on your hands, you might not want to reindex each week; however, it is a good idea to do this after a week of heavy trades, releases, injuries, or other roster moves).
- **Play file** - the master file of Weekly Scoring Plays and Updated NFL Rosters.
- **Franchise file** - this file stores all the owner information of each franchise in your league.
- **Division file** - this file stores your league's divisional setup.
- **Roster Transaction file** - this file keeps track of your league's roster moves throughout the season.

A. *FSPI® BULLETIN BOARD SERVICE UPDATE*

Through the FSPI® Service, your league can subscribe to receive the weekly scoring updates via download for use with the Franchise Football League's Fantasy Football game. All you need for this service is any standard communication software, such as Procomm Plus®, which is available from any major software dealer, and a modem. In some cases you may be able to purchase both as part of a special offer bundle. **To subscribe**, just **call 1-800-872-0335** and we will set up your account. You can then download an entire season's worth of stats each Monday and Tuesday to update your league in just minutes.

How Does It Work?

Once you have installed your communication software, follow these steps on how to log onto the FSPI Public Bulletin Board Service. To obtain further information about the FFL and to subscribe to the Weekly Scoring Update service, contact:

Four BBS Phone Lines: 703-893-7002

Hours of Operation: 3pm - 12pm EST (21 hours/day)
(Subject to change without notice)

Settings: N - Parity
               8 - Data Pits
               1 - Stop Bits

Baud Rates: 1200 - 14,400

After your communication software has called our **Fantasy Sports BBS**, you will see the welcome screen followed by prompts asking you to enter your **first name**, **last name**, and

your password. Your first time on, you can create whatever password you wish. Write it down so that you don't forget it because you will need to enter it every time you sign on to the **Fantasy Sports BBS**.

From here, a menu will appear on the screen for you to choose from. Depending on your security level (which vary according to which services you have paid for), you have access to download the FFL Weekly Statistics about three hours after the final Sunday and Monday games.

The first stat file will be available on Sunday, September 4, 1994.

For new members just signing on to the bulletin board system, you can read all about **FSPI**, the upcoming **1995** version of the **FBL**, and future programs in **Fantasy Hockey** and **Fantasy Basketball**. You will be able to download full working demo versions of these programs as well as other sports-related information. All users will be able to download modifications or changes made throughout the 1994 seasons of **National Football League** or the **Major League Baseball**.

After you have downloaded the **FFLWK01.EXE** file, which is the compressed Week #1 stat file, you will need to copy it from the directory of your communication software to the FFL directory of our program.

For example, if you are using **Procomm Plus** software to download stats, you might type at the C:\FFL prompt:
Copy C:\pcplus\FFLWK01.EXE [Enter]

In this case, the **PCPLUS** is the standard directory name for the Procomm Plus software. Once this has been done you will need to decompress the file by typing at the C:\FFL prompt:

FFLWK01 [Enter]

Now start the FFL program and when you enter **the Update Weekly Scoring** section, the program will look for and import these stats. If all goes well with the update, you can delete the **FFLWK01.EXE** file to save space.

B. PRODIGY® SERVICE UPDATE

Through the PRODIGY® Service, your league can subscribe to receive the weekly scoring updates via download for use with the Franchise Football League's Fantasy Football game. All you need for this service is your PRODIGY® Service Start-Up Kit, which is available from any Sears location or any major software dealer, and a modem. In some cases you may be able to purchase both as part of a special offer bundle.

How Does It Work?

Once you have installed your PRODIGY® Service software and logged on to the service, follow these steps to obtain further information about the FFL and how to subscribe to the Weekly Scoring Update service:

When the **PRODIGY® Service HIGHLIGHTS** screen appears,

Type: **J [Enter]** key

and then when the box appears,

Type: **FFL [Enter]**

Answer the questions under the ordering section. You will need a major credit card (VISA, Mastercard) to charge your enrollment fee which covers the entire season of weekly downloads. You can also arrange to pay by check, but you will need to contact a Prodigy Customer Services Representative for more information. Each week of the NFL season, scoring updates and NFL game results will be available via PRODIGY®

Service download around three hours after the last Sunday and Monday games (subject to statistics availablity).

The first download will be available on Sunday September 4, 1994. Once the season has started, each week's stat file will be labeled and kept on-line all season long for you to download. Once you have selected the week you wish to download, the system will prompt you with the default FFL directory and that week's file name, so that you can change either the directory name or the disk drive (C: is the default drive setting) you wish the file to be copied to.

For example, in Week 4 of the season you may be asked if this is the path you wish to use when copying the stat file to your computer:

\FFL\FFLPLAY.4

which would copy the Week 4 scoring file to the FFL directory on your C: drive.

Once you have exited PRODIGY® Service and are now at your **C:\FFL** prompt start your FFL program and **SET CURRENT WEEK** to Week 4 (in this case), and the program will look for and read the **"FFLPLAY.4"** stat file containing the scoring plays for that week. Now, you are ready to update your league's stats.

C. FACSIMILE UPDATE SERVICE

This method will provide you with the weekly FFL scoring plays. The FFL scoring plays will be sent via fax 3-4 hours following the Monday Night Football game so that you will have them waiting for you first thing Tuesday morning. This will save you a lot of time in not having to fumble through the Monday and Tuesday sports pages for the box scores. You will be able to easily enter all the week's scoring plays into the

Scoring Plays Entry Screen (see **G. Update Weekly Scoring**) right from this fax.

D. Next/Second Day Diskette Update Service

Through this method, you will receive the weekly scoring updates on diskette on the **Wednesday** (for **Next Day** Service) or **Thursday** (for **Second Day** Service) following that Monday night's game.

III. FREQUENTLY ASKED QUESTIONS

- **Can I run more than one league using this software?** Yes, all you will need to do is to install the software in a separate directory for each league you want to run. For example, the first league will be in C:\FFL and the second might be in C:\FFL2, etc.

- **Will this software run on a Macintosh computer?** Only if it is set up to run DOS programs with a program such as SoftPC. However, we do not offer technical support for those who choose to run this program on a Macintosh.

- **Can I run this program from Windows?** No! This program is not meant to be run from *any* menu system. If you try to run it from Windows, it will crash and you may lose important data that is unrecoverable, forcing you to start the entire season over.

- **Can I customize the reports my league wants to see each week?** Yes, from the Weekly Reports menu you can select all the reports you want to see every week to print at the same time.

- **How can I back up all my league's data each week?** If you are running MS-DOS 5.0 or earlier you can type this from the C:\FFL prompt: **Backup *.* a: [ENTER]**

If you using MS-DOS 6.0 or later, there is a menu system that will appear if you type **BACKUP** at the C:\FFL prompt and press **[ENTER]**. You will need to consult your DOS User's Manual for further information.

In any case, these backup proceedures require the use of your floppy disk drives and will require that more disks be used as the season progresses.

IV. SOFTWARE TROUBLESHOOTING

IMPORTANT: Please read the following section on software troubleshooting. Although we do not anticipate any errors occurring in your FFL program, any problems you may experience should be minor and easily correctable.

Here are the most commonly asked questions and their solutions:

- **My program won't start or run properly when I start it from Windows or a menu?** The FFL program is not meant to be run from any menu system. If you try to run it from Windows, it will crash and you may lose important data that is unrecoverable, forcing you to start the entire season over. It also is not designed to run on a network.
- **What do I do if I get error codes across the top of the screen in certain places of the program?** First, re-index the Play file and/or Player file, then try the task again. Also, make sure you are not running the FFL program from a menu program such as DOS- Shell or Windows. (*Consult*

your menu software manual on how to exit the menu to the DOS prompt.) Also check your CONFIG.SYS file, located in the main root directory on your computer's hard drive, to make sure these settings appear:

Files=50
Buffers=30

If you need to make changes to this file, *consult your computer's operating system manual* on how to make these modifications. You can also use a Boot-Diskette to bypass these menus without making major changes to your software.

- **How do I set up a Boot-Disk for my computer?** First, place a blank diskette in the A: drive of your system and type from the DOS prompt of C:\

    Format a:/s then press **[ENTER]**

    The computer will format the diskette and copy the file necessary to enable your computer to start up from the diskette, instead of the hard disk drive. Press **[ENTER]** when you are asked to label the diskette, and type **N** for no when asked if you would like to format another. Now, again type from the DOS prompt of C:\

    Copy Con A:\Config.sys [ENTER]

    You will then see a blank line after you press **[ENTER]**, so now type

    Files=50 [ENTER]
    Buffers=30 [ENTER]
    ^Z [ENTER]

    (hold **[CTRL]** key and **Z** down at the same time.) You should now see the message of "1 File(s) copied" and then the C:\ prompt again. Now leave the diskette in the disk drive and hold the **[CTRL][ALT]** and **[Del]** keys down at the same time to re-boot your computer. You should see the computer access the A:\ drive with the diskette in it, then the DOS prompt of A:\ appear on the screen when it is done. Now type

C:\ [ENTER]
(or the drive in which the FFL game is located)
CD\FFL [ENTER]
Now try the FFL program again.

- **I get "out of memory" errors while running the FFL program!** Make sure you are not running any memory resident programs at the same time as the FFL program, such as menus, or other TSR (terminate-stay-resident) programs. You should be able to bypass this error if you use the boot-disk discussed earlier. If you are using DOS 5.0 or higher, consult your DOS maunal on how to load your operating system and other device drivers into upper memory.

- **None of the reports will print out!** Make sure all power and cable connections between the printer and the computer are tightly plugged in. Turn the printer off then back on, and make sure you see the "Ready" or "On-line" light activate on the front of your printer showing that it is ready. Now, try to print again.

- **When I print reports I either get just the heading and nothing else, double-spaced information, or garbage?** You need to make sure that your printer is set up for Epson emulation. Please consult your printer's documentation and Owner's Manual on how to check on this.

- **How can I conserve space from each week after I have finished updating that weeks scores?** From the League Setup Menu, select the Purge Plays option. This will erase all the index files the program used to update that weeks scores and recreate the "FFLPLAY.1" file, including any changes you have made to the scoring plays. After you have updated successfully for a given week and are satisfied with the results, you can copy that week's FFLPLAY.# file to a floppy disk for backup and delete it from your hard drive. This can save as much as 40K of space per week.

Also, you can reduce more space each week by deleting all the .PRN and .RPT files that are created when you generate/view any reports.

This can be done by typing at the C:\FFL prompt:
Erase *.prn [ENTER]
Erase *.rpt [ENTER]

V. INFORMATION HOTLINES

The **FFL Technical Support Lines** are open from **10am - 6pm (EST) Monday through Friday**. If you need support with the latest version of the program, be sure you have first looked through the previous section on **Software Troubleshooting** to see if there is a solution listed for your situation. After that, if you still can't resolve your situation, give us a call.

You **must** have these few items of information so we may help you correct any problem:

- Brand name or model of the computer you are using (Compaq, IBM, NEC, Tandy, etc.)
- The processor and speed of your computer (386SX, 16mhz, etc.)
- Amount of RAM your computer has (640K, 2MB, etc.)
- Operating system version number (DOS 5.0, DOS 3.3, etc.)
- Type of disk drive you are using (3.5" High Density 1.44 or Double-Sided Doubled Density 720K)
- Make and model of printer (HP LaserJet IIP, NEC P5200 dot matrix, etc.)
- What steps you were performing right before the error occurred
- **The contents of your CONFIG.SYS file**

> **Fantasy Football**
> **Technical Support Line:**
> **1-703-893-4861**
> **Monday-Friday (10am - 6pm EST)**

Technical Support Bulletin Board: Leave a message for the System Operator (SysOp) on the FSPI Bulletin Board. Be sure to include any and all important information so we can respond to your problem promptly. You may also leave us e-Mail on the Prodigy Service. Write to us by typing:

[JUMP]:sports bb and selecting **Football-Fantasy** or directly to our **Technical Support** ID# **GDXS68F**.

Please be advised:
Due to reductions in the number of staff working on the BBS and Prodigy, this is a much slower method of getting your questions answered than calling for support.

Write to: Franchise Football League
Technical Support Department
P.O. Box 9805
McLean, VA   22102

**FFL Order Processing Department
1-800-872-0335**

Write to: Fantasy Sports Properties, Inc.
Order Processing Department
P.O. Box 9805
McLean, Virginia   22102

APPENDIX A
1994 NFL SCHEDULE

WEEK ONE
Seattle at Washington
Atlanta at Detroit
Cleveland at Cincinnati
Houston at Indianapolis
Kansas City at New Orleans
Minnesota at Green Bay
Philadelphia at NY Giants
Tampa Bay at Chicago
Arizona at LA Rams
Dallas at Pittsburgh
New England at Miami
NY Jets at Buffalo
San Diego at Denver
LA Raiders at San Francisco,
MON

WEEK THREE
Washington at NY Giants
Arizona at Cleveland
Buffalo at Houston
Green Bay at Philadelphia
Indianapolis at Pittsburgh
Minnesota at Chicago
New England at Cincinnati
New Orleans at Tampa Bay
NY Jets at Miami
LA Raiders at Denver
San Diego at Seattle
San Francisco at LA Rams
Kansas City at Atlanta
Detroit at Dallas, MON

WEEK TWO
Washington at New Orleans
Buffalo at New England
Detroit at Minnesota
Indianapolis at Tampa Bay
LA Rams at Atlanta
Miami at Green Bay
Pittsburgh at Cleveland
San Francisco at Kansas City
Cincinnati at San Diego
Denver at NY Jets
Houston at Dallas
Seattle at LA Raiders
NY Giants at Arizona
Chicago at Philadelphia, MON

WEEK FOUR
Atlanta at Washington
Cleveland at Indianapolis
LA Rams at Kansas City
Miami at Minnesota
Tampa Bay at Green Bay
Cincinnati at Houston
New England at Detroit
New Orleans at San Francisco
Pittsburgh at Seattle
San Diego at LA Raiders
Chicago at NY Jets
Denver at Buffalo, MON
(Open Date: Arizona, Dallas,
 NY Giants, Philadelphia)

WEEK FIVE
Dallas at Washington
Detroit at Tampa Bay
Green Bay at New England
NY Jets at Cleveland
Seattle at Indianapolis
Atlanta at LA Rams
Buffalo at Chicago
Minnesota at Arizona
NY Giants at New Orleans
Philadelphia at San Francisco
Miami at Cincinnati, MON
(Open Date: Denver, Kansas
City, LA Raiders, San Diego)

WEEK SIX
Washington at Philadelphia
Indianapolis at NY Jets
LA Rams at Green Bay
Miami at Buffalo
New Orleans at Chicago
San Francisco at Detroit
Tampa Bay at Atlanta
Arizona at Dallas
Denver at Seattle
Kansas City at San Diego
LA Raiders at New England
Minnesota at NY Giants, MON
(Open Date: Cincinnati,
Cleveland, Houston, Pittsburgh)

WEEK SEVEN
Cleveland at Houston, THU
Arizona at Washington
Cincinnati at Pittsburgh
Indianapolis at Buffalo
LA Raiders at Miami
New England at NY Jets
San Francisco at Atlanta
NY Giants at LA Rams
Philadelphia at Dallas
San Diego at New Orleans
Kansas City at Denver, MON
(Open Date: Chicago, Detroit,
Green Bay, Minnesota, Seattle,
Tampa Bay)

WEEK EIGHT
Green Bay at Minnesota, THU
Washington at Indianapolis
Chicago at Detroit
Cincinnati at Cleveland
LA Rams at New Orleans
Pittsburgh at NY Giants
Seattle at Kansas City
Atlanta at LA Raiders
Dallas at Arizona
Denver at San Diego
Tampa Bay at San Francisco
Houston at Philadelphia, MON
(Open Date: Buffalo, Miami,
New England, NY Jets)

WEEK NINE

Philadelphia at Washington
Dallas at Cincinnati
Detroit at NY Giants
Kansas City at Buffalo
Miami at New England
Cleveland at Denver
Houston at LA Raiders
Minnesota at Tampa Bay
NY Jets at Indianapolis
Seattle at San Diego
Pittsburgh at Arizona
Green Bay at Chicago, MON
(Open Date: Atlanta, LA
Raiders, New Orleans, San
Francisco)

WEEK TEN

San Francisco at Washington
Chicago at Tampa Bay
Detroit at Green Bay
Indianapolis at Miami
New England at Cleveland
New Orleans at Minnesota
Pittsburgh at Houston
San Diego at Atlanta
Arizona at Philadelphia
Buffalo at NY Jets
Cincinnati at Seattle
Denver at LA Rams
LA Raiders at Kansas City
NY Giants at Dallas, MON

WEEK ELEVEN

Arizona at NY Giants
Atlanta at New Orleans
Chicago at Miami
Cleveland at Philadelphia
Houston at Cincinnati
Minnesota at New England
San Diego at Kansas City
Dallas at San Francisco
LA Raiders at LA Rams
NY Jets at Green Bay
Seattle at Denver
Tampa Bay at Detroit
Buffalo at Pittsburgh, MON
(Open Date: Indianapolis,
Washington)

WEEK TWELVE

Washington at Dallas
Cleveland at Kansas City
Detroit at Chicago
Green Bay at Buffalo
Indianapolis at Cincinnati
Miami at Pittsburgh
San Diego at New England
Atlanta at Denver
New Orleans at LA Raiders
NY Jets at Minnesota
Philadelphia at Arizona
Tampa Bay at Seattle
LA Rams at San Francisco
NY Giants at Houston, MON

WEEK THIRTEEN

Buffalo at Detroit, THU
Green Bay at Dallas, THU
NY Giants at Washington
Houston at Cleveland
Miami at NY Jets
Philadelphia at Atlanta
Tampa Bay at Minnesota
Chicago at Arizona
Cincinnati at Denver
Kansas City at Seattle
LA Rams at San Diego
Pittsburgh at LA Raiders
New England at Indianapolis
San Francisco at New Orleans, MON

WEEK FOURTEEN

Chicago at Minnesota, THU
Washington at Tampa Bay
Dallas at Philadelphia
Green Bay at Detroit
NY Jets at New England
Pittsburgh at Cincinnati
Arizona at Houston
Atlanta at San Francisco
Denver at Kansas City
Indianapolis at Seattle
New Orleans at LA Rams
NY Giants at Cleveland
Buffalo at Miami
LA Raiders at San Diego, MON

WEEK FIFTEEN

Detroit at NY Jets, SAT
Cleveland at Dallas, SAT
Washington at Arizona
Chicago at Green Bay
Cincinnati at NY Giants
Indianapolis at New England
LA Rams at Tampa Bay
Minnesota at Buffalo
Philadelphia at Pittsburgh
Denver at LA Raiders
San Francisco at San Diego
Seattle at Houston
New Orleans at Atlanta
Kansas City at Miami, MON

WEEK SIXTEEN

Minnesota at Detroit, SAT
Denver at San Francisco, SAT
Tampa Bay at Washington
Atlanta at Green Bay
Cleveland at Pittsburgh
LA Rams at Chicago
Miami at Indianapolis
New England at Buffalo
San Diego at NY Jets
Cincinnati at Arizona
Houston at Kansas City
NY Giants at Philadelphia
LA Raiders at Seattle
Dallas at New Orleans, MON

WEEK SEVENTEEN
Washington at LA Rams, SAT
Arizona at Atlanta, SAT
Buffalo at Indianapolis, SAT
Dallas at NY Giants, SAT
Green Bay at Tampa Bay, SAT
New England at Chicago, SAT
Philadelphia at Cincinnati, SAT
Seattle at Cleveland, SAT
Kansas City at LA Raiders, SAT
New Orleans at Denver, SAT
NY Jets at Houston, SAT
Pittsburgh at San Diego, SAT
Detroit at Miami, SUN
San Francisco at New Orleans, MON

FRANCHISE FOOTBALL LEAGUE'S - 1993 FINAL FANTASY RANKINGS

	Player	Pos	Team	Passing			Rushing			Receiving			Field Goals			PATs	Def.-ST TDs	Total TDs	Total Fantasy Pts.
				'1-9	'10-39	'40+	'1-9	'10-39	'40+	'1-9	'10-39	'40+	'10-39	'40-49	'50+				
1	YOUNG, Steve	QB	San Francisco	11	13	5	1	1										31	273
2	ELWAY, John	QB	Denver	10	13	2												25	201
3	HOSTETLER, Jeff	QB	LA Raiders	4	7	3	4	1										19	189
4	HEBERT, Bobby	QB	Atlanta	13	8	3												24	186
5	JACKE, Chris	K	Green Bay										19	6	6	35			182
6	FAVRE, Brett	QB	Green Bay	5	12	2	1											20	174
7	JAEGER, Jeff	K	LA Raiders										25	6	4	27			172
8	ERICKSON, Craig	QB	Tampa Bay	3	9	6												18	171
9	MOON, Warren	QB	Houston	12	7	2	1											22	171
10	HANSON, Jason	K	Detroit										24	7	3	28			165
11	DEL GRECO, Al	K	Houston										21	4	4	39			162
12	KELLY, Jim	QB	Buffalo	4	11	3												18	159
13	MURRAY, Ed	K	Dallas										17	8	3	38			159
14	BEUERLEIN, Steve	QB	Phoenix	6	8	4												18	156
15	ELAM, Jason	K	Denver										18	4	4	41			155
16	CARNEY, John	K	San Diego										22	7	2	31			152
17	ANDERSEN, Morten	K	New Orleans										16	11	1	33			146
18	RICE, Jerry	WR	San Francisco							7	6	1						16	144
19	BUTLER, Kevin	K	Chicago										19	3	5	21			143
20	JOHNSON, Norm	K	Atlanta										17	7	2	34			140
21	ESIASON, Boomer	QB	NY Jets	7	8	1												17	138
22	DAVIS, Greg	K	Phoenix										13	4	4	37			136
23	AIKMAN, Troy	QB	Dallas	5	6	4	1											15	132
24	STOYANOVICH, Pete	K	Miami										18	4	2	37			131
25	ALLEN, Marcus	RB	Kansas City				11	1			3							15	129
26	BLEDSOE, Drew	QB	New England	7	5	2					1							15	129
27	KASAY, John	K	Seattle										16	4	3	29			127
28	LOWERY, Nick	K	Kansas City										15	7	1	37			127
29	ANDERSON, Gary	K	Pittsburgh										23	5		32			126
30	SIMMS, Phil	QB	NY Giants	5	8	2												15	126
31	CHRISTIE, Steve	K	Buffalo										16	6	1	36			124
32	MIRER, Rick	QB	Seattle	8	3	1	3											15	123
33	RISON, Andre	WR	Atlanta							6	7							15	123
34	TESTAVERDE, Vinny	QB	Cleveland	5	7	2												14	117
35	COFER, Mike	K	San Francisco										12	4		59			115
36	REVEIZ, Fuad	K	Minnesota										21	3	1	27			115
37	PELFREY, Doug	K	Cincinnati										15	7	2	13			113
38	ZENDEJAS, Tony	K	LA Rams										10	7	6	23			113
39	BRISTER, Bubby	QB	Philadelphia	6	7	1	1											14	111
40	HARBAUGH, Jim	QB	Chicago	1	5	1	4											11	111

FRANCHISE FOOTBALL LEAGUE'S - 1993 FINAL FANTASY RANKINGS

#	Player	Pos	Team	Pass '1-9	Pass '10-39	Pass '40+	Rush '1-9	Rush '10-39	Rush '40+	Rec '1-9	Rec '10-39	Rec '40+	FG '10-39	FG '40-49	FG '50+	PATs	Def.-ST TDs	Total TDs	Total Fantasy Pts.
41	TREADWELL, David	K	NY Giants										21	4		28			111
42	HUMPHRIES, Stan	QB	San Diego	2	8	2												12	108
43	MONTANA, Joe	QB	Kansas City	4	8	1												13	108
44	WILSON, Wade	QB	New Orleans	1	10	1												12	108
45	BIASUCCI, Dean	K	Indianapolis										22	3		15			106
46	MITCHELL, Scott	QB	Miami	4	5	3												12	105
47	STOVER, Matt	K	Cleveland										9	6	1	36			103
48	HUSTED, Michael	K	Tampa Bay										10	3	3	27			102
49	O'DONNELL, Neil	QB	Pittsburgh	9	4	1												14	102
50	SHARPE, Sterling	WR	Green Bay							3	7	1						11	93
51	BLANCHARD, Cary	K	NY Jets										12	5		31			92
52	BYARS, Keith	RB	Miami				2			1	2							7	90
53	MARINO, Dan	QB	Miami	1	4	3	1											9	90
54	WATTERS, Ricky	RB	San Francisco				8	2		1								11	90
55	WILLIAMS, Calvin	WR	Philadelphia							3	6	1						10	84
56	LOHMILLER, Chip	K	Washington										14	1	1	24			81
57	EVERETT, Jim	QB	LA Rams	2	2	4												8	78
58	KIRBY, Terry	RB	Miami				1	2		1	1	1						6	78
59	SMITH, Emmitt	RB	Dallas				6	2		1	1							10	78
60	BENNETT, Edgar	RB	Green Bay				8	1		1								10	75
61	BROWN, Gary	RB	Houston				3	3		1	1							8	75
62	BROWN, Tim	WR	LA Raiders							1	5	1					1	8	75
63	SHARPE, Shannon	TE	Denver							4	3	2						9	75
64	METCALF, Eric	RB	Cleveland				1				1	1					2	5	72
65	BAHR, Matt	K	Philadelphia										11	2		28			71
66	FOSTER, Barry	RB	Pittsburgh				7	1		1								9	69
67	MCMAHON, Jim	QB	Minnesota	4	5													9	69
68	MILLER, Anthony	WR	San Diego							1	3	3						7	69
69	RUBLEY, T.j.	QB	LA Rams	1	7													8	69
70	RYPIEN, Mark	QB	Washington	1	3		3											7	69
71	WILLIAMS, Kevin	WR	Dallas				1	1		1	1						2	6	69
72	CARTER, Cris	WR	Minnesota							5	4							9	66
73	JACKSON, Michael	WR	Cleveland							3	4							8	66
74	KRAMER, Erik	QB	Detroit	3	4	1												8	66
75	PEETE, Rodney	QB	Detroit	1	4	1	1											7	66
76	COATES, Ben	TE	New England								5							6	63
77	DAVIS, Willie	WR	Kansas City							4	3	1						8	63
78	IRVIN, Michael	WR	Dallas							2	3	2						7	63
79	KOSAR, Bernie	QB	Cleveland	3	5													8	63
80	MOORE, Ron	RB	Phoenix				6	3										9	63

FRANCHISE FOOTBALL LEAGUE'S - 1993 FINAL FANTASY RANKINGS

	Player	Pos	Team	Passing			Rushing			Receiving			Field Goals			PATs	Def.- ST TDs	Total TDs	Total Fantasy Pts.
				'1-9	'10-39	'40+	'1-9	'10-39	'40+	'1-9	'10-39	'40+	'10-39	'40-49	'50+				
81	PROEHL, Ricky	WR	Phoenix							2	3	2						7	63
82	SALISBURY, Sean	QB	Minnesota	6	3													9	63
83	SISSON, Scott	K	New England										12	2		15			61
84	EARLY, Quinn	WR	New Orleans							6								6	60
85	GEORGE, Jeff	QB	Indianapolis	5	2	1												8	60
86	Houston	DT	Houston														6	6	60
87	REED, Andre	WR	Buffalo								4	2						6	60
88	CARRIER, Mark	WR	Cleveland					1			3						1	5	57
89	CUNNINGHAM, Randall	QB	Philadelphia	2	1	2	1											6	57
90	Cleveland	DT	Cleveland														5	5	57
91	DEBERG, Steve	QB	Tampa Bay	3	3	1												7	57
92	MEANS, Natrone	RB	San Diego				6	1	1									8	57
93	New Orleans	DT	New Orleans														5	5	57
94	San Francisco	DT	San Francisco														5	5	57
95	Buffalo	DT	Buffalo														5	5	54
96	CENTERS, Larry	RB	Phoenix				1				2							3	54
97	HOGE, Merril	RB	Pittsburgh				1				4							5	54
98	JACKSON, Keith	TE	Miami							2	2	2						6	54
99	KRIEG, Dave	QB	Kansas City	4	2	1												7	54
100	MEGGETT, David	RB	NY Giants				1				1						1	3	54
101	MOORE, Herman	WR	Detroit							1	4	1						6	54
102	WALKER, Herschel	RB	Philadelphia				1			1	2							4	54
103	WARREN, Chris	RB	Seattle				4	2	1									7	54
104	WORKMAN, Vince	RB	Tampa Bay				2		1		1							4	54
105	Philadelphia	DT	Philadelphia														5	5	52
106	BETTIS, Jerome	RB	LA Rams				5	1	1									7	51
107	FRIESZ, John	QB	San Diego	2	3	1												6	51
108	FRYAR, Irving	WR	Miami								3	2						5	51
109	HARPER, Alvin	WR	Dallas							2	3							5	51
110	INGRAM, Mark	WR	Miami							2	3	1						6	51
111	JEFFIRES, Haywood	WR	Houston							2	3	1						6	51
112	MITCHELL, Johnny	TE	NY Jets							2	3	1						6	51
113	PRITCHARD, Mike	WR	Atlanta							4	3							7	51
114	TAYLOR, John	WR	San Francisco								3	2						5	51
115	DELPINO, Robert	RB	Denver				8											8	48
116	PICKENS, Carl	WR	Cincinnati							2	4							6	48
117	CARLSON, Cody	QB	Houston	1	1		1	1										4	45
118	COPELAND, Horace	WR	Tampa Bay								1	3						4	45
119	GREEN, Eric	TE	Pittsburgh							1	3	1						5	45
120	LOGAN, Marc	RB	San Francisco				6	1										7	45

FRANCHISE FOOTBALL LEAGUE'S – 1993 FINAL FANTASY RANKINGS

#	Player	Team	Pos	Passing			Rushing			Receiving			Field Goals			PATs	Def.-ST TDs	Total TDs	Total Fantasy Pts.
				'-9	'10-39	'40+	'-9	'10-39	'40+	'-9	'10-39	'40+	'10-39	'40-49	'50+				
121	PHILCOX, Todd	Cleveland	QB	1	3		1											5	45
122	Phoenix		DT														4	4	45
123	Washington		DT														4	4	45
124	BAVARO, Mark	Philadelphia	TE							4	2							6	42
125	BAXTER, Brad	NY Jets	RB				7											7	42
126	BROOKS, Bill	Buffalo	WR							1	4							5	42
127	CROSS, Howard	NY Giants	TE							1	4							5	42
128	CULVER, Rodney	Indianapolis	RB				3			1							1	5	42
129	Chicago		DT														5	5	42
130	HAWKINS, Courtney	Tampa Bay	WR							2	2	1						5	42
131	JOHNSON, Johnny	NY Jets	RB				2		1		1							4	42
132	JOHNSON, Vance	Denver	WR							1	4							5	42
133	KLINGLER, David	Cincinnati	QB	4	2													6	42
134	MARTIN, Kelvin	Seattle	WR							2	2	1						5	42
135	MILBURN, Glyn	Denver	RB							2	1							3	42
136	RUSSELL, Leonard	New England	RB				7											7	42
137	WILLIAMS, John L.	Seattle	RB				1	2			1							4	42
138	ALLEN, Eric	Philadelphia	DB														4	4	42
139	ANDERSON, Willie	LA Rams	WR							1	1	2						4	39
140	DAVIS, Kenneth	Buffalo	RB				5	1										6	39
141	Detroit		DT														4	4	39
142	RUZEK, Roger	Philadelphia	K										7	1		13			39
143	SCHROEDER, Jay	Cincinnati	QB	2	3													5	39
144	CARTER, Anthony	Minnesota	WR							3	2							5	36
145	CLARK, Gary	Phoenix	WR								4							4	36
146	EVANS, Vince	LA Raiders	QB			3												3	36
147	GANNON, Rich	Washington	QB	1	2		1											4	36
148	GIVINS, Ernest	Houston	WR							1	2	1						4	36
149	HARMON, Ronnie	San Diego	RB								2							2	36
150	HARRIS, Jackie	Green Bay	TE							1	2	1						4	36
151	HUGHES, Tyrone	New Orleans	DB														3	3	36
152	JETT, James	LA Raiders	WR									3						3	36
153	LEE, Amp	San Francisco	RB				1			1	1							3	36
154	MARSHALL, Arthur	Denver	WR		1					1	2							4	36
155	MOORE, Derrick	Detroit	RB				3											3	36
156	Miami		DT														3	3	36
157	RUSSELL, Derek	Denver	WR							1	2	1						4	36
158	THOMAS, Thurman	Buffalo	RB				6											6	36
159	VARDELL, Tommy	Cleveland	RB				3			1								4	36
160	WRIGHT, Alexander	LA Raiders	WR							1	2	1						4	36

FRANCHISE FOOTBALL LEAGUE'S - 1993 FINAL FANTASY RANKINGS

#	Player	Pos	Team	Pass '1-9	Pass '10-39	Pass '40+	Rush '1-9	Rush '10-39	Rush '40+	Rec '1-9	Rec '10-39	Rec '40+	PATs	FG '10-39	FG '40-49	FG '50+	Def.-ST TDs	Total TDs	Total Fantasy Pts
161	DRAYTON, Troy	TE	LA Rams							1	3							4	33
162	Dallas	DT	Dallas														3	3	33
163	HAMPTON, Rodney	RB	NY Giants				4	1										5	33
164	HILL, Randal	WR	Phoenix							2	1	1						4	33
165	JACKSON, Mark	WR	NY Giants							2	1	1						4	33
166	MCCARDELL, Keenan	WR	Cleveland							1	3							4	33
167	SANDERS, Ricky	WR	Washington							1	3							4	33
168	SLAUGHTER, Webster	WR	Houston							4	1							5	33
169	BEEBE, Don	WR	Buffalo								2	1						3	30
170	BROOKS, Reggie	RB	Washington				1		2									3	30
171	BROWN, Derek	RB	New Orleans				2				1							3	30
172	BUCK, Mike	QB	New Orleans	3		1												4	30
173	BURKETT, Chris	WR	NY Jets							2	2							4	30
174	COBB, Reggie	RB	Tampa Bay				3					1						4	30
175	CONKLIN, Cary	QB	Washington	2	2													4	30
176	GARY, Cleveland	RB	LA Rams				1					1						2	30
177	HAYNES, Michael	WR	Atlanta							3		1						4	30
178	JOHNSTON, Daryl	RB	Dallas				3					1						4	30
179	LEWIS, Nate	WR	San Diego							2	2							4	30
180	MARTIN, Eric	WR	New Orleans								2	1						3	30
181	MARTIN, Tony	WR	Miami								2	1						3	30
182	O'BRIEN, Ken	QB	Philadelphia	2	2													4	30
183	Pittsburgh	DT	Pittsburgh														3	3	30
184	STONE, Dwight	WR	Pittsburgh				2	1										3	30
185	BUTTS, Marion	RB	San Diego				3	1										4	27
186	CHANDLER, Chris	QB	Phoenix		3													3	27
187	Kansas City	DT	Kansas City														3	3	27
188	LANGHORNE, Reginald	WR	Indianapolis							1	1	1						3	27
189	MCGEE, Tim	WR	Washington								3							3	27
190	OBEE, Terry	WR	Chicago							1	1	1						3	27
191	QUERY, Jeff	WR	Cincinnati							3	1							4	27
192	THOMPSON, Darrell	RB	Green Bay				1	1	1									3	27
193	TOLLIVER, Billy Joe	QB	Atlanta	1	1	1												3	27
194	Seattle	DT	Seattle														3	3	25
195	ANDERSON, Neal	RB	Chicago				4											4	24
196	Atlanta	DT	Atlanta														2	2	24
197	BERNSTINE, Rod	RB	Denver				4											4	24
198	BUNCH, Jarrod	RB	NY Giants				2			1								3	24
199	CALLOWAY, Chris	WR	NY Giants							1	2							3	24
200	CARTER, Dexter	RB	San Francisco						1								1	2	24

#	Player	Pos	Team	Passing '1-9	Passing '10-39	Passing '40+	Rushing '1-9	Rushing '10-39	Rushing '40+	Receiving '1-9	Receiving '10-39	Receiving '40+	FG '10-39	FG '40-49	FG '50+	PATs	Def.-ST TDs	Total TDs	Total Fantasy Pts
201	CASH, Keith	TE	Kansas City							4								4	24
202	CLAYTON, Mark	WR	Green Bay							1	2							3	24
203	CRAIG, Roger	RB	Minnesota				1				1							2	24
204	DAVIS, Eric	DB	San Francisco														2	2	24
205	HILLIARD, Dalton	RB	New Orleans				2			1								3	24
206	JONES, Brent	TE	San Francisco							1	2							3	24
207	MCDUFFIE, OJ	WR	Miami														2	2	24
208	METZELAARS, Pete	TE	Buffalo							4								4	24
209	NY Giants	DT	NY Giants														2	2	24
210	RIVERS, Reggie	RB	Denver				1				1							2	24
211	SANDERS, Barry	RB	Detroit				1	2										3	24
212	SHERRARD, Mike	WR	NY Giants									2						2	24
213	THIGPEN, Yancey	WR	Pittsburgh							1	2							3	24
214	TURNER, Kevin	RB	New England							2								2	24
215	BAILEY, Johnny	RB	Phoenix					1			1							2	21
216	BLADES, Brian	WR	Seattle							2	1							3	21
217	Cincinnati	DT	Cincinnati														2	2	21
218	ELLARD, Henry	WR	LA Rams								1	1						2	21
219	GREEN, Willie	WR	Detroit								1	1						2	21
220	Green Bay	DT	Green Bay														2	2	21
221	LA Raiders	DT	LA Raiders														2	2	21
222	MITCHELL, Brian	RB	Washington				2	1										3	21
223	Minnesota	DT	Minnesota														2	2	21
224	PEGRAM, Erric	RB	Atlanta				2	1										3	21
225	THOMAS, Lamar	WR	Tampa Bay								1	1						2	21
226	TILLMAN, Lewis	RB	NY Giants				2	1										3	21
227	WILLIAMS, Aeneas	DB	Phoenix														2	2	21
228	ANDERS, Kimble	RB	Kansas City								1							1	18
229	ANDERSEN, Gary	RB	Tampa Bay								1							1	18
230	BIRDEN, J.J.	WR	Kansas City							1		1						2	18
231	CASH, Kerry	TE	Indianapolis							3								3	18
232	CHAFFEY, Pat	RB	NY Jets															1	18
233	CLAY, Willie	DB	Detroit														2	2	18
234	CONWAY, Curtis	WR	Chicago								2							2	18
235	DUNCAN, Curtis	WR	Houston							3								3	18
236	GARDNER, Carwell	RB	Buffalo								1							1	18
237	GRAHAM, Scottie	RB	Minnesota				3											3	18
238	HEBRON, Vaughn	RB	Philadelphia				3											3	18
239	HIGGS, Mark	RB	Miami				3											3	18
240	Indianapolis	DT	Indianapolis														2	2	18

FRANCHISE FOOTBALL LEAGUE'S – 1993 FINAL FANTASY RANKINGS

	Player	Pos	Team	Passing '1-9	Passing '10-39	Passing '40+	Rushing '1-9	Rushing '10-39	Rushing '40+	Receiving '1-9	Receiving '10-39	Receiving '40+	PATs	FG '10-39	FG '40-49	FG '50+	Def.-ST TDs	Total TDs	Total Fantasy Pts
241	JEFFERSON, Shawn	WR	San Diego								2							2	18
242	LASSIC, Derrick	RB	Dallas				3											3	18
243	MATHIS, Terance	WR	NY Jets					1										1	18
244	McCAFFERY, Ed	WR	NY Giants								2							2	18
245	McCALLUM, Napoleon	RB	LA Raiders				3											3	18
246	MUSTER, Brad	RB	New Orleans				3											3	18
247	NOVACEK, Jay	TE	Dallas				1			1								2	18
248	RATHMAN, Tom	RB	San Francisco				3											3	18
249	THOMPSON, Leroy	RB	Pittsburgh				3											3	18
250	TIMPSON, Michael	WR	New England								2							2	18
251	TOMCZAK, Mike	QB	Pittsburgh		2													2	18
252	WALSH, Steve	QB	New Orleans	1		1												2	18
253	YOUNG, Mike	WR	Philadelphia							1	1							2	18
254	BRISBY, Vincent	WR	New England							1	1							2	15
255	HOLMAN, Rodney	TE	Detroit							1	1							2	15
256	JONES, Ernie	WR	LA Rams							1	1							2	15
257	KINCHEN, Brian	TE	Cleveland							1	1							2	15
258	MONK, Art	WR	Washington							1	1							2	15
259	PERRIMAN, Brett	WR	Detroit							1	1							2	15
260	REICH, Frank	QB	Buffalo	1	1													2	15
261	SMITH, Robert	RB	Minnesota				1	1										2	15
262	THORNTON, Jim	TE	NY Jets							1	1							2	15
263	TILLMAN, Cedric	WR	Denver							1	1							2	15
264	TRUDEAU, Jack	QB	Indianapolis	1	1													2	15
265	Tampa Bay	DT															2	2	15
266	WORLEY, Tim	RB	Pittsburgh				1	1										2	15
267	YOUNG, Duane	TE	San Diego							1	1							2	15
268	BAILEY, Vic	WR	Philadelphia															1	12
269	BAKER, Myron	LB	Chicago														2	2	12
270	BALDWIN, Randy	RB	Cleveland				1											1	12
271	BLOUNT, Eric	WR	Phoenix				1											1	12
272	BONO, Steve	QB	San Francisco	2														2	12
273	BROOKS, Robert	WR	Green Bay				1											1	12
274	BROUSSARD, Steve	RB	Atlanta														1	1	12
275	CLARK, Vinnie	DB	Atlanta				1											1	12
276	COLEMAN, Lincoln	RB	Dallas				2											2	12
277	COLLINS, Mark	DB	NY Giants														1	1	12
278	COPELAND, Russell	WR	Buffalo														1	1	12
279	CRITTENDEN, Ray	WR	New England						1									1	12
280	DISHMAN, Chris	DB	Houston														1	1	12

#	Player	Pos	Team	Passing '1-9	Passing '10-39	Passing '40+	Rushing '1-9	Rushing '10-39	Rushing '40+	Receiving '1-9	Receiving '10-39	Receiving '40+	PATs	FG '10-39	FG '40-49	FG '50+	Def.-ST TDs	Total TDs	Total Fantasy Pts
281	EDMUNDS, Ferrell	TE	Seattle							2								2	12
282	EDWARDS, Anthony	WR	Phoenix									1						1	12
283	FRANK, Donald	DB	San Diego														1	1	12
284	GOUVEIA, Kurt	LB	Washington														1	1	12
285	GRAY, Mel	WR	Detroit														1	1	12
286	GREEN, Darrell	DB	Washington														1	1	12
287	HANKS, Merton	DB	San Francisco														1	1	12
288	ISMAIL, Raghib	WR	LA Raiders									1						1	12
289	JOHNSON, A.J.	DB	Washington														1	1	12
290	JOHNSON, Tracy	RB	Seattle							1								1	12
291	JONES, Henry	DB	Buffalo														1	1	12
292	JOSEPH, James	RB	Philadelphia							1								1	12
293	LEWIS, Darryl	DB	Houston														1	1	12
294	LINCOLN, Jeremy	DB	Chicago														1	1	12
295	LYNCH, Eric	RB	Detroit				2											2	12
296	LYNCH, Lorenzo	DB	Phoenix														1	1	12
297	MCDOWELL, Anthony	RB	Tampa Bay							1								1	12
298	MCGRIGGS, Lamar	DB	Minnesota														1	1	12
299	MCNAIR, Todd	RB	Kansas City				2											2	12
300	MIDDLETON, Ron	TE	Washington							2								2	12
301	MUSTAFAA, Najee	DB	Cleveland														1	1	12
302	NEAL, Lorenzo	RB	New Orleans						1									1	12
303		DT	NY Jets														1	1	12
304	OLIVER, Louis	DB	Miami														1	1	12
305	ROBERTSON, Marcus	DB	Houston														1	1	12
306	SECULES, Scott	QB	New England	2														2	12
307	SHERMAN, Heath	RB	Philadelphia				2											2	12
308	SMITH, Irv	TE	New Orleans							2								2	12
309	SMITH, Tony	RB	Atlanta							1								1	12
310		DT	San Diego														2	2	12
311	TALLEY, Darryl	LB	Buffalo														2	2	12
312	THOMAS, Derrick	LB	Kansas City														1	1	12
313	TILLMAN, Spencer	RB	Houston														1	1	12
314	WASHINGTON, Brian	DB	NY Jets														1	1	12
315	WHITE, Lorenzo	RB	Houston				2											2	12
316	WILLIAMS, Darryl	DB	Cincinnati														1	1	12
317	WOLFLEY, Ron	RB	Cleveland							1								1	12
318	WOODSON, Rod	DB	Pittsburgh														1	1	12
319	WORD, Barry	RB	Minnesota				2											2	12
320	DALUISO, Brad	K	NY Giants													1			10

FRANCHISE FOOTBALL LEAGUE'S – 1993 FINAL FANTASY RANKINGS

#	Player	Pos	Team	Passing '1-9	Passing '10-39	Passing '40+	Rushing '1-9	Rushing '10-39	Rushing '40+	Receiving '1-9	Receiving '10-39	Receiving '40+	FG '10-39	FG '40-49	FG '50+	PATs	Def.-ST TDs	Total TDs	Total Fantasy Pts
321	ELLIOTT, Lin	K	Dallas										1	1		2			10
322	ARMSTRONG, Tyji	TE	Tampa Bay								1							1	9
323	BEACH, Sanjay	WR	San Francisco								1							1	9
324	BRENNER, Hoby	TE	New Orleans								1							1	9
325	BRIM, Michael	DB	Cincinnati														1	1	9
326	BUTLER, Leroy	DB	Green Bay														1	1	9
327	CARRIER, Mark	DB	Chicago														1	1	9
328	CARTER, Pat	TE	LA Rams								1							1	9
329	COLEMAN, Monte	LB	Washington														1	1	9
330	CROEL, Mike	LB	Denver														1	1	9
331	DAWKINS, Sean	WR	Indianapolis								1							1	9
332	DOWDELL, Marcus	WR	New Orleans								1							1	9
333	DRONETT, Shane	DT	Denver														1	1	9
334	EVANS, Byron	LB	Philadelphia														1	1	9
335	HALL, Ron	TE	Tampa Bay								1							1	9
336	HARRIS, Leonard	WR	Houston								1							1	9
337	HAYES, Jon	TE	Kansas City								1							1	9
338	HESTER, Jessie	WR	Indianapolis								1							1	9
339	JACKSON, Steve	DB	Houston														1	1	9
340	JAMISON, George	LB	Detroit														1	1	9
341	JONES, Dante	LB	Chicago														1	1	9
342	JORDAN, Steve	TE	Minnesota								1							1	9
343	KINCHEN, Todd	WR	LA Rams								1							1	9
344	KIRKLAND, Levon	LB	Pittsburgh														1	1	9
345	MACK, Milton	DB	Tampa Bay														1	1	9
346	MCDANIEL, Terry	DB	LA Raiders														1	1	9
347	MCGRUDER, Michael	DB	San Francisco														1	1	9
348	MCGWIRE, Dan	QB	Seattle		1													1	9
349	MCKELLER, Keith	TE	Buffalo								1							1	9
350	MCMILLIAN, Audrey	DB	Minnesota														1	1	9
351	MCNEAL, Travis	TE	LA Rams		1													1	9
352	MILLER, Chris	QB	Atlanta															1	9
353	MILLS, Sam	LB	New Orleans														1	1	9
354	MOORE, Dave	TE	Tampa Bay								1							1	9
355	MOORE, Stevon	DB	Cleveland														1	1	9
356	MURRELL, Adrian	RB	NY Jets					1										1	9
357	NED, Derrick	RB	New Orleans					1										1	9
358	NEWMAN, Patrick	WR	New Orleans								1							1	9
359	ODOMES, Nathaniel	DB	Buffalo														1	1	9
360	ORLANDO, Bo	DB	Houston														1	1	9

FRANCHISE FOOTBALL LEAGUE'S - 1993 FINAL FANTASY RANKINGS

	Player	Pos	Team	Passing '1-9	Passing '10-39	Passing '40+	Rushing '1-9	Rushing '10-39	Rushing '40+	Receiving '1-9	Receiving '10-39	Receiving '40+	Receiving '50+	FG '10-39	FG '40-49	FG '50+	PATs	Def.-ST ST TDs	Total TDs	Total Fantasy Pts
361	RASHEED, Kenyon	RB	NY Giants					1											1	9
362	SMITH, Kevin	DB	Dallas															1	1	9
363	TILLMAN, Lawyer	WR	Cleveland								1								1	9
364	WADDLE, Tom	WR	Chicago								1								1	9
365	WALKER, Derrick	TE	San Diego								1								1	9
366	WASHINGTON, Mickey	DB	Buffalo															1	1	9
367	WETNIGHT, Ryan	WR	Chicago								1								1	9
368	BALL, Eric	RB	Cincinnati				1												1	6
369	BARNETT, Tim	WR	Kansas City							1									1	6
370	BATY, Greg	TE	Miami							1									1	6
371	BAXTER, Fred	TE	NY Jets							1									1	6
372	BELL, Nick	RB	LA Raiders				1												1	6
373	BIENIEMY, Eric	RB	San Diego				1												1	6
374	BLACKMON, Robert	DB	Seattle															1	1	6
375	BOYKIN, Deral	DB	LA Rams															1	1	6
376	BYNER, Earnest	RB	Washington				1												1	6
377	COOK, Marv	TE	New England							1									1	6
378	CROOM, Corey	RB	New England				1												1	6
379	FENNER, Derrick	RB	Cincinnati				1												1	6
380	GALBRAITH, Scott	TE	Dallas							1									1	6
381	GASH, Sam	RB	New England				1												1	6
382	GLOVER, Andrew	TE	LA Raiders							1									1	6
383	GREEN, Paul	WR	Seattle							1									1	6
384	HEARST, Garrison	RB	Phoenix				1												1	6
385	HERROD, Jeff	LB	Indianapolis															1	1	6
386	HORTON, Ethan	TE	LA Raiders							1									1	6
387	ISMAIL, Qadry	WR	Minnesota							1									1	6
388	JOHNSON, Anthony	RB	Indianapolis				1												1	6
389	JOHNSON, Reggie	TE	Denver							1									1	6
390		DT	LA Rams															1	1	6
391	LEWIS, Albert	DB	Kansas City															1	1	6
392	MACK, Kevin	RB	Cleveland				1												1	6
393	MADDOX, Tommy	QB	Denver	1															1	6
394	MCAFEE, Fred	RB	New Orleans				1												1	6
395	MCMURTRY, Greg	WR	New England							1									1	6
396	MILES, Ostell	RB	Cincinnati				1												1	6
397	MILLS, Ernie	WR	Pittsburgh							1									1	6
398	MIMS, David	WR	Atlanta							1									1	6
399	MOORE, Rob	WR	NY Jets							1									1	6
400	REEVES, Walter	TE	Phoenix							1									1	6

FRANCHISE FOOTBALL LEAGUE'S - 1993 FINAL FANTASY RANKINGS

	Player	Pos	Team	Passing			Rushing			Receiving			Field Goals			PATs	Def.-ST TDs	Total TDs	Total Fantasy Pts.
				'1-9	'10-39	'40+	'1-9	'10-39	'40+	'1-9	'10-39	'40+	'10-39	'40-49	'50+				
401	ROBINSON, Greg	RB	LA Raiders				1											1	6
402	ROLLE, Butch	TE	Phoenix							1								1	6
403	ROYSTER, Mazio	RB	Tampa Bay				1											1	6
404	SINGLETON, Nate	WR	San Francisco							1								1	6
405	SMALL, Torrance	WR	New Orleans							1								1	6
406	STEPHENS, John	RB	Green Bay				1											1	6
407	STEPHENS, Rod	LB	Seattle				1										1	1	6
408	THOMAS, Blair	RB	NY Jets				1											1	6
409	THOMPSON, Craig	TE	Cincinnati							1								1	6
410	TICE, Mike	TE	Minnesota							1								1	6
411	TURNER, Floyd	WR	New Orleans							1								1	6
412	VERDIN, Clarence	WR	Indianapolis																6
413	WARE, Andre	QB	Detroit	1															6
414	WELLMAN, Gary	WR	Houston							1								1	6
415	WILLIAMS, Jamie	TE	San Francisco							1								1	6
416	LATHON, Lamar	LB	Houston																4
417	NOBLE, Brian	LB	Green Bay																4
418	PAUP, Bryce	LB	Green Bay																4

FRANCHISE FOOTBALL LEAGUE'S
1993 ALL FANTASY ROSTER

FIRST TEAM

Over all Rank	Player	Pos	Team	Passing '1-9	'10-39	'40+	Rushing '1-9	'10-39	'40+	Receiving '1-9	'10-39	'40+	Field Goals '10-39	'40-49	'50+	PATs	Def.-ST TDs	Total TDs	Total Fantasy Pts.
1	YOUNG, Steve	QB	San Francisco	11	13	5	1	1										31	273
25	ALLEN, Marcus	RB	Kansas City				11	1			3							15	129
52	BYARS, Keith	RB	Miami		1		2		1		2	2						7	90
18	RICE, Jerry	WR	San Francisco						1	7	6	2						16	144
33	RISON, Andre	WR	Atlanta							6	7	2						15	123
50	SHARPE, Sterling	WR	Green Bay							3	7	1						11	93
63	SHARPE, Shannon	TE	Denver							4	3	2						9	75
5	JACKE, Chris	K	Green Bay										19	6	6	35			182
86	Houston	DT															6	6	60
	Totals:			11	14	5	14	2	2	21	28	7	19	6	6	35	6	6	1,169

SECOND TEAM

Over all Rank	Player	Pos	Team	Passing '1-9	'10-39	'40+	Rushing '1-9	'10-39	'40+	Receiving '1-9	'10-39	'40+	Field Goals '10-39	'40-49	'50+	PATs	Def.-ST TDs	Total TDs	Total Fantasy Pts.
2	ELWAY, John	QB	Denver	10	13	2	8	2										25	201
54	WATTERS, Ricky	RB	San Francisco				1	2			1	1						11	90
58	KIRBY, Terry	RB	Miami							1	1	1						6	78
55	WILLIAMS, Calvin	WR	Philadelphia							3	6	1						10	84
62	BROWN, Tim	WR	LA Raiders							1	5	1					1	8	75
68	MILLER, Anthony	WR	San Diego							1	3	3						7	69
76	COATES, Ben	TE	New England							4	3	1						8	63
7	JAEGER, Jeff	K	LA Raiders										25	6	4	27			172
90	Cleveland	DT	LA Raiders														5	5	57
	Totals:			10	13	2	9	4	0	10	18	6	25	6	4	27	5	5	889

1993 FFL Season Totals:	Passing '1-9	'10-39	'40+	Rushing '1-9	'10-39	'40+	Receiving '1-9	'10-39	'40+	Field Goals '10-39	'40-49	'50+	PATs	Def.-ST TDs	Total TDs	Total Fantasy Pts.
	194	249	74	246	44	13	190	249	73	476	135	61	876	161	1,493	16,632

1992 FFL Season Totals:	Passing '1-9	'10-39	'40+	Rushing '1-9	'10-39	'40+	Receiving '1-9	'10-39	'40+	Field Goals '10-39	'40-49	'50+	PATs	Def.-ST TDs	Total TDs	Total Fantasy Pts.
	166	262	89	268	54	12	161	262	89	394	130	37	936	214	1,577	17,262

1991 FFL Season Totals:	Passing '1-9	'10-39	'40+	Rushing '1-9	'10-39	'40+	Receiving '1-9	'10-39	'40+	Field Goals '10-39	'40-49	'50+	PATs	Def.-ST TDs	Total TDs	Total Fantasy Pts.
	176	242	92	283	52	23	174	244	92	440	141	42	918	150	1,528	16,920

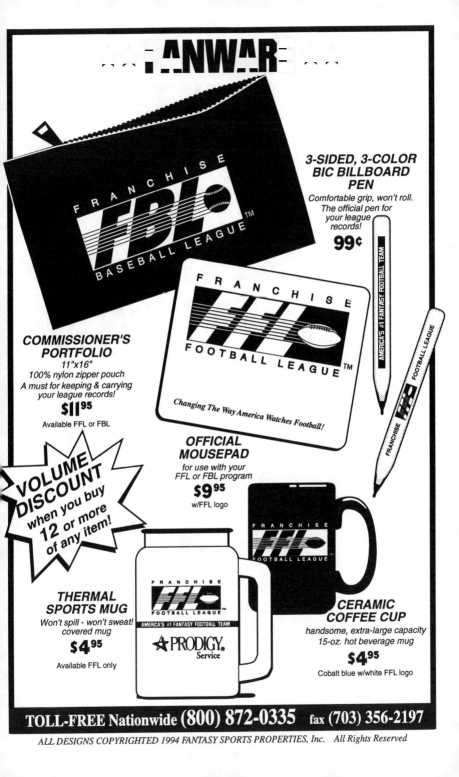

1994/1995 FANTASY SPORTS ORDER FORM

SOFTWARE

	QTY	PRICE	TOTAL
1994 FFL Fantasy Football Software (3.5")	_____	@ $ 34.95 (plus $ 5.00 S & H) ea.	_____
1995 FBL Fantasy Baseball Software (3.5")	_____	@ $ 34.95 (plus $ 5.00 S & H) ea.	_____
**For 5.25" Diskettes, add	_____	@ $ 5.00	_____

JOURNALS

1994 FFL Fantasy Football Journal	_____	@ $ 9.95 (plus $ 3.00 S & H) ea.	_____
Additional Football Journals	_____	@ $ 3.95 (plus $ 1.00 S & H) ea.	_____
1995 FBL Fantasy Baseball Journal	_____	@ $ 9.95 (plus $ 3.00 S & H) ea.	_____
Additional Baseball Journals	_____	@ $ 3.95 (plus $ 1.00 S & H) ea.	_____

SOFTWARE/JOURNAL COMBO PACKAGES

1994 FFL Software and FFL Journal	_____	@ $ 39.95 (plus $ 6.00 S & H) ea.	_____
All additional FFL Journals	_____	@ $ 3.95 (plus $ 1.00 S & H) ea.	_____
1995 FBL Software and FBL Journal	_____	@ $ 39.95 (plus $ 6.00 S & H) ea.	_____
All additional FBL Journals	_____	@ $ 3.95 (plus $ 1.00 S & H) ea.	_____

WEEKLY UPDATE SERVICES

		FBL		FFL
Fantasy Sports Properties Weekly Statistical Updates				
Download via modem from the FSPI BBS	_____ @ $119.95		_____ @ $79.9	
PRODIGY downloads must be purchased online				
JUMP:FBL or FFL on PRODIGY for more info.	@ $149.95*		@$99.9!	
Fantasy Sports Properties Weekly Diskette Service				
Next Day Diskettes (FBL--Tues./FFL--Weds.)	_____ @ $ 329.00		_____ @ $249.	
2nd Day Diskettes (FBL--Weds./FFL--Thurs.)	_____ @ $ 229.00		_____ @ $179.	
Franchise Football League Facsimile Service	*Not Available for FBL*		_____ @ $129.	

MERCHANDISE

	QTY			QTY		TOTALS
FFL Billboard Pens	_____	@ $ .99ea.	or	_____ doz	@ $ 9.99/doz	_____
FFL Sports/Travel Mugs	_____	@ $ 4.95ea.	or	_____ doz	@ $ 49.95/doz	_____
FFL Coffee Cups	_____	@ $ 4.95ea.	or	_____ doz	@ $ 49.95/doz	_____
FFL Mouse Pads	_____	@ $ 9.95ea.	or	_____ doz	@ $ 99.95/doz	_____
FFL Baseball Caps	_____	@ $ 9.95ea.	or	_____ doz	@ $ 99.95/doz	_____
FBL Baseball Caps	_____	@ $ 9.95ea.	or	_____ doz	@ $ 99.95/doz	_____
FFL Commissioner's Portfolio	_____	@ $11.95ea.	or	_____ doz	@ $ 119.95/doz	_____
FBL Commissioner's Portfolio	_____	@ $11.95ea.	or	_____ doz	@ $ 119.95/doz	_____
FFL 100% Cotton T-Shirts	__M __L __XL	**XXL** ($ 14.95ea. or $ 149.95/doz)				_____
FBL 100% Cotton T-Shirts	__M __L __XL	**XXL** ($ 14.95ea. or $ 149.95/doz)				_____
FFL Crew Neck Sweatshirt	__M __L __XL	**XXL** ($ 24.95ea. or $ 249.95/doz)				_____
FBL Crew Neck Sweatshirt	__M __L __XL	**XXL** ($ 24.95ea. or $ 249.95/doz)				_____
FFL Golf Shirts	__M __L __XL	**XXL** ($ 29.95ea. or $ 299.95/doz)				_____
FBL Golf Shirts	__M __L __XL	**XXL** ($ 29.95ea. or $ 299.95/doz)				_____
FFL Hooded Sweatshirt	__M __L __XL	**XXL** ($ 34.95ea. or $ 349.95/doz)				_____
FBL Hooded Sweatshirt	__M __L __XL	**XXL** ($ 34.95ea. or $ 349.95/doz)				_____

**(add $ 2.00 each for XXL garments)

Merchandise Subtotal _____

(For Merchandise Shipping/Handling, Add 10% of Merchandise Subtotal) _____

Mail, Fax or Call your order in today!!

Grand Total for Entire Order $_____

NAME_____

ADDRESS_____

CITY_____STATE_____ZIP_____

PHONE NUMBER (____)_____FAX (____)_____

METHOD OF PAYMENT: (circle one) VISA MC CHECK#_____

CREDIT CARD #_____EXP:_____